Immigration for Startups
A Guide for Founders

IMMIGRATION FOR STARTUPS

A GUIDE FOR FOUNDERS

Jason Susser & Greg Siskind

ALAN HOUSE PUBLISHING

Printed in the United States of America
First Printing: 2020

ISBN: 978-1-7320271-6-9; ISBN 10: 1-7320271-6-1
Library of Congress Control Number: 2020913554

Alan House Publishing
1028 Oakhaven Road
Memphis, TN 38119

In memory of my father, Alan Siskind, and my brother, Joel Siskind, who embodied all of the best characteristics of entrepreneurship. You are missed every day.

Greg Siskind

To my heroes, Shmuel and Lynn Susser; and to my beloved wife and daughter, Courtney and Sunny: you two are my world.

Jason Susser

About the Authors

Jason Susser is an attorney at Siskind Susser PC, where his practice focuses exclusively on immigration and nationality law. Jason works extensively with entrepreneurs to find creative immigration solutions for startup companies in the United States. He often works with foreign founders to develop immigration strategies that balance the needs of an early-stage business with the challenges of the immigration system.

As many of these companies go through rounds of funding and begin to scale, Jason helps them develop immigration policies and assists in the immigration needs of their employees. He works with companies ranging from the solo entrepreneur to the Fortune 500. He also advises startup accelerators and universities working with entrepreneurial students.

Jason has authored several articles and regularly speaks about startups and immigration. He is a member of the American Immigration Lawyers Association and currently serves as treasurer of the organization's Midsouth chapter.

Since its inception, Siskind Susser has been internationally recognized for its legal technology. Jason has continued that tradition of innovation by helping to develop expert systems and apps for clients, staff, and other attorneys who desire to use AI-based software to approach immigration issues more efficiently.

Greg Siskind is a founding partner of Siskind Susser PC and is one of America's best-known immigration attorneys. Greg is a past chair of the International Medical Graduate Taskforce (IMG Taskforce) (www.imgtaskforce.org), a physician immigration bar organization in the United States. Greg also serves as a member of the Board of Governors of the American Immigration Lawyers Association (www.aila.org).

Greg is a man of many firsts. He created the first immigration law firm website in 1994 followed by the first lawyer blog in 1997. He also was the first immigration lawyer ever to grace the cover of the *American Bar Association Journal*. And he is one of the first immigration lawyers to develop artificial intelligence-based software applications for clients.

Greg has been practicing law since 1990. He received his bachelor's degree from Vanderbilt University and his law degree from the University of Chicago.

Siskind Susser PC (www.visalaw.com) is internationally known for advising startups on immigration matters. The firm has worked with some of the top accelerator programs in the country, represented countless award-winning entrepreneurs, and worked with top universities to help foreign students start companies after graduation. Siskind Susser has one of the largest health care immigration practices in the United States and represents many of the nation's hospitals and health care systems across the country, as well as smaller health care employers, individual health care professionals, and other medical institutions.

SUMMARY OF CONTENTS

Acknowledgments

I want to thank my co-author, Greg Siskind. I appreciate the opportunity to work on this together, and all the advice you have given me from marketing to technology to career development and beyond. I would also like to thank Tatia Gordon-Troy for your guidance and work putting this book together, and Lori Cox for your work editing early versions. Also, thank you to my mentor, "Superman" Sam.

No thank you would be big enough for my mother and mentor, Lynn Susser. You have taught me how to be a lawyer, manager, and parent. Your concern for our clients and love for this work is infectious and felt by the entire Siskind Susser family.

To my other hero, my dad, Shmuel: thank you for all your guidance, confidence, and love. I am also grateful for my brothers, Daniel and Ian, and brother-in-law Tim, for your support, as well as my grandparents, Elliot and Diana Saunders.

With a less than 1-year-old daughter at home, my wife, Courtney, asked me what I was thinking about one night, and I told her that I really wanted to write this book. Despite just finishing a master's, starting a new position, and us barely sleeping, Courtney immediately told me to do it. I am forever grateful to her for her love, partnership, and encouragement; and to Sunny, for her laughter and the joy she brings me every day.

I, like many Americans, am a product of hardworking and entrepreneurial immigrants, from Europe to the Middle East to Canada and the United States. This book is in honor of all of them, and I hope it helps someone else create a life for their children in this country as fortunate as the one that was created for me.

Jason Susser

August 2020

As an immigration lawyer who is also an entrepreneur, I've always had an affinity for my clients who have rolled the die and tried to make a go at launching and sustaining a venture. It can be scary, exhilarating, and exhausting to make a go at being an entrepreneur. Bearing the additional stress of complying with immigration law makes me admire these clients even more. And it is to these clients whom I've gotten to know over the last 30 years that I initially want to express my thanks.

My colleagues always have had patience with me as I've pursued writing projects like this book; and they have been there for me when I've needed feedback or just some encouragement. That is especially true of my law partner and business co-founder, Lynn Susser, who has been there in good times and bad.

It has been a pleasure collaborating on this book with Jason Susser. You understand the immigration issues faced by startups better than any lawyer I know, and that experience is reflected in this book. I am grateful to have you as my co-author.

Finally, my wife, Audrey, my daughters, Eden, Lily and Noa, and my mother, Karen, have been there for me and I owe everything to them.

Greg Siskind

August 2020

CONTENTS

INTRODUCTION

America is a country created by immigrants. This is clear in our culture, demographics, and economy. The chronicles of U.S. business are filled with endless stories of foreign entrepreneurs risking it all to build some of the most quintessential American companies and products: Andrew Carnegie, Levi Strauss, Sergey Brin, Peter Thiel, Elon Musk, and so on; not to mention the millions of small businesses created by immigrants in communities throughout the country.

The Brookings Institute found that in 2017, 43 percent of the companies in America's Fortune 500 were founded or co-founded by an immigrant or the child of an immigrant.[1] A Harvard study found that although immigrants only make up 15 percent of the American work force, 35 percent to 40 percent of new firms have at least one immigrant co-founder, and 31 percent of venture capital–backed founders are immigrants.[2]

The unfortunate reality is that the U.S. immigration system is not commensurate with the role foreign-born entrepreneurs play in building American companies and employing U.S. workers. Instead, U.S. immigration law favors the foreign-born employee coming to work for a U.S. company.

Aside from a few visa categories limited to people of specific nationalities, the average foreign entrepreneur will have a hard time figuring out which visa will allow him or her to build a company in the United States.

The purpose of *Immigration for Startups: A Guide for Founders* is to help foreign-national founders build America's next great company. Whether you are reading this from abroad, in the United States as a student, or currently here working as

[1] The Brookings Institute study can be found at https://bit.ly/brookings17.

[2] The Harvard University study can be found at https://bit.ly/HarvardStudy2016.

a traditional employee of a U.S. company, our goal is to help you navigate the U.S. immigration system and understand your options. If you are filled with the entrepreneurial spirit and determined to build a company in the United States, we hope this book will demystify the path to self-employment.

1

AN OVERVIEW OF THE U.S. IMMIGRATION SYSTEM

The U.S. immigration system is one of the most complicated in the world. The thousands of pages of statutes, rules, policy manuals, and case law are not only vast, but rapidly changing. This book focuses on the major immigration strategies available to entrepreneurs, but it will help to have some context and a basic understanding of how the U.S. immigration system works before diving in.

Many people in the United States are U.S. citizens either by birth or as a result of naturalization; however, under the U.S. immigration system, foreign-born individuals who are not naturalized citizens will have one of the following statuses:

- **Nonimmigrant status**: Persons in the United States in a nonimmigrant classification are said to have nonimmigrant status. These individuals are granted a nonimmigrant visa to enter the United States for a temporary purpose, such as a pleasure trip, to enroll in or attend a school, or to work. Individuals can seek a nonimmigrant visa to enter the United States at a U.S. consulate abroad and then present that visa at a port of entry to be admitted for a defined period of time (which may be different from the expiration date on the visa in the passport). Some nonimmigrant visas can be renewed indefinitely while others have defined time periods during which they can be used. Also, some individuals can seek admission as nonimmigrants at a port of entry in the United States without a visa.
- **Immigrant status**: An individual seeking to remain permanently in the United States can seek permanent residency, also known as a "green card." Individuals can process immigrant visa applications abroad and have an immigrant visa issued by a U.S. consulate or they can apply from within the United States through a process called "adjustment of status."
- **Asylees and other special groups**: Some individuals can enter and remain legally in the United States in statuses that are distinct from nonimmigrant visas, such as political asylum/refugee status, temporary protected status (for people from countries facing disasters or wars), and "parole," which is a dis-

cretionary status U.S. Citizenship and Immigration Services (USCIS) can use to grant individuals the right to stay and work in the United States on a case-by-case basis. There is also a category called "entrepreneur parole," which is discussed later in this handbook.

- **Undocumented status or unlawfully present**: There are several reasons why individuals might fall into this category: (1) they entered the United States without inspection; (2) they overstayed their authorized stay in the United States; or (3) they otherwise violated their nonimmigrant status.

For most would-be entrepreneurs, an immigration strategy will typically involve first coming to the United States as a nonimmigrant and then eventually moving on to immigrant status and then to citizenship.

A nonimmigrant typically will seek a visa at a U.S. consulate, which is run by the U.S. Department of State. There are some cases where a person does not need a visa to enter. For example, Canadians can often enter the United States without a visa and simply get inspected at a port of entry and admitted as a nonimmigrant. For nationals of dozens of countries, admission under the Visa Waiver Program (often referred to as ESTA) is possible for up to 90 days without the need for a visa.

After securing a visa at a consulate, most would-be nonimmigrants seek admission at a port entry—usually an airport in the United States or a land port of entry or a cruise ship port of entry. The person seeking entry as a nonimmigrant will present the U.S. Customs and Border Protection (CBP) officer with his or her passport and visa stamp and the officer will make a determination regarding whether the person can be admitted to the United States. If so, the person will be given an I-94 (downloadable from the CBP website) and a stamp in the passport stating the nonimmigrant classification the person is admitted under and how long the person's authorized stay will be.

Once in the United States in nonimmigrant status, the individual must comply with the rules of his or her visa category and can potentially seek to amend the approval, change employers, or extend status. Those changes typically require the filing of an application with U.S. Citizenship and Immigration Services.

Immigrants

Entrepreneurs do not typically enter the United States with immigrant status, but it is certainly possible. The person may have a close U.S. relative (such as a citizen spouse); the person might win the green card lottery; or the person could enter the United States in an employment-based green card category, such as the EB-1C category for multinational corporate transfers.

The strategy is more often to wait on permanent residency. For one, the general green card process takes many months. Many green card categories have restrictive quotas that are limited further by country of birth, so some applicants might be looking at decades to get a green card in a particular category. In the employment categories, the green card backlogs hit Indian, Chinese, and Filipino nationals particularly hard.

In some cases, a person needs to develop the business and have a successful track record before a green card becomes a realistic option.

In other cases, a green card may not ever be a consideration. This could be the case, for example, if a person only wants to be in the United States for part of the year and wishes to avoid being designated a resident of the United States for tax purposes.

To qualify for permanent residency, a person can choose to start at a U.S. consulate and enter the United States on an immigrant visa. Or, if the person is in the United States legally and a visa number is available (*i.e.*, he or she is not subject to a backlog in a particular green card category), the person may apply to adjust status and get the green card at the end of that process. That will often involve the entrepreneur continuing to work as a nonimmigrant while waiting on the adjustment-of-status application to be adjudicated. The person also can secure a temporary employment authorization document and an advance parole travel document as part of the adjustment-of-status application.

Visa Strategies

Immigration for Startups: A Guide for Founders is designed to educate you on the various immigration categories and strategies typically used by entrepreneurs seeking residency in the United States. Often, a person's immigration journey will involve being in multiple nonimmigrant categories before eventually procuring a green card and then citizenship.

Here are two examples of how the journey might unfold:

- Jill initially enters the United States on a B-2 visitor visa to visit universities. She then leaves and applies for admission to an MBA program in the United States and when she is admitted, she procures an F-1 student visa and enters in that status.
- After receiving the MBA, Jill gets "optional practical training" while working for a year to gain experience in her field.

- After a year, she converts the status to an H-1B after her application through her employer is accepted in the annual H-1B lottery.
- She then decides to make the jump to starting her own business and gets an E-2 visa based on a commercial investment treaty between the United States and her home country.
- When her business takes off, Jill successfully self-petitions for a green card as an EB-1, based on demonstrating extraordinary ability in business.
- After five years as a permanent resident, Jill becomes eligible for citizenship and naturalizes.

Another path might look like this:

- Jack runs a business outside the United States that is doing well and he decides he wants to branch out to having an operation in the United States.
- He initially enters the United States on a B-1 visitor visa to scope out locations, talk to potential customers, negotiate with vendors, and take additional steps to get the business set up.
- Jack secures an L-1 visa, which allows him to transfer from his overseas company to the United States (while the overseas company continues to run).
- After the business in the United States is running successfully for a year, Jack gets an extension of his L-1 status and then pursues a green card as an EB-1, based on being a multinational executive/manager.
- Jack chooses not to become a citizen because his home country does not recognize dual citizenship and he wishes to retain his nationality.

There are a number of other paths an entrepreneur can take to acquire residency; and given the precarious state of the global economy, it is easy to see legislative and administrative changes coming in the not-too-distant future to make it easier for job-creating startup founders to work in the United States.

But given the long track record of the United States, do not expect immigration to go smoothly and easily. The system has many agencies involved in the process, byzantine application processes, and hostile politics.

The more you know about the system, the more likely you will navigate it successfully.

2

B-1/B-2 VISAS AND THE VISA WAIVER PROGRAM

Individuals coming to the United States temporarily for certain business purposes may seek entry with a B-1 visa. Those coming for tourism, pleasure, or visiting will seek entry with a B-2 visa. Those doing both on the same trip may get a designation as B-1/B-2. The B-1 visa can be useful to an entrepreneur, particularly in the early stages of a business.

B-1/B-2 Visitor Visas: Immigrant Intent

An overriding requirement governing B-1 visas and several others is contained in Section 214(b) of the Immigration and Nationality Act. It states that every person shall be "presumed to be an immigrant until he establishes to the satisfaction of the consular officer at the time of application for a visa, and the immigration officers at the time of application for admission, that he is entitled to a nonimmigrant status…"

In short, if an officer finds that the applicant either intends to immigrate or the officer does not believe the person is going to comply with the terms of the visa, the visa will be denied. This section is cited in the vast majority of B-1 denials.

The B-1 applicant must possess the following:

- ✓ A residence in a foreign country, which he or she does not intend to abandon;
- ✓ The intent to enter the United States for a limited period of time; and
- ✓ The sole purpose of engaging in legitimate activities relating to business.

Having a residence abroad means one's place of general abode. It can be one's own home or the home of someone else if the B-1 applicant resides in the household of another (such as a parent). The applicant must demonstrate meaningful ties to the home country, such as permanent employment, meaningful business or financial connections, close family relationships, or social or cultural ties indicating a strong connection to the home country and an intention to return.

Generally, having a pending green card application to remain permanently in the United States would be a highly negative factor since it would indicate that one does not have an intention to return to the home country. However, such an application may not be fatal if an immigrant visa number is not available and an applicant can demonstrate that he or she does not intend to remain in the United States waiting on the immigrant visa to become available.

Intending to remain in the United States for a limited period of time does not come with a bright line test. The maximum period of entry on a B-1 is typically six months. However, consular officers are instructed by the U.S. Department of State's *Foreign Affairs Manual* that the key to showing nonimmigrant intent is demonstrating that the intended stay has an actual time limitation and is not *indefinite* in nature.

It is possible to get a visitor visa even if the intended period of time in the United States exceeds six months; an example of this is a domestic partner accompanying a nonimmigrant to the United States for a work assignment that may last more than six months. Also, the period of time the applicant states as needed for the visit must be consistent with the purpose of the trip. Finally, the applicant must have specific and realistic plans for the entire period of the contemplated visit, which means being prepared to provide a detailed itinerary.

A common requirement is that the purpose of the visit *not* be to engage in employment in the United States. It can be hard in some cases to determine whether this line is crossed, but a key factor in this discernment is whether the principal place of business and actual accrual of profits comes from outside the United States.

A good example would be the Board of Immigration Appeals case, *Matter of Hira*; this case involved a tailor who came to the United States to measure customers for custom suits that were made outside the United States. In that case, the B-1 visa was considered appropriate because the work was largely conducted outside the United States (perhaps the result would have been different had the suits been tailored in the United States following the measurements).

The *Foreign Affairs Manual* lays out in detail the types of acceptable activities in which B-1 visitors may engage, which are based on the *Hira* decision:

9 FAM 402.2-5(B) (U) Aliens Traveling to United States to Engage in Commercial Transactions, Negotiations, Consultations, Conferences, Etc.

- Engaging in commercial transactions, which do not involve gainful employment in the United States (such as taking orders from customers for goods and services provided abroad)
- Negotiating contracts
- Consulting with business associates
- Participating in scientific, educational, professional, or business conventions, conferences or seminars;
- Undertaking independent research (which may include market research, as an example);

9 FAM 402.2-5(C)(3) (U) Members of Board of Directors of U.S. Corporation

- Coming to the United States to attend a meeting of a board of directors of a U.S. corporation or to perform other functions resulting from membership on the board;

9 FAM 402.2-5(C)(7) (U) Investor Seeking Investment in United States

- Coming to the United States to seek an investment (including an investment that may later require a work visa if the applicant intends to work in the business as long as the applicant refrains from working in the business on the visit or actively participating in the management of the business while in the United States in B status).

9 FAM 402.2-5(E)(3) (U) Clerkship

- Individuals coming to the United States to observe the conduct of business activity provided the individual pays his or her own expenses.

9 FAM 402.2-5(F) (U) Aliens Normally Classifiable H-1 or H-3

- In some cases, an individual coming to the United States to perform work that would normally be classified as appropriate for an H-1B visa (discussed later) may be granted a "B visa in lieu of H-1B visa" if the source of pay for the work is from a foreign source and the worker is customarily employed by the company outside the United States. The State Department will deny the visa if it appears that a U.S. entity is routing payment for the worker's services through a foreign entity. The State Department has issued various memos on the subject of "B-1 in lieu of H" over the years and clarified that Section 214(b) *does not* apply to the B-1 in lieu of H category. That's because the category is intended to mimic the H-1B category which is because, as will be explained in the section on H-1Bs, that visa category is governed by a concept called "dual intent" where one can have intentions to immigrate and still qualify for the visa. Also, the work must be intended to last less than six months and the normal H-1B requirements—working in a specialty occupation, for example—apply.

Note that some consulates are less familiar with the B-1 in lieu of H category and applicants need to be thoroughly prepared to explain in 30 seconds or less why they are applying for the category and should have an attorney cover letter with the application explaining eligibility while citing to and providing the Department of State memoranda on the subject. A B-1 or B-2 visa is the one type of visa that one can normally have in addition to another visa.[1]

An activity not listed in the *Foreign Affairs Manual* still can be an acceptable basis for a B-1 visa if the general tests for the B-1 are otherwise met. However, officers are instructed to seek an Advisory Opinion from the Department of State's Advisory Opinions Division in the United States (which obviously means a decision will be delayed).

Some activities likely *not* to be considered acceptable for B-1 purposes are the following:

- Supervising or directing staff in the function of their work;
- Providing services directly to a U.S. employer;
- Representing a U.S. employer to others or with the same organization;
- Making and implementing decisions that affect the U.S. operations;
- Any activity that a U.S. worker would typically be paid to perform.

B-1 nonimmigrants are eligible to file change-of-status applications with U.S. Citizenship and Immigration Services (USCIS) to convert to other visa types or to extend their B-1 status. But a few notes of caution are warranted.

First, USCIS may scrutinize applications to look for evidence of fraud, particularly in the forthrightness (or lack thereof) regarding the purpose of the original application. If, for example, the purpose of the B-1 visa is to come to the United States to engage in startup activities prior to a business becoming operational but the intention to file for a work visa when those activities ended was not noted at the time of visa entry, USCIS may view the application negatively.

---

[1] In May 2018, U.S. Citizenship and Immigration Services (USCIS) Director Francis Cissna noted in a letter to Congressman Paul Mitchell that USCIS is working on a new regulation in coordination with the State Department governing B-1 visas including reviewing B-1 in lieu of H policies.

Second, USCIS typically will look very closely at B-1 extension requests if it believes the applicant is either not planning to stay for a short duration or has intentions contrary to B-1 purposes (such as having liquidated all assets outside the United States, sold a foreign residence, etc.).

Spouses and children may accompany the B-1 visa holder; however, because the activities while in the United States on a B-1 visa are to be for a very limited duration, it should not surprise the applicant if questions are asked about why the family is accompanying the visitor.

The Visa Waiver Program

B-1 and B-2–eligible individuals from certain countries are authorized to enter the United States without a visa stamp under the Visa Waiver Program (VWP). The program, created in 1986, allows people from designated countries who have low visa denial rates and low visa overstay rates to enter the United States to pursue B-1 and B-2 activities without having to get a visa stamp from a U.S. consulate.

Citizens of the following 38 countries are eligible to participate in the Visa Waiver Program:

Andorra
Australia
Austria
Belgium
Brunei
Chile
Czech Republic
Denmark
Estonia
Finland
France
Germany
Greece
Hungary
Iceland
Ireland
Italy
Japan
Latvia
Liechtenstein
Lithuania
Luxembourg
Malta
Monaco
Netherlands
New Zealand
Norway
Portugal
San Marino
Singapore
Slovakia
Slovenia
South Korea
Spain
Sweden
Switzerland
Taiwan
United Kingdom

The United Kingdom is limited to those British citizens who have the unrestricted right to reside in England, Scotland Wales, Northern Ireland, the Channel Islands, and the Isle of Man.

To enter under the VWP, an individual must be a citizen of one of the above-listed eligible countries and complete an Electronic System for Travel form (ESTA) via the Department of State's website.[2] That application includes biographic and travel information, as well as disclosures on prior criminal convictions, and must be completed at the time travel is booked and no later than 72 hours prior to the intended date of travel. ESTA verification is limited to two years or the date of expiration of the passport, if that date is earlier than two years. Applicants also must obtain a new ESTA for changes to name, gender, country of citizenship, or changes to a response to any of the screening questions on ESTA.

Upon completion of an ESTA application, the applicant receives an instantaneous response of one of the following:

1. Authorization Approved—travel authorized
2. Travel Not Authorized—applicant must apply for a visa at an embassy or consulate prior to travel to the United States
3. Authorization Pending—traveler will need to check the ESTA website within 72 hours to receive a final response

Applicants who are denied ESTA authorization are still eligible to apply for a B-1 or B-2 visa at a consulate. Re-applications are permitted after a minimum 10-day wait. Also, a visa refusal for any reason could result in an ESTA authorization denial.

There are a few key restrictions on VWP entrants that don't apply to B-1 and B-2 visa holders. First, stays are limited to 90 days (versus a normal 180-day maximum for people entering on B-1 and B-2 visas). Second, VWP entrants may not apply for an extension of stay or a change of status to another nonimmigrant or immigrant classification (except adjustment-of-status applications for permanent residency are permitted in very limited circumstances).

VWP entrants are normally unable to apply for a new visa at a U.S. consulate in Mexico or Canada; and leaving the United States for one of those countries and then re-entering from those countries will not entitle the person to an additional VWP entry. However, travel to Canada, Mexico, or nearby islands is permitted during a VWP trip and re-entry is permitted for the duration of the original 90 days still unused in the country.

Finally, the VWP entrant must have a return or onward ticket, have a permitted machine-readable passport, and not be inadmissible to the United States. Just as a

---

[2] https://esta.cbp.dhs.gov/esta.

visa refusal can result in ESTA denial, it also can result in being denied entry at a port of entry under the VWP.

In 2015, Congress changed the VWP program to prohibit travelers in several categories from using the VWP:

- VWP country nationals who have traveled to or been present in Iran, Iraq, Libya, Somalia, Sudan, Syria, or Yemen on or after March 1, 2011, (with limited exceptions for diplomatic or military travel in the service of a VWP country); and
- Nationals of VWP countries who are also nationals of Iran, Iraq, Sudan, or Syria.

Possession of a machine-readable passport (or e-Passport) has created confusion, as some VWP countries have not transitioned all of their passports to meet the new requirement. Acceptable passports will have an expiration date that is less than 180 days away and have machine-readable lines, *see Figure 1.*

The passport must also be embedded with an electronic chip that can be scanned to match the traveler's identification to the passport. The symbol on the cover from the International Civil Aviation Organization indicates that the passport qualifies, *see Figure 2.* Temporary and emergency passports must still be qualifying e-Passports.

Canadian visitors do not participate in the VWP and are exempt from getting a visa; they are permitted stays up to 180 days similar to B-1 and B-2 visa holders.

FIGURE 1: Machine-readable Passport

FIGURE 2: Passport Cover Showing ICAO Symbol

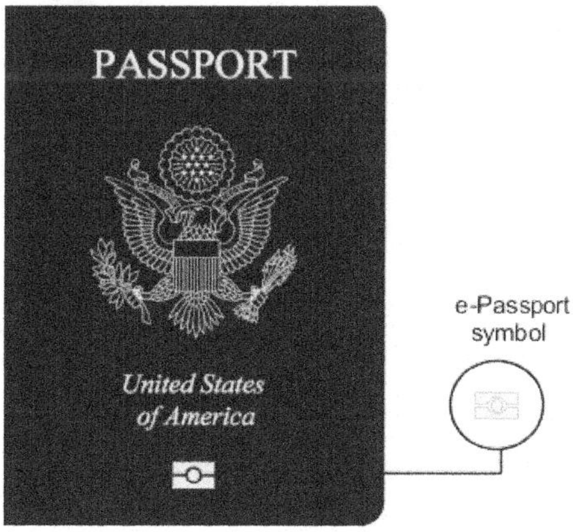

3

Entering the United States as a Student: The F-1 Visa

One of the immigration paths that entrepreneurs can follow is entering the United States on a student visa. This allows the subject to pursue studies leading to a degree and take advantage of employment programs available to international students in the United States. Studying in the United States can provide an excellent way to gain education and skills helpful in establishing and running a business, as well as providing access to alumni networks and startup funding channels.

In this chapter, we discuss student visas that allow for pre– and post-graduation employment opportunities (as opposed to categories of study that *do not* allow employment). There are three types of student visas available in the United States that enable these opportunities: the F-1, the M-1, and the J-1 visas. For employment to be permitted in any of these categories, the student must be studying full-time and, in the case of F-1 and J-1 visas, be pursuing a college or university degree.

- **F-1 visas** are, by far, the most common type of student visa used by entrepreneurs. These are available to individuals who are students pursuing a full course load and who pursue studies at a college or university approved by the U.S. Department of Homeland Security to accept F-1 students. F-1s are used for various types of study, but for those interested in employment opportunities, a full-time degree program is necessary.
- **M-1 visas** are available to students at vocational and other recognized nonacademic institutions (other than language training programs) approved to accept M-1 students by the Department of Homeland Security.
- **J-1 exchange visitor visas** can be used for a variety of purposes (including interning and training opportunities) and include student programs. A J-1 student must be pursuing a full course of study leading to or culminating in the award of a degree from an accredited college or university under an approved J-1 exchange program (which is typically the college or university's own J-1

student program). J-1 student programs must be financed directly or indirectly by the U.S. government, the government of the student's home country, an international organization of which the United States is a member by treaty or statute, or supported by funding from any source other than personal or family funds. J-1 visa holders are often required to return to their home countries for two years upon the completion of their time on a J-1 visa.

The M-1 category is limited to a small number of institutions and the programs are typically not in fields of interest to entrepreneurs starting businesses in the United States. The J-1 student programs are restrictive in terms of financing (as well as the home residency requirement, which will be covered in Chapter 8); therefore, the vast majority of entrepreneurs coming to the United States as students use the F-1 category. For that reason, this chapter focuses on F-1 status.

Finding a School That Accepts F-1 Students

There are more than 4,500 accredited institutions comprising the higher education system in the United States. For a college or university to sponsor an international student, the school must be approved by U.S. Immigration and Customs Enforcement's Student and Exchange Visitor Program[1] (SEVP). One can search by geographic location and filter by program type; importantly, there is also an option to filter institutions based on their authorization to accept F-1 students.

Note that to qualify for "optional practical training," which will allow employment after graduation, a student must be enrolled in a college or university and be pursuing at least an associate's degree.

After locating a school that accepts F-1 students, the applicant should visit the school's website to find its requirements for admission. These include the school's standardized testing requirements, English language requirements, and whether prior education will be recognized. Also, note the school's admission calendar, as many schools require applications far in advance of the date coursework will begin.

Applicants should be sure to understand the costs of studying. Some colleges and universities, particularly those that are government-owned (referred to as "public" colleges and universities), charge a substantially reduced tuition to residents of the state where they are located. International students are charged as non-residents at a higher

---

[1] To find out whether a school is authorized to accept F-1 students, go to https://studyinthestates.dhs.gov/school-search.

level. Most private universities charge all students the same price regardless of residency or visa status.

Average Fees at U.S. Universities, 2018-19				
	Public two-year colleges	Public four-year colleges (in-state fees)	Public four-year colleges (out-of-state fees)	Private non-profit four-year colleges
Tuition and other fees	$3,660	$10,230	$26,290	$35,830
Room and board	$8,660	$11,140	$11,140	$12,680
Total (per year)	$12,320	$21,370	$36,430	$48,510
Source: https://trends.collegeboard.org/college-pricing/figures-tables/average-published-undergraduate-charges-sector-2018-19				

Students will need to demonstrate the ability to cover tuition and room and board for a university to admit you as an F-1 student. U.S. colleges and universities *do* offer financial incentives for some international students, such as scholarships, in-state tuition benefits, and waived application fees. Receiving such benefits is not an impediment to receiving a student visa. Consulates will look at many factors in deciding whether to issue a student visa, and one may be the likelihood the student will work without authorization while studying because he or she is unable to afford the cost of studying; for this reason, scholarships based on financial need are often withheld from potential international students.

Many schools have a separate process for international students to apply and applicants should follow that process closely. For example, some schools require prior college course work to be evaluated by a company that specializes in such comparisons and an acceptable result on an English proficiency examination. In addition, undergraduate and graduate degree programs often require all applicants to take a standardized exam appropriate for the degree being sought, an application (typically completed online), an essay, and recommendation letters.

After admittance to a college or university, the school will register the student in the Student and Exchange Visitor Information System (SEVIS). SEVIS is a web-based system that the U.S. Department of Homeland Security uses to maintain information on schools under SEVP as well as U.S. Department of State-designated Exchange Visitor Program sponsors, F-1 students, M-1 students, and J-1 Exchange Visitor Program participants.

SEVIS, created in the wake of the 9/11 terror attacks, is used to keep track of international students from the date of acceptance in an educational program through the end of studies and post-graduation training/employment.

Once registered in SEVIS, the school's Designated Student Officer (DSO) will verify the student's financial means to cover the expenses of attending. He or she will then issue the student a Form I-20 (Certificate of Eligibility for Nonimmigrant Student Status). Form I-20 lists the applicant's educational program, including the degree type, state, and anticipated end date. It also documents the student's expected costs for studying and living in the United States, as well as the source of funds to pay those costs.

Information on a student's dependent spouse and children are also listed if applicable, but sections regarding employment and travel outside the United States after studies commence can be completed later on. The student's I-20 is a critical document the student will need to apply for a visa initially, as well as to document the fact that the student is maintaining student status in the United States.

After the student is registered in SEVIS, the student will be required to pay a fee using online Form I-901.[2] The current fee for F-1 applicants is $200. F-1 applicants are required to pay the fee before attending the visa interview at a U.S. consulate or embassy. The applicant does not have to pay the fee at the time of scheduling the visa appointment; however, it might take up to three business days for the SEVIS fee to be received and verified.

The student must print a receipt demonstrating payment of the I-901 SEVIS fee, which will be needed for the visa interview (see below). The student should confirm that all the details of his or her entry in SEVIS are correct, including spelling or a change in the school to be attended. If these or other changes are required, the student can email a request to: FMJfee.sevis@ice.dhs.gov.

Student visas are approved directly at a U.S. consulate in the student's home country and, unlike other visa categories, no preliminary approval is required from U.S. Citizenship and Immigration Services (USCIS). While the process of applying for a U.S. visa is generally similar across the world, consult the website of the respective U.S. consulate to learn about local variations. Not all consulates handle every type of visa application.

---

[2] www.fmjfee.com/i901_fee/index.html.

Links to all U.S. consulates around the world can be found online.[3] Consular web pages also provide information on appointment scheduling, which can vary significantly from country to country.

Items required for applying for a student visa at a U.S. consulate:

- A passport valid for at least six months beyond the intended period of stay in the United States.
- A Nonimmigrant Visa Application (Form DS-160) confirmation page after completing the form online. The application requires information on the applicant's travel plans, prior trips to the United States, where the applicant has resided for the past five years, any work and education history, and information on dependents. The applicant will be asked to provide the SEVIS ID and the address of the school (each is listed on the I-20). A photo must be uploaded meeting specific requirements, such as having a white background, being less than six months old, and meeting certain measurements.
- Application fee payment receipt (see the instructions on the local consulate web page).
- The Form I-20.

Consular officers may also ask for documentation regarding academic preparation; this can include transcripts, diplomas, and standardized test results. They also may want to see documentation regarding the applicant's ability to pay the costs of studying in the United States.

One common basis for denying a student visa is failure to demonstrate nonimmigrant intent. If an applicant is likely to face closer scrutiny of his or her immigrant intentions, the applicant should be prepared to demonstrate the following:

- Financial ties to the home country—this can be demonstrated through proof of property ownership, investments in businesses and institutions in the home country, and letters or financial statements from a bank or accountant;
- The likelihood of employment in the home country upon completion of studies—this can be indicated through a letter from a current employer guaranteeing re-employment, or a similar letter from a prospective employer along with a statement of how the U.S. education will benefit the employer;
- An immigration history that shows the applicant is not a risk (such as a passport that shows travel to other countries with no overstaying).

Because those who are applying for student visas are often young, providing proof of their family's assets or ties to the home country, if they do not have their own, is recommended.

---

[3] www.usembassy.gov.

Other red flags that would cause closer scrutiny of a student visa could be: having close family members living in the United States; prior U.S. visa denials; and whether the particular consulate has a history of denying F-1 visa applications.

If the consular officer is satisfied the applicant has met the requirements for a student visa, the applicant will be issued a machine-readable visa on his or her passport. The length of the visa will vary depending on the length of the academic program and the rules of reciprocity between the home country and the United States. Some countries' nationals, for example, will be granted multiple entry visas for longer periods of time, while other nationals will be granted single entry visas that expire after a brief period, possibly only a few days or weeks after issuance.

At the port of entry, the visa will be presented to a U.S. Customs and Border Protection officer who will determine whether the student is eligible for entry and the length of stay permitted for the particular trip to the United States. This is done via the creation of an I-94 arrival/departure record that is available online.

Note that while most nonimmigrants are given I-94s with specific expiration dates, students are generally granted I-94s with the notation "D/S" instead of an expiration date. "D/S" means "duration of status" and students are permitted to remain as long as they are maintaining their student status and have a valid and unexpired I-20.

The "D/S" I-94 has been a key benefit for international students because it simplifies the process for remaining in valid status in the United States. It also has meant that students are generally not subject to bars on readmission to the United States as a result of visa overstays because the overstay determination is based on the I-94 expiration date. Note, however, that in 2018, USCIS issued a policy memorandum holding that F-1 students and J-1 exchange visitors can be subjected to re-entry bars based on violations of their status and not just based on the I-94. That memorandum resulted in a lawsuit filed by several universities; and as of the publication date of this edition, the lawsuit is pending and the memorandum remains in place (with no time being accumulated toward overstay bars).

If a Customs and Border Protection officer at the port of entry is not satisfied with the information the applicant has provided, the applicant may be sent to an interview room for a "secondary inspection." If an officer is not satisfied after that, the applicant may be denied admission to the United States, or, in the alternative, an officer may issue the student a Form I-515A allowing for temporary admission to the United States for 30 days during which time the student must address the issues identified in the I-515A.

A student may enter the United States up to 30 days ahead of the start date for studies listed on the I-20 and the student must report to the school during that period.

In order to maintain status, a student must:

- Attend and pass all classes; and
- Maintain a full course of study (typically, at least 12 course hours per semester).

Students who study full-time for at least one semester are eligible for an annual vacation (typically a summer recess) *if* the student intends to enroll full-time in the academic term following the vacation. Students are permitted to take courses during the vacation period.

Transfers to another school are permitted if an F-1 student has maintained his or her status at the current school and the student goes through USCIS's transfer process.

Once a program is completed (including post-graduation work authorization—see discussion below), F-1 students must depart the United States within 60 days of the expiration *or* apply for an extension for additional studies *or* change to another nonimmigrant status. The transfer must be noted in SEVIS with the current school's DSO, ergo moving responsibility to the new school's DSO; this must be done before the transfer can take place. Also, note that work authorization at the student's current institution ends as soon as the transfer release date happens. The new school's DSO should be consulted regarding employment at the new institution.

Employment

Students on F-1 visas pursuing degrees are eligible to accept employment during their studies (and in the period immediately following their studies) under the following circumstances:

On-Campus Employment

Employment on a college or university's campus or at an off-campus location affiliated with a school is permitted. On-campus employment may begin up to 30 days before the start of classes and may be for up to 20 hours per week when school is in session and full-time during vacation periods. Unlike other employment programs, on-campus employment is considered "incident to status" and does not require the DSO's approval or notation in SEVIS. However, the student will need to apply for a Social Security number and will need to present to the Social Security Administration a letter from the DSO and documentation from the on-campus employer proving the student is engaging in on-campus employment. Note that on-campus employment *cannot take place* during the 60-day grace period following studies.

Employment Based on Severe Economic Conditions

F-1 students who have been maintaining their status for a year and who suffer a severe economic hardship can seek off-campus employment if they can show the following:

- The need is caused by circumstances beyond their control;
- The employment on-campus is unavailable or insufficient to meet the financial needs that have arisen; and
- The off-campus employment will not interfere with the student's ability to maintain a full course load.

If the DSO determines that the above requirements are met, the DSO will update SEVIS with a recommendation to approve employment authorization and generate a new I-20 containing the DSO's recommendation.

The student will then need to submit the following:

- An I-765 form to USCIS along with the requisite filing fee ($495 as of the time of publication);
- A copy of the newly annotated I-20;
- Two photos of the applicant (meeting size and background requirements);
- A copy of the student's I-94; and
- Evidence regarding the hardship and circumstances.

If USCIS agrees the requirements are met, it will grant employment authorization in one-year increments or until the program's end-date, whichever ends first. The employment can be in any job and need not be related to the course of study.

There is also a separate set of rules that allows the Department of Homeland Security (DHS) to offer relief to students from parts of the world facing "emergent circumstances," including allowance for DHS to change the rules regarding duration of status, maintaining a full course of study, and being eligible to work.

Practical Training

DHS regulations permit "practical training" for F-1 students who have been lawfully enrolled on a full-time basis in a SEVP-approved school. There are two types of practical training—curricular practical training and optional practical training. Each is discussed below.

Curricular Practical Training

F-1 students may participate in a curricular practical training (CPT) program that is an integral part of an established curriculum. Work may include alternative work/study, internships, cooperative education, or any other type of required internship or practicum that is offered by sponsoring employers through cooperative agreements with the school. The work must be closely related to the student's major field of study.

CPT is normally available after a student has completed one academic year, though exceptions can be made for graduate students in programs that require immediate curricular training for all of the program's students.

CPT must first be approved and recorded by a DSO who will enter in SEVIS the employer, location, and period approved for employment and issue a new I-20 endorsed to permit CPT. Employment is limited to a specific employer and a specific position and may be approved in increments of up to one year.

Until 2018, there was no cumulative maximum; however, in late 2018, USCIS took the position that total full-time practical training (both CPT and Optional Practical Training (OPT)) is limited to one year and the agency began denying changes to H-1B status in the United States for those previously approved by their schools for extensions *beyond* one year. This has been viewed as a misinterpretation of the law by USCIS and has led to litigation that has not yet been resolved.

Many people have avoided these denials by filing prospective nonimmigrant status applications through consular processing instead of requesting a change of status with USCIS. The schools are also able to provide students with significant documentation regarding the scope of the CPT that has allowed many people with requests for additional evidence regarding this issue to still ultimately have their changes of status approved (though some cases have resulted in denials based on the agency's new interpretation).

Students can be approved for part-time CPT (up to 20 hours per week) or full-time (over 20 hours per week). Part-time CPT does not affect eligibility for OPT. CPT students are expected to maintain a full course of study during the period of employment.

There is no minimum salary requirement for CPT, but the job must still meet federal and state employment law requirements including minimum wage requirements.

CPT does not require approval from USCIS and students need only present their CPT-endorsed I-20 form to the employer whose name is approved by the DSO and is on the I-20. Also, using CPT at one educational level does not affect use of OPT at a higher level.

For entrepreneurs, OPT rather than CPT may be more attractive because it can have greater flexibility when it comes to the entrepreneur having an ownership interest in the employing business.

Optional Practical Training

The strategy often employed by entrepreneur students transitioning into running their startups is optional practical training or OPT. This is a work program that allows students to engage in temporary employment to gain practical experience in their fields of study.

Students using OPT can start and run a business as long as the student otherwise abides by business law requirements (such as having an appropriate license) and the business is related to what the student studied.

OPT can be used before the student's coursework is finished or after the student's studies are completed. Up to one year of OPT is available generally (see below, however, for special rules relating to Science, Technology, Engineering, and Mathematics (STEM) students). Also, as previously mentioned, USCIS is taking the position that one year of practical training *in total* is available to students, and time spent in CPT would be *subtracted* from available OPT time.

OPT is available only after the student has competed a full academic year. Time spent outside the United States in study abroad programs will not disrupt the counting of a full academic year.

Unlike CPT, OPT employment may not begin unless USCIS has approved an employment authorization document following the approval of an application submitted using Form I-765. If OPT is used while the student is still in school, the student is limited to 20 hours per week of employment during school sessions and full-time work during vacation periods (assuming the student intends to enroll in the next term). Full-time studies must be maintained by those using pre-completion OPT. Students who have completed their coursework and are in the period when they are working on a thesis or dissertation are eligible for part-time pre-completion OPT or full-time post-completion OPT.

For students who elect to use their OPT after completing their programs, full-time work is permitted, and students are expected to complete their 12 months of OPT during the 14-month period following the completion of their studies. For students using OPT before graduation, their part-time work will be deducted from their one year of OPT eligibility at a 50 percent rate. For example, if the student works for six months using pre-completion OPT, then he or she will be considered to have used three months of OPT allotment.

While non-STEM OPT is limited to 12 months, it is for a particular educational level. If a student goes on to pursue a higher degree, then 12 more months of OPT become available. For example, if 12 months of OPT are used after receiving a bachelor's degree and then the student goes on to receive a master's degree, 12 more months of OPT would be available.

Also, the 12 months of eligibility at a particular educational level can be split between programs. For example, a student can use six months of OPT for a bachelor's degree and then if the student enrolls in another bachelor's program, he or she could use the remaining six months.

Unlike CPT, OPT does not require employment to be arranged ahead of time. However, the student is expected to be employed during the OPT period and unemployment is limited to an aggregate of 90 days. Additional rules on unemployment apply to STEM OPT periods and are discussed below.

To secure OPT, the student must work through the school's DSO, who determines the eligibility of the student for OPT. If the DSO decides that the student qualifies, he or she will recommend OPT in SEVIS. The student then submits Form I-765 to USCIS to secure an employment authorization document and the student can begin work after receiving employment authorization and after the start date listed on the employment authorization document. There are also additional requirements for STEM OPT extensions (discussed below).

The I-765 can be filed up to 90 days before being enrolled for one full academic year as long as the period of employment will not start before the completion of the academic year. The I-765 must be filed no later than 60 days after the program's scheduled end date as long as that date is no later than 30 days after the DSO enters the OPT recommendation in SEVIS.

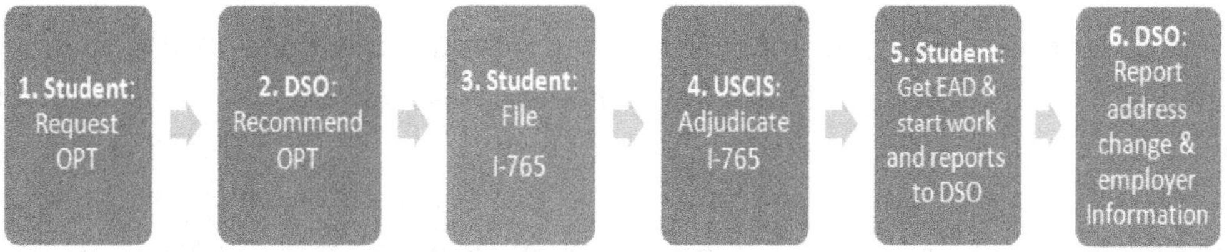

Source: https://studyinthestates.dhs.gov/sevis-help-hub/student-records/fm-student-employment/f-1-optional-practical-training-opt

After post-completion OPT begins, the student must inform the DSO of any changes in the student's name and address, as well as his or her employer's name and address, and the DSO must update SEVIS accordingly within 21 days of being notified. STEM OPT students have additional notification requirements discussed below.

A key issue for entrepreneurs in OPT who desire to remain in the United States and run their companies is the avoidance of a gap in employment authorization when they transition to an H-1B visa, one of the most common routes used to maintain the ability to work in the United States. Students typically graduate in April or May and H-1B start dates begin in October, so it is common for OPT to end with a multi-month period remaining before H-1B status can begin.

Congress has solved this problem by creating something called the "*cap-gap*," which allows students with expiring employment authorization under OPT (who have timely applied for a change to H-1B status and cannot begin work on the H-1B until October 1 because the H-1B allotment of visas for the current year has been used) to have their work authorization automatically extended until October 1 (when new H-1B visas are available) or until the change-of-status petition is rejected.

F-2 spouses and children will have their F-2 status extended during the cap-gap period. If an H-1B application is pending beyond October 1, a student can remain in the United States based on the time it takes for the change-of-status petition to be resolved. However, employment authorization ends on September 30.

F-1 students whose employment authorization expires but are still in legal status (if they are in their 60-day grace period, for example), may not work during the cap-gap period, but their "duration of status" period *is* extended.

F-1s who take advantage of the cap-gap need to request a new "cap-gap" Form I-20 from their DSO that shows eligibility for the extension. The student also must maintain contact with the employer to know if the H-1B petition has been accepted or rejected. The cap-gap I-20 is the document that demonstrates the F-1 student remains in status.

Travel during the cap-gap period is permitted if a student has a valid employment authorization document. But once that document has expired, returning to the United States is risky and DHS recommends not traveling at all, since USCIS will consider the H-1B change-of-status application to be abandoned and re-entry is not permitted until the H-1B is approved by a consulate abroad near the October 1 start date.

As noted above, OPT can be highly useful to an entrepreneur because one can start a company and work for the business while in OPT. The flexibility available with the OPT doesn't last forever—the student will need to convert to another status (like an

H-1B) after a year. But the authors have seen many successful businesses start while the founders were in F-1 OPT status.

STEM OPT

In 2008, U.S. Citizenship and Immigration Services released a rule permitting F-1 students studying in certain science, technology, engineering, and mathematics fields to have the option of obtaining an additional 17 months of OPT beyond the 12 months available to other F-1 students. In March 2016, USCIS modified the rule to allow for up to 24 months OPT for STEM F-1s if an employer can meet additional restrictions. All new STEM OPT applicants filing after March 2016 are covered under the 2016 rules.

The following requirements must be met for the student to qualify for STEM OPT:

1. The student must be in the post-completion 12-month standard OPT period. The STEM OPT extension is permissible even if the student is still working on a thesis or dissertation.
2. The student's degree must be in a qualifying STEM field.[4]
3. The student must have a prospective employer who completes a Form I-983 Training Plan, which must be provided by the student to the DSO.
4. The employer must have an Employer Identification Number and be enrolled in E-Verify.
5. The employment must be paid and for at least 20 hours per week (note this is different from standard post-completion OPT). Students may have more than one STEM OPT employer but must work at least 20 hours per week for each employer.
6. If the DSO determines that the STEM OPT requirements are met, the DSO will update SEVIS and generate a new 24-month Form I-20 with the extension recommendation.
7. The student will submit the following to USCIS within 60 days of the SEVIS update: Form I-765, the I-765 filing fee, the new STEM OPT Form I-20, and evidence of having obtained the STEM degree.

[4] To determine this, the student can consult the DSO (also note that the DHS STEM Designated Degree Program list is online at https://bit.ly/25Jd9hZ).

The qualifying STEM degree can be a degree received previously, so long as it was obtained in the last 10 years and was granted by a U.S. institution. For example, an MBA student with a bachelor's degree in mathematics might qualify for STEM OPT following completion of the MBA. However, if a prior degree is the basis for STEM OPT, the student must have completed the thesis or dissertation and not just the coursework. A second STEM OPT extension is also permitted if a student returns to school and completes a higher-level STEM degree.

The STEM OPT period begins immediately after the date of expiration of the standard OPT period. It is not unusual with an I-765 for the extension period to still be pending at that point. Fortunately, a student is authorized to continue being employed for 180 days after the standard OPT employment authorization period ends.

The employer is required to be enrolled in E-Verify, but perhaps the most intimidating requirement for an employer involves the training plan requirement. The plan must be described on Form I-983 and must address the following:

1. How are the student's assignments with the employer related to the student's STEM degree?
2. How will the assignments with the employer contribute to the student making progress toward professional goals and objectives?
3. How will the employer evaluate the student?
4. How will the employer supervise the student?

The SEVIS instructions for the DSO note that the I-983 training plan description should address the following:

- Explains how the training is directly related to the student's qualifying STEM degree.
- Identifies goals for the STEM practical training opportunity, including specific knowledge, skills, or techniques that will be imparted to the student and explains how those goals will be achieved through the work-based learning opportunity with the employer.
- Describes a performance evaluation process.
- Describes methods of oversight and supervision.

Students on a STEM extension *are* permitted to start businesses and be employed by that business. DHS noted in the 2016 rule's preamble:

> The rule also requires that a student must have a bona fide employer-employee relationship with an employer to obtain a STEM OPT extension. In response to comments received, DHS clarifies that students may be employed

> by start-up businesses, but all regulatory requirements must be met and the student may not provide employer attestations on his or her own behalf.[5]

In other words, students should register their businesses with E-Verify and work full-time. The student should be prepared to show that the business is licensed and the business should relate to the student's degree. Someone else in the business other than the F-1 student will need to sign attestations on behalf of the employer.

The job that serves as the basis for STEM OPT must be for at least 20 hours per week, be directly related to the student's degree, and will assist the student in reaching his or her training goals. It *cannot* be a volunteer or unpaid position. However, the preamble to the 2016 rule states that "alternative compensation may be allowed during a STEM OPT extension as long as the F-1 student can show that he or she is a bona fide employee and his or her compensation, including any ownership interest in the employer entity (such as stock options), is commensurate with the compensation provided to other similarly situated U.S. workers."

The ability to be paid with stock or something similar will, of course, be of interest to some startups. The job's pay and work conditions must be "commensurate with terms and conditions applicable to the employer's similarly situated U.S. workers in the area of employment" and the STEM OPT worker cannot replace a full– or part-time, temporary or permanent U.S. worker.

In the preamble of the 2016 final STEM OPT rule, DHS opined further on the ability of startup businesses to hire STEM OPTs:

> DHS also clarifies that F-1 students seeking STEM OPT extensions may be employed by new 'start-up' businesses so long as all regulatory requirements are met, including that the employer adheres to the training plan requirements, remains in good standing with E-Verify, will provide compensation to the STEM OPT student commensurate to that provided to similarly situated U.S. workers, and has the resources to comply with the proposed training plan. For instance, alternative compensation may be allowed during a STEM OPT extension as long as the F-1 student can show that he or she is a bona fide employee and that his or her compensation, including any ownership interest in the employer entity (such as stock options), is commensurate with the compensation provided to other similarly situated U.S. workers.[6]
>
> In addition, a STEM OPT extension must involve a bona fide employer-employee relationship. Finally, DHS clarifies that under this final rule stu-

[5] 81 Fed.Reg. 13072 (Mar. 11, 2016) par. 447.

[6] 81 Fed. Reg. 13079 (Mar. 11, 2016) par. 523.

> dents may seek practical training opportunities with start-up businesses, so long as all regulatory requirements are met. Such students may not provide employer attestations on their own behalf.[7]

One area that remains fluid at the time of writing this chapter is whether STEM OPT can be used by F-1s being placed at third-party worksites by an employer. In January 2018, USCIS changed its website to add numerous new restrictions on such employment. Shortly after announcing the policy, the agency was sued and the case has not been decided. The reader is advised to consult counsel before accepting a position that involves placement at third-party sites.

DHS states in the 2016 rule preamble that F-1 students in STEM OPT extensions (including those whose application for STEM OPT extension is pending) may travel abroad and seek re-entry to the United States during the extension period as long as they have a valid, unexpired F-1 visa and a current I-20 endorsed for re-entry by the DSO within the last six months.

STEM OPT F-1s must submit a "validation report" to their school's DSO every six months after beginning STEM OPT and when ending F-1 status (1) upon leaving the United States, (2) changing to another nonimmigrant or immigrant category, (3) changing educational levels at the same institution, (4) transferring institutions, or (5) upon the end of the OPT period, whichever comes first. The report must be submitted by the student within 10 days of each six-month validation due date. The DSO will then update SEVIS noting the submission of the report.

The report must contain the following:

- The student's full legal name;
- The student's SEVIS ID number;
- The student's current mailing and residential address;
- The name and address of the student's current employer; and
- The date the student began working for the current employer.

Additionally, the student has 10 days to report changes in name and address and if the student stops working for an employer or starts working for a new employer. If there are material changes to the training plan submitted on Form I-983, the student must notify the DSO "at the earliest available opportunity."[8]

---

[7] 81 Fed. Reg. 13079 (Mar. 11, 2016) par. 517.

[8] 8 Code of Federal Regulations (CFR) §214.2(f)(10)(ii)(C)(9)(ii).

Employers are required to notify the DSO within five days of the termination or departure of a student. Like the student, the employer must notify the DSO "at the earliest available opportunity"[9] when there are material changes to the training plan.

Unemployment

Finally, there are restrictions on a STEM OPT F-1's unemployment. While a job offer is not a requirement for standard post-completion OPT, both standard and STEM OPT rules restrict *how long* an F-1 may be unemployed during the OPT periods.

The rules are as follows:

- During *standard* post-completion OPT, the student can be unemployed for no more than 90 days in aggregate; and
- During the 24-month STEM OPT period, the limit is raised to an aggregate of 150 days, which includes both the standard and the STEM OPT period.

Closures during holidays and weekends are not considered unemployment and being outside the United States does not normally toll the unemployment limits.

Dependents

A spouse and any unmarried children *under the age of 21* can be admitted in F-2 status as dependents of an F-1 student if they are accompanying the F-1. They can also follow to join after the F-1's entry.

To qualify, the F-2 applicant must present evidence of the following to a Department of State consular officer and a Customs and Border Protection port-of-entry officer:

- The applicant is the spouse of the F-1 (via a marriage certificate) or the unmarried minor child of the F-1 (via a birth certificate);
- The applicant has sufficient funds to cover his or her expenses or that other arrangements have been made to cover those expenses;
- The F-2 will be accompanying or following-to-join the F-1 and that the F-1 is enrolled in a full course of study or is working in approved practical training; and
- The F-2 intends to depart the United States upon the termination of F-1 student status.

---

[9] *Id.*

U.S. immigration law recognizes same-sex marriages and the same documentation is required of a same-sex spouse as a heterosexual spouse. However, civil unions and other arrangements that are not legally recognized as a marriage will not qualify a person for F-2 status. In such cases, the Department of State has had a longstanding policy of allowing people in such relationships to petition for a visitor visa. Under 9 *Foreign Affairs Manual* (FAM) 402.2-4(B)(5), the B-2 classification is appropriate for people who are "members of the household of another alien in long-term nonimmigrant status, but who are not eligible for derivative status under that alien's visa classification." Note that this also covers elderly parents and other family members who are not spouses or unmarried minor children.

F-2 students are issued their own I-20s by a DSO and have a separate record in SEVIS. The F-2 I-20s must be presented to a consular officer and a port-of-entry officer at the time of the visa application and at the arrival at a port of entry. The F-2s will also have a separate I-94 that is typically marked "duration of status" like the F-1. F-2s may travel and be readmitted using a valid, unexpired visa and along with the F-2's I-20, and with documentation that the F-1 is maintaining status.

F-2s are not authorized to work. An F-2 who wishes to work *must obtain a change of status to another visa category that is appropriate for work.* F-2s are also not permitted to engage in a full course of study unless they change status to F-1. However, an F-2 spouse or F-2 child may enroll in less than a full course of study (typically 12+ hours a semester and charged at a full course rate by the school) even if that coursework leads to a degree. F-2 children are, however, permitted to study full-time in any elementary or secondary school (kindergarten through 12th grade).

Maintaining Status

Finally, it is worth reminding readers that maintaining student status is now more critical than ever. In August 2018, USCIS released a memorandum changing its policy on how it treats students who have failed to maintain their student status. Prior to August 2018, students were not subject to the three– and ten-year bars on re-entering the United States if they had "D/S" noted on their I-94. D/S, as mentioned previously, means "duration of status."

People who overstay by 180 days to a year are subject to a three-year bar from re-entering the United States, while those who overstay for more than a year are subject to a ten-year bar from re-entering. The three– and ten-year bars have largely not been an issue for most students because their I-94s do not have an actual expiration date that serves as the basis for determining if the bars apply.

USCIS is seeking to start the clock for the bars based on when a student violates his or her status. This would be the case even if the violation is based on something that was the school's fault (such as making a mistake in SEVIS). The policy was prevented from taking effect because of a lawsuit, though readers should be aware in case the agency ultimately prevails in litigation

Some issues can be corrected in SEVIS by the DSO and some the DSO can request of DHS via SEVIS. Students can sometimes get their status reinstated by USCIS if a violation has occurred.

USCIS may reinstate a student's status if the student:

- Has not been out of status for more than five months at the time of filing a request for reinstatement;
- Does not have a record of repeated or willful violations of immigration regulations;
- Is currently pursuing, or intending to pursue, a full course of study in the immediate future at the school that issued the Form I-20;
- Has not engaged in unauthorized employment;
- Is not deportable on any ground other than overstaying or failing to maintain status; and
- Establishes that the violation resulted from circumstances beyond the student's control (such as serious illness or injury, closure of the institution, a disaster, or an oversight on the part of the DSO).

If USCIS reinstates the student's status, USCIS will endorse the student's copy of the Form I-20 indicating that the status has been reinstated. USCIS will update SEVIS to reflect the decision.

The need to reinstate one's status is more critical than ever given the new policy on re-entry bars. In the past, departing the United States and re-entering might have "cleaned up" a status violation and the student could resume studies without consequence. Now, departing may trigger a three– or ten-year bar on re-entering. On the other hand, applying for reinstatement and getting denied also carries the risk of the student being placed in removal proceedings; therefore, students are advised to consult immigration counsel regarding risks of the various options.

4

ENTERING THE UNITED STATES FOR EMPLOYMENT: THE H-1B VISA

The H-1B is likely the most well-known employment-based visa category. This program allows for U.S. companies (*petitioners*) to employ foreign nationals (*beneficiaries*) in what are known as *specialty occupations*. These are positions that require theoretical and practical application of highly specialized knowledge and also require a bachelor's degree (or equivalent) as the minimum requirement for entry into the occupation.

It is the position itself, and not the individual, that must meet the threshold specialty occupation requirements. The regulations[1] explain that these occupations are often in the following categories, but not limited to:

- architecture
- engineering
- mathematics
- physical sciences
- social sciences
- medicine and health
- education
- business specialties
- accounting
- law
- theology
- the arts

Many requirements of the H-1B make it a less desirable visa option for founders and key members of early-stage startups. However, every entrepreneur in the United States, particularly in Science, Technology, Engineering, and Mathematics (STEM)

[1] 8 Code of Federal Regulations (CFR) §214.2(h)(4)(ii).

fields, should be familiar with the H-1B since it will come up frequently with employees as you seek to recruit and develop top international talent.

The Lottery

The Immigration and Nationality Act requires that 65,000 applicants receive H-1Bs each fiscal year,[2] as well as an additional 20,000 persons holding U.S. master's degrees.[3] Far more than 85,000 people apply each year; therefore, U.S. Citizenship and Immigration Services (USCIS) *randomly selects* from the applications it receives in March each year in what is known as the H-1B lottery.[4] In the 2019 fiscal year (April 2018), USCIS received 190,098 applications (down from 199,000 the year before, and 236,000 in 2016). If a person's application is chosen in the lottery, the case is then adjudicated, though not necessarily approved.

When considering if an H-1B is the right option, it is important to consider that the H-1B is based on the government's fiscal year, which starts October 1. Even if selected and approved, new employees could not begin their time in H-1B status until that date at the earliest. There is one exception, however. F-1 students working on optional practical training (OPT) at the time their H-1B petitions are filed as *a change of status* can continue to work due to what is known as a *cap gap*, where F-1 status and work authorization are automatically extended to September 30 so long as the H-1B remains pending or is approved.[5]

It is important to note that a person only has to be selected in the lottery *once*. If selected in the lottery on a petition from Company A, that person can later be petitioned by Company B without having to go through the lottery again, simply by transferring the H-1B.

Some employers are exempt from the H-1B lottery altogether. In most cases, they must fit in one of the following categories:[6]

- Institutions of higher education.

---

[2] Immigration and Nationality Act (INA) §214(g)(1)(A).

[3] INA §214(g)(1)(A)(5)(C).

[4] For fiscal year 2021 (October 2020 through September 2021), USCIS instituted a new H-1B lottery process. For prior years, applicants submitted complete H-1B petitions during the first week of April prior to the start of the fiscal year. For FY 2021, applicants filled out an online form in March 2020 requesting an H-1B number and, if selected, could submit an actual H-1B petition beginning in April 2020. The new process is described at https://bit.ly/LotteryProcess.

[5] *USCIS Handbook for Employers* M-274, 7.4.5 Cap-Gap www.uscis.gov/i-9-central/745-cap-gap.

[6] 8 CFR §214.2(h)(8)(ii)(F).

- Nonprofit entities related to or affiliated with an institution of higher education if one of the following is true:
  - The nonprofit entity is connected to or associated with an institution of higher education through shared ownership or control by the same board or federation;
  - The nonprofit entity is operated by an institution of higher education;
  - The nonprofit entity is attached to an institution of higher education as a member, branch, cooperative, or subsidiary; or
  - The nonprofit entity has entered into a formal written affiliation agreement with an institution of higher education that establishes an active working relationship between the nonprofit entity and the institution of higher education for the purposes of research or education, and a fundamental activity of the nonprofit entity is to directly contribute to the research or education mission of the institution of higher education.

Cap Exempt versus Cap Subject

Cap-exempt institutions may file H-1B petitions *anytime of the year* with start dates at any time. This is a huge advantage compared to *cap-subject* employers who can only put their employees in the H-1B lottery in April of each year and hope they are randomly selected. Working on a cap-exempt H-1B does not allow the recipient to then transfer to a cap-subject employer though, because the recipient has not been counted against the cap. Even a founder who has never been through the lottery may be working on an H-1B at a cap-exempt employer, but then will still need to go through the lottery to begin working at his or her own startup (since it will be cap-subject).

On the other hand, an employee may have more than one *concurrent* H-1B, so if one H-1B is for a *cap-exempt* H-1B employer, that employee may also work for a *cap-subject* employer without being selected in the lottery—so long as they maintain the cap-exempt employment. In this scenario, the person is able to apply the cap-exempt status to all his or her H-1Bs, based on the one cap-exempt employer.

This scenario can be used in the startup context as more universities have begun initiating incubator and accelerator programs affiliated with the university. The university is generally cap-exempt, so founders may join programs like that in roles such as Entrepreneur-in-Residence, and then file a concurrent H-1B with their own startup so they have the ability to both work with the school's accelerator and the their own company.

Also, entrepreneurs working closely with universities should explore ways to take advantage of cap exemption. If students from a local university are gaining credited experience in education or research at a company, a formal affiliation agreement may make them a cap-exempt employer.

Each specific affiliation is worth analyzing before committing to the lottery. Keep in mind, though, that any claim of cap-exemption needs to be thoroughly explained and documented for USCIS approval. This usually involves submitting the contract or affiliation agreement between the organization and the university.

Whether employees are cap-subject or cap-exempt, H-1Bs will be approved for a period of *no more than three years*. Further, every person is limited to *a total of six years* of H-1B time *unless* there is an approved I-140 (employment-based green card petition).

I-140s are covered in more detail in the chapters addressing permanent residence, but it is important to note that an approved I-140 provides eligibility for unlimited three-year H-1B extensions beyond the normal six-year cap. Only days spent *inside the United States* in H-1B or L-1 status count toward the six years. A person may recapture anytime spent outside of the United States or in the United States in another status. For example, if a person comes back and forth as a visitor or spends time vacationing outside the United States, those days can be recaptured and added back on to the six years.

Dependent Status

The spouses and children of an H-1B holder are entitled to *H-4* status. The derivative family members' status in the United States, however, is tied to the H-1B maintaining his or her lawful H-1B status (this is done by staying employed, complying with the terms of the H-1B, etc.). In most cases, H-4s are not eligible for work authorization. The exception to the rule is that when an H-1B holder has an approved I-140, his or her spouse may apply for and receive work authorization, known as H-4 employment authorization.[7]

The H-4 employment authorization document option tends to be used by individuals who are facing backlogs rather than those with current priority dates. People from countries for which visas are generally available, who have an approved I-140, can simply file their green card applications and complete the process of becoming permanent residents. The green card process is covered in more depth in Chapter 11.

[7] 8 CFR §214.2(h)(9)(iv).

Specialty Occupation

In order to qualify for an H-1B, much of the scrutiny is on the position itself—not just the foreign national, since the position must be established as a *specialty occupation*. According to the regulation:

> Specialty occupation means an occupation which requires theoretical and practical application of a body of highly specialized knowledge in fields of human endeavor including, but not limited to, architecture, engineering, mathematics, physical sciences, social sciences, medicine and health, education, business specialties, accounting, law, theology, and the arts, and which requires the attainment of a *bachelor's degree or higher in a specific specialty*, or its equivalent, as a minimum for entry into the occupation in the United States.[8] [Emphasis applied].

In 2018, the Trump administration began attacking H-1B applications, claiming that positions (not the individuals) do not qualify as specialty occupations if they do not require a degree in a *specific* field. This claim is based on the language in the above regulation requiring "the attainment of a bachelor's degree or higher in a *specific* specialty."[9]

According to the regulation, there are four ways to prove a position qualifies as a specialty occupation. The regulations list the test in the alternative, meaning only one of the four must be met. However, the Trump administration is suggesting all four prongs should be met. As per the regulation, to qualify as a specialty occupation, the position must meet one of the following criteria:

1. A baccalaureate or higher degree or its equivalent is normally the minimum requirement for entry into the particular position;
2. The degree requirement is common to the industry in parallel positions among similar organizations or, in the alternative, an employer may show that its particular position is so complex or unique that it can be performed only by an individual with a degree;
3. The employer normally requires a degree or its equivalent for the position; *or*

[8] 8 CFR §214.2(h)(4)(ii).

[9] *Id.*

4. The nature of the specific duties is so specialized and complex that knowledge required to perform the duties is usually associated with the attainment of a baccalaureate or higher degree. [10]

The practical effect of the Trump-era interpretation that all four criteria must be met is that USCIS now challenges H-1B applications where companies will accept multiple degrees for the position. For example, a startup may be petitioning its founder and chief technology officer (CTO) and lists the acceptable degrees for the position as Computer Science, Management Information Systems (MIS), or Engineering. USCIS would now argue that the job does not qualify as a specialty occupation because there is no specific degree required; instead there are a number of possible degrees. To make matters worse, USCIS will argue that Engineering and Business are too broad and nonspecific since there are many subfields of engineering or business.

While this is frustrating for all H-1B employers and visa holders, this problem is made worse for founders because they often wear many hats and have executive roles with broad responsibilities, such as chief executive officer (CEO), chief operating officer (COO), or chief technology officer (CTO).

A baccalaureate or higher degree or its equivalent is normally the minimum requirement for entry into the particular position

Under the first prong of the specialty occupation test, USCIS determines the "normal" minimum requirements of a position by looking to the Department of Labor's (DOL) *Occupational Outlook Handbook* (OOH) for guidance. This is despite DOL explicitly stating that is not the intended purpose of the OOH. The OOH is the database of information on categories of occupations created by the U.S. Bureau of Labor and Statistics, which is part of DOL.

The OOH has individual pages for *some* occupations and within those pages there is a section on "How to Become One." These subpages often have some generalized information on the degrees people earn before moving into the given position, or degrees people should pursue if trying to get into the field. The issue is that if the OOH is vague in its description of a given position, USCIS will then claim that no *specific* degree is "normally" required for the position. The example affecting founders most frequently is the OOH page for top executives. The OOH states:

[10] 8 CFR §214.2(h)(4)(iii)(A).

> Many top executives have a bachelor's or master's degree in business administration or in an area related to their field of work. Top executives in the public sector often have a degree in business administration, public administration, law, or the liberal arts. Top executives of large corporations often have a master's degree in business administration (MBA).[11]

The OOH is clearly making a general observation of the normal degrees held by America's Top Executives. However, USCIS would take this to mean that any number of degrees could prepare someone to be a CEO; therefore, no specific degree is "normally" required, meaning it fails this prong of the specialty occupation test. This reading of the regulations and manipulation of the OOH is despite court rulings that say otherwise. For example, the court in *Residential Finance Corp. v. USCIS* held:

> [T]here is no apparent requirement that the specialized study need be in a single academic discipline as opposed to a specialized course of study in related business specialties. Defendant's implicit premise that the title of a field of study controls ignores the realities of the statutory language involved and the obvious intent behind them. The knowledge and not the title of the degree is what is important. Diplomas rarely come bearing occupation-specific majors. What is required is an occupation that requires highly specialized knowledge and a prospective employee who has attained the credentialing indicating possession of that knowledge.[12]

For this reason, founders may have an easier time qualifying for an H-1B if they hold technical degrees and work on the technical side of operations. For example, the co-founder CTO with a *computer science degree* may be able to demonstrate that his or her duties are most closely related to those of a *software developer*. According to the OOH:

> Software developers usually have a bachelor's degree in computer science and strong computer programming skills.[13]

In some cases, the OOH is just not going to have pertinent information due to its limited number of entries, or the language will be too vague. While USCIS might jump to consider this conclusive, remember that there are still three other ways to establish a position as a specialty occupation.

---

[11] https://bit.ly/OOHMgmt.

[12] *Residential Finance Corp. v. USCIS*, 839 F. Supp. 2d 985 (S.D. Ohio 2012).

[13] https://bit.ly/OOHIT.

The degree requirement is common to the industry in parallel positions among similar organizations or, in the alternative, an employer may show that its particular position is so complex or unique that it can be performed only by an individual with a degree

Some founders may turn to the second possible prong.[14] This can also be a frustrating test under current USCIS trends because it requires evidence of what comparable companies are requiring and how they are similar. This is most commonly accomplished by pulling ads for job openings from major job websites. However, USCIS will then want proof that the companies are actually similarly situated. It is helpful to include company bios showing they are within the same industry, same geographic area, and have a similar number of employees.

Affidavits can be obtained from other people in the industry attesting to the normal requirements for similar positions within the industry; or expert opinion letters can be used from objective outside writers, such as professors or recruiters, attesting to what is normal for that type of position in the given industry."

The employer normally requires a degree or its equivalent for the position

The third prong is normally a strong argument."[15] For founders, however, there is probably not another CEO, so there will not be evidence that everyone in the same position holds the same degree. Nonetheless, evidence that everyone, including the founder, holds a degree in the specific field closely related to his or her position can be presented. This can be done by presenting an organization chart accompanied by either copies of the whole team's diplomas or a statement listing everyone's education credentials signed by the company.

The nature of the specific duties is so specialized and complex that knowledge required to perform the duties is usually associated with the attainment of a baccalaureate or higher degree

The fourth option[16] is usually a strong argument for a founder, given the wide-range of complex duties, and is presented by using a letter of support from a co-founder or member of the board of directors detailing the duties and responsibilities. Providing samples of the specialized work product whenever possible is helpful, as

[14] 8 CFR §214.2(h)(4)(iii)(A)(2).

[15] 8 CFR §214.2(h)(4)(iii)(A)(3).

[16] 8 CFR §214.2(h)(4)(iii)(A)(4).

is explaining how the founder's education provides the specialized knowledge needed to perform such work.

The Trump-era attack on "specialty occupation" needs to be considered from the outset when deciding whether an H-1B makes sense for a startup. Take into consideration that USCIS disfavors general MBAs, which many founders have, because they argue these are general business degrees and not specialized. If a founder with an MBA is trying to qualify for an H-1B, it may be wise to look to the underlying degree as the qualifying degree, and the MBA as additional evidence. For example, co-founder of a biotech company with a *bachelor's in biomedical engineering* and a *master's in business administration* could rely on the undergraduate degree. Or, co-founder of a fintech company with a *bachelor's in finance* and a *master's in business administration* could do the same.

Wage Requirements

Once an entrepreneur has identified a position as a specialty occupation, he or she should consider that H-1Bs have wage requirements unlike most other nonimmigrant visa categories. This factor may be unattractive to founders wanting to take a low salary to keep burn rate low; and the compensation the founder is receiving in equity is not factored into the prevailing wage. Therefore, it is important to determine at the outset whether it makes sense to pay the beneficiary at least the prevailing wage paid to workers in similar occupations (but not necessarily at a startup) in the geographic area.

The prevailing wage can be researched in the U.S. Department of Labor's Foreign Labor Certification Data Center Online Wage Library.[17]

Once the geographic location is selected, occupations are broken down into DOL's *Standard Occupational Classification* (SOC) System, which collects data on occupations by category. The SOC system contains 867 occupations but still struggles to stay current with technology and modern industry. This can be challenging for many startups since there are obvious missing occupation categories for today's workforce, such as *Data Scientist* or *Product Manager*.

In cases where there is not an obvious fit, the duties of the position—rather than the title—should be the primary factor in selecting an appropriate SOC code. Employers can opt to file a *Prevailing Wage Request* with DOL and have DOL determine the proper SOC code and wage level. The advantage here is that USCIS will

---

[17] www.flcdatacenter.com/oeswizardstart.aspx.

not likely come back and argue that the wrong SOC code or wage level was selected since the determination was made by DOL instead of the petitioner. These determinations regularly take three to five months, so they are rarely practical for H-1B filings. Employers may pay to have private wage surveys performed to determine an appropriate wage.

Aside from narrowing down the correct occupation category, employers must identify the correct wage level for the given position. Every SOC code has a wage level of I–IV.

- **Level I** wages represent entry-level positions.
- **Level II** wages are for positions that require more independent decision-making and complex tasks.
- **Level III** wages are for more experienced staff members who may supervise others.
- **Level IV** wages are for employees in supervisory or managerial positions with sufficient experience.[18]

In 2017, the Trump administration began attacking Level I filings, claiming that many jobs could not be both specialty occupations and entry level. This is, of course, untrue since first-year lawyers, for example, typically fill entry-level attorney positions but still meet (if not exceed) the threshold baccalaureate requirements. While many Level I challenges were ultimately overcome, many people have become much more intentional on selecting the appropriate wage level.

Some Level II positions have seen challenges as well, particularly when USCIS believes that the petitioner is simply picking the highest wage level that the salary can satisfy. Thought should go into the strategy of picking the correct SOC code and wage level at the very beginning of the H-1B process in order to not haunt the petition down the road.

This process can be a bigger challenge for co-founders and very early-stage startups for the following reasons: (1) similar to the specialty occupation discussion, founders often paint themselves into a bit of a corner due to the SOC code and wage level processes; (2) most founders hold job titles such as founder, CEO, COO, or something along those lines; and (3) as entrepreneurs, founders tend to wear many hats ranging from general management to technical research and product development.

[18] Employment and Training Administration Prevailing Wage Determination Policy Guidance Nonagricultural Immigration Programs Revised November 2009.

For these reasons, it can be difficult to find an occupation code other than *Chief Executive* and *General Operations Manager*. Both of these job codes come with very broad duties and very high prevailing wages. The CEO of an early stage startup, however, almost never has a salary comparable to the CEOs of the banks and large companies in the same geographic area.

For example, the prevailing wage for a *General and Operations Manager* in San Francisco, CA, at Level III is $159,182 per year, and at Level IV is $202,030 per year.[19] This may lead people to want to select lower wage levels like Level I or Level II, but these are rarely appropriate and often challenged since the job duties entail managing people, operations, fundraising, hiring, firing, etc.

Furthermore, most early-stage ventures are focused on keeping spending low and extending their runway. The prevailing wage requirements of the H-1B are not very conducive to conserving cash flow when it comes to company executives. Equity and other benefits need to be disclosed in the H-1B petition, but they are not factored into whether the beneficiary's salary is equal to or greater than the prevailing wage. Similar to other pros and cons of H-1Bs for startup founders, the wage requirements may make more sense for the co-founder who is spending most of his or her time on the technical side instead of the business side.

Labor Condition Applications

Whether filing a cap case in the lottery, a cap-exempt petition, an extension for a person already in H-1B status, or the transfer of a new hire's H-1B, the process will begin by filing a labor condition application (LCA) with DOL. In order to submit an LCA, the company must first provide its Federal Employer Identification Number (FEIN) to the Office of Foreign Labor Certification for verification.

The LCA (Form ETA 9035) contains specifics of the position including: title, start date, worksite location, the wage to be paid, and the prevailing wage for the SOC code and wage level that was chosen. The form is then submitted online and DOL typically certifies the LCA within seven business days. A certified and signed copy of the LCA is eventually submitted to USCIS as part of the H-1B petition. Once certified, an LCA is valid for *up to three years*. An H-1B cannot be approved without a valid LCA, so mistakes on the LCA can be costly.

---

[19] https://bit.ly/OESdata.

Additionally, the employer must post a Notice of Filing Labor Condition Application. The posting is to inform all employees of the company that an LCA has been or will be filed for an H-1B worker.

The notice must include the following information:

- job title;
- salary;
- start date;
- end date; and
- work location.

This notice must be *posted for 10 business days* at work locations.[20] Furthermore, one must list the dates that the notice was posted and removed, and it must be signed and dated by a company official.

The LCA is intended to serve two related purposes: (1) ensuring that U.S. wages are not depressed by the hiring of foreign labor; and (2) that foreign workers are not exploited. On this document, the employer makes specific representations regarding the conditions under which the foreign worker was hired and will be employed. These attestations are as follows:

- The employer will pay the required wage, which is the greater of the prevailing wage or the actual wage paid to other employees in the same position.
- The employment of H-1B workers will not adversely affect the working conditions of U.S. workers.
- When the LCA was filed, there was no strike, lockout or other work stoppage because of a labor dispute.
- The H-1B worker will be given a copy of the LCA, and the employer has notified the bargaining representative if the job is unionized, or if not, has posted in a conspicuous place notice that an LCA was filed.

The Public Access File

Within one business day of filing the LCA, the employer must establish a public access file (PAF) that may be viewed by any person. The PAF must contain the following items:[21]

- A copy of the filed LCA and cover pages (once the LCA is certified in about a week after filing, you will add a copy of the signed certified LCA to the PAF).
- A copy of the LCA Instructions (10 pages).

---

[20] 20 CFR §655.734(a)(1)(ii).

[21] 20 CFR §655.760.

- Documentation of the wage rate to be paid and a copy of the documentation used to establish the prevailing wage which explains how the employer calculated the prevailing wage used in the LCA.
- A memorandum from the employer documenting that the H-1B beneficiary will be paid an amount equal to or higher than the actual wage paid to other employees with similar experience and qualifications and explaining the system used to determine the actual wage.
- Acknowledgment that the H-1B employee has received a copy of the LCA.
- Documentation that the LCA has been provided to the Collective Bargaining Representative OR documentation that the LCA was posted at the work site or provided to employees' electronically.
- A summary of the benefits offered to the employer's U.S. workers in the same occupational classification as the H-1B worker. Any differences in benefits need to be explained.
- If the employer undergoes a change in corporate structure (such as a merger), a sworn statement from a responsible officer of the new employing entity that it accepts all the obligations, liabilities and undertakings under the LCAs filed by the predecessor employer, together with a list of each affected LCA, their date of certification and a description of the actual wage system and the Federal Employer ID Number of the new employer.
- Where the employer uses the Internal Revenue Service (IRS) definition of a "single employer," a list of any entity included as part of the single employer when making H-1B determinations.
- For employers who are H-1B dependent or a "willful violator" and it indicates an employee is exempt from the dependency requirements on account of wage or degree, a list of exempt H-1B employees and a summary of recruitment methods used and the time frames of recruitment of U.S. workers.

The PAF may be stored in print and/or electronically and must be made available to any "interested or aggrieved" party who has "notified DOL of his or her/its interest or concern in the administrator's determination." The employer may also need to demonstrate maintenance of a PAF if DOL audits the employer.

The PAFs must be retained at the employer's place of business *in the United States* or at the place of employment for *a period of one year beyond the last date on which any H-1B nonimmigrant covered in the LCA is employed* (whether the employee quits or is terminated).[22] If no H-1B workers were actually employed under the LCA (such as if the worker chooses a different employer or the application is not selected in the H-1B lottery), the PAF must be retained for *one year from the date the LCA either expired or was withdrawn.* Also, there are no exceptions when an employee becomes a permanent resident.

[22] 20 CFR §655.760(c).

Required payroll records for H-1B employees and similarly employed U.S. workers must be retained for *a period of three years from the date of the creation of the records.*[23] If there is a DOL enforcement action, all payroll records must be retained until the enforcement proceeding is completed.

If more than one LCA has been filed for a worker, separate PAFs must be created and the retention clock on each will run independently. If one of the LCAs is not used, the employer could withdraw the LCA and the one-year clock for retention would begin at that point.

If an LCA was filed, but no H-1B petition was filed with USCIS relying on the LCA, the retention rules still apply. The employer could withdraw the LCA and wait a year before destroying the PAF. Otherwise, the PAF must be retained until *one year after the LCA expires.*

Once the LCA has been certified and the public access file created, the actual H-1B petition needs to be filed with USCIS using Form I-129. The I-129 contains the information on the petitioner, beneficiary, and LCA for USCIS.

The Filing

The forms themselves might seem like a formality, with decisions really being based on the evidence in the petition, but there are serious decisions to be made in how they are completed. Most notably, a decision has to be made on whether the beneficiary will complete a *change of status* upon approval or if the beneficiary should *consular process*. If a foreign national is *already in* the United States in a lawful status, he or she may file for a change of status. In this case, if the H-1B petition is approved, then the approval will contain a *new* I-94 documenting that the foreign national's status has automatically been changed from the previous status to H-1B status. For example, a student completing OPT would change status from F-1 to H-1B upon receiving the approval with the new I-94.

If the foreign national is *not in* the United States at the time of filing, a change of status cannot be completed. Furthermore, if a person files for a change of status but leaves the United States while it is pending, he or she abandons the change of status even though the person does not abandon the underlying H-1B petition. In these circumstances and many others, the beneficiary will need to consular process upon approval.

---

[23] *Id.*

When an H-1B is approved for consular processing, USCIS issues the approval notice but not a new I-94. From there, the beneficiary must apply to the Department of State for a new visa that will be processed at a U.S. consulate or embassy abroad. Once the physical H-1B visa has been approved at the consulate and printed in the beneficiary's passport, he or she can travel to the United States and be admitted using that visa. Once entered, the person will have a new I-94 showing he or she has entered the United States in H-1B status.

A case-by-case analysis should be used in deciding whether a petition should be submitted as a *change of status* or *consular processing*. The foreign national's location, family members, current status, immigration history, travel plans, employer needs, and many more factors need to be considered. [24]

Most startup co-founders will become familiar with the H-1B as they try to hire top talent in the United States. For many employees, it will be a well-suited visa category, particularly in professional industries such as technology, engineering, finance, and medicine.

Employer-Employee Relationship

H-1Bs require the petitioner and beneficiary have an Employer-Employee relationship. In its simplest form, this means the petitioner may hire, pay, fire, supervise, or otherwise control the work of the foreign national. This raises some distinct challenges for the founder of a company seeking an H-1B as an employee. In 2010, USCIS issued a memo further expanding on what an Employer-Employee relationship is for H-1B purposes.[25] The memo, commonly referred to as "*The Neufeld Memo*," explained that many factors would be considered in determining whether a qualifying relationship exists, including the following (with no one factor being decisive):

- Does the petitioner supervise the beneficiary and is such supervision off-site or on-site?

[24] As the authors were completing this book, the Trump administration released a Proclamation that dramatically changed the calculation regarding consular processing or changing status in the United States. Proclamation 20052 (signed June 22, 2020) barred the issuance of certain H-1B, H-2B, J-1, and L-1 visas as well as dependent visas in those categories. The order expires December 31, 2020, and it is not clear if the measure will survive litigation. The order may also die either because President Donald Trump chooses not to extend it or the inauguration of a new president leads to the order being rescinded (a near certainty if Vice President Joe Biden wins the 2020 presidential election).

[25] "Determining Employer-Employee Relationship for Adjudication of H-1B Petitions, Including Third Party Placements," (*posted* Jan. 8, 2010) AILA Doc. No. 10011363.

- If the supervision is off-site, how does the petitioner maintain such supervision, *i.e.*, weekly calls, reporting back to main office routinely, or site visits by the petitioner?
- Does the petitioner have the right to control the work of the beneficiary on a day-to-day basis if such control is required?
- Does the petitioner provide the tools or instrumentalities needed for the beneficiary to perform the duties of employment?
- Does the petitioner hire, pay, and have the ability to fire the beneficiary?
- Does the petitioner evaluate the work-product of the beneficiary, *i.e.*, progress/performance reviews?
- Does the petitioner claim the beneficiary for tax purposes?
- Does the petitioner provide the beneficiary any type of employee benefits?
- Does the beneficiary use proprietary information of the petitioner in order to perform the duties of employment?
- Does the beneficiary produce an end-product that is directly linked to the petitioner's line of business?
- Does the petitioner have the ability to control the manner and means in which the work product of the beneficiary is accomplished?

The Neufeld memorandum was challenged and in June 2020, USCIS ended up rescinding the memorandum. In a new memorandum, the agency states:

> The officer should apply the existing regulatory definition in assessing whether an employer and a beneficiary have an employer-employee relationship. The officer should consider whether the petitioner has established that it meets at least one of the 'hire, pay, fire, supervise, or otherwise control the work of" factors with respect to the beneficiary … The officer may not apply the prior rescinded guidance.[26]

Founders and majority shareholders will face challenges, however, if they cannot show an "outside entity which can exercise control over the beneficiary." The most common solution to this problem is the creation of a board of directors that has the power to control the founder as an employee. This solution is one of many examples where a strong conflict may exist between smart *business strategy* and smart *immigration strategy*. Giving other people the ability to fire the founder from the company he or she created is a decision that should not be taken lightly—no matter the possible immigration benefit.

To satisfy this requirement for the business owner with a majority (or a large percentage) of the share, many boards of directors consist of the beneficiary co-founder, co-founder, and advisor, all with *equal* voting power. Each person has to

[26] USCIS Policy Memorandum, PM-602-0114, June 17, 2020.

assess his or her comfort with a set-up like the one described above, and discussions with a business lawyer are advised. Notwithstanding, a three-person board of directors given the authority by majority vote to control employees in the ways described above can be sufficient for H-1B purposes and can establish a successful Employer-Employee relationship.

Given the Neufeld memo's existence for 10 years as well as the new lawsuit-driven rescission that happened just as this book was being completed, it is too early to say how strict the agency will adjudicate H-1Bs where the beneficiary is a founder of the company. The authors believe that the new guidance should be an easier burden for entrepreneurs to meet since other co-founders or a board of directors should be able to more easily show one of factors in the new memo: "hire, pay, fire, supervise, or otherwise control the work of…"

In submitting persuasive evidence of the employer-employee relationship, there are still certain criteria from the longstanding Neufeld era that could be helpful for co-founder H-1Bs, such as showing the company is withholding taxes on the beneficiary's paystubs or providing employee benefits (usually pretty easy to demonstrate). Ultimately, the board or other founders' ability to remove the beneficiary is still the most persuasive evidence of an employer-employee relationship.

Ability to Pay

The next challenge many startup petitioners will see relates to the ability to pay the beneficiary the prevailing wage. A company does not have to be profitable at the time it files a petition for an employee, but USCIS will want evidence that the wage listed on the LCA can be paid to the beneficiary. In general, audited financials or the most recent corporate tax return will suffice. If the founder is still bootstrapping, he or she may provide company bank statements showing enough cash to support the LCA. If closing a round of funding, the petitioner may provide the convertible notes, the Simple Agreement for Future Equity (SAFE), or a copy of the term sheet to show the coming infusion of cash. There are many ways to address ability to pay, but the key is addressing it in the *initial filing* or one can expect to receive a *Request for Evidence* (RFE) on the subject.

Other H-1B Startup Challenges

Sufficient Work

USCIS often requests additional evidence that startups have sufficient specialty occupation work available for the beneficiary. This is particularly true when the startup does not submit company financials showing significant sales, as mentioned above, leaving the adjudicator to wonder whether work will exist for the entire period requested (often three years). Employers can work to prevent this issue (or respond to an RFE if the issue arises) by submitting formation documents to show the company is, in fact, real. Marketing materials or pitch decks to show what the company does can be submitted as well. It is helpful to provide samples of valid contracts with customers to show ongoing or upcoming work, or even signed commitments to work together once there is a product to market. If the company is not yet showing sales, provide IRS Form 941 (Employer's Quarterly Federal Tax Returns) to show that the company is maintaining a workforce.

Office Space

USCIS also still loves to see traditional businesses with office leases despite the realities of how business today is done. It is not uncommon to see an RFE where USCIS questions the "legitimacy of your business," because it exists in a shared workspace, university campus, or home office. However, there is no requirement that an H-1B petitioning company *not* be located in a shared office space. If challenged on this issue, it is helpful to add context—*i.e., this address is a high-level research laboratory provided by a university for startups in its accelerator programs*. Then provide pictures of the facilities and any lease or terms that the company has with the owner of the space.

Validation

Another hurdle startups may face is USCIS trying to verify the company is real using its Validation Instrument for Business Enterprise (VIBE) system. USCIS relies on Dun and Bradstreet (D&B) as its independent information provider (IIP) to determine a bona fide job offer exists. New companies may register with D&B or simply provide enough evidence to demonstrate the petitioner is legitimate. Especially early-stage companies with less-obvious presence can submit formation documents, bank account information, or IRS documents such as proof of EIN (Employer Identification Number) or IRS Form 941.

Transfers, Extensions, and Amendments

As your company grows and begins recruiting, it will likely come across exceptional candidates who are on H-1Bs with their current employer. For him or her to come join the team, the H-1B must be transferred to your company. Once the LCA is certified and the H-1B petition is filed with USCIS, the recruit can begin work with the new employer.

However, many H-1B holders will be understandably hesitant to leave Employer #1 until the H-1B transfer to Employer #2 is approved. The concern is that they could leave their secure H-1B employment with Employer #1 and start working for Employer #2, only to find out the case has been denied and they are stuck without an approved H-1B. *Premium processing* is a USCIS service that allows employers to pay an additional amount of money ($1,440[27] as of December 2019) for 15-day processing of the petition. If USCIS sends a Request for Evidence or RFE, the petitioner will be given up to *87 days* to respond; however, upon filing the response, USCIS is still confined to a new 15-day window to adjudicate. In most cases, Employer #2 can submit the H-1B transfer with *premium processing* and have an approval in a few weeks, thereby allowing the employee the security to put in his or her two weeks' notice with Employer #1.

In September 2018 and again in March 2020, the Trump administration suspended *premium processing* of H-1B transfers making this transition much more difficult. Without *premium processing*, transfers were known to take two to four months.[28]

In some cases, H-1Bs must be amended to reflect changes in the H-1B employment. H-1B amendments require certification of a new LCA and then a new filing with USCIS. Amendments are necessary when there are material changes to the position, or the worksite location is changed to a location outside of the *metropolitan statistical area* (MSA) listed on the LCA. Material changes are often changes in the position, such as promotion to a significantly more managerial role or a lateral promotion to a position with different job duties. Receiving a raise or a change in title *only* does not necessitate the filing of an H-1B amendment. When there are changes to an H-1B position, an immigration attorney should analyze whether an amendment is necessary.

[27] As this book was being completed, USCIS proposed increasing filing fees by several hundred more dollars. That issue is being fought and it is not clear yet whether the fee increase will happen.

[28] In June 2020, premium processing resumed at USCIS.

If an H-1B employee quits or is terminated, he or she has a *60-day grace period* to file an H-1B transfer to a new employer, change to a status other than H-1B, or leave the United States. An exception is a person who has *less* than 60 days left in H-1B status (*i.e.*, his or her I-94 has less than 60 days remaining), in which case the person is entitled to a grace period in *the amount of time remaining on the I-94.*

A person is only allowed to use the 60-day grace period one time. For example, if a person is terminated and then during his or her 60-day grace period has an H-1B filed to join a new company, and that petition is then denied, he or she does not get an additional 60-day grace period. Also note that the 60-day grace period applies to an H-4 dependent.

If an H-1B holder is not able to transfer to a new employer or change to another status within the grace period, that person may still leave the United States and at a later date and have an H-1B filed on his or her behalf and consular process the new visa.[29] If the H-1B holder stays in the United States beyond the grace period, they will have to disclose that overstay on all future visa applications. Overstays of any nonimmigrant visa status (including H-1B) of 180 days or more trigger a three-year bar to admission to the United States, and an overstay of a year or more triggers a ten-year bar.

Mergers and Acquisitions

Entrepreneurs will need to consider their H-1B employees in the case of mergers, acquisitions, or corporate restructuring. In general, if there are material corporate changes, all H-1Bs employees at the company will need to have H-1B amendments filed on their behalf. The amendments are accompanied by new LCAs with the new company information for DOL. The main exception to this rule is when the new H-1B employing company succeeds the interest and obligations of the original H-1B employing company, and there are no other changes in the terms of employment.

In successor-in-interest cases, the new or acquiring company can assume the *public access files* of the original company and add a memo documenting:[30]

- Each affected LCA number and its date of certification;
- A description of the new employing entity's actual wage system applicable to H-1B nonimmigrant(s) who become employees of the new employing entity;
- The FEIN of the new employing entity; and

[29] As noted previously in this chapter, consular processing as of the date of completion of this book is not available for many H-1B applicants because of President Trump's June 22, 2020, Proclamation.

[30] 8 U.S. Code (USC) §1184(c)(10).

- A sworn statement expressly acknowledging the successor's assumption of all obligations, liabilities, and undertakings arising from or under the attestations made in each certified and effective LCA filed by the predecessor.

Any company undergoing a merger, acquisition, or corporate restructuring needs to have an attorney review whether an amendment is required or a memo to the PAF. Company owners should take into consideration the extra time this immigration analysis and potential subsequent filings will take and how it will affect key team members on H-1Bs. Otherwise, the new H-1B employing entity could find itself with employees who have gaps in their employment authorization.

5

Entering the United States as a Treaty Trader or Investor: The E-1 and E-2 Visas

The Immigration and Nationality Act provides treaty trader/investor nonimmigrant status for a national of any of the countries with which an appropriate treaty of commerce and navigation exists (see chart below). An individual who wishes to go to the United States to carry on substantial trade, principally between the United States and his or her own country, may apply for a *treaty trader visa* (*E-1*). Someone who is going to the United States to develop and direct the operations of an enterprise in which he or she has invested, or is actively in the process of investing, a substantial amount of capital may apply for a *treaty investor visa* (*E-2*). E-1 and E-2 visas are available for the following treaty countries at the time this writing:[1]

Country	Classification
Albania	E-2
Argentina	E-1 / E-2
Armenia	E-2
Australia	E-1 / E-2
Austria	E-1 / E-2
Azerbaijan	E-2
Bahrain	E-2
Bangladesh	E-2
Belgium	E-1 / E-2
Bolivia	E-1 / E-2
Bosnia & Herzegovina	E-1 / E-2
Brunei	E-1

[1] http://bit.ly/DOStreatycountries.

Bulgaria	E-2
Cameroon	E-2
Canada	E-1 / E-2
Chile	E-1
Chile	E-2
China (Taiwan)	E-1 / E-2
Colombia	E-1 / E-2
Congo (Brazzaville)	E-2
Congo (Kinshasa)	E-2
Costa Rica	E-1 / E-2
Croatia	E-1 / E-2
Czech Republic	E-2
Denmark	E-1 / E-2
Ecuador	E-2
Egypt	E-2
Estonia	E-1 / E-2
Ethiopia	E-1 / E-2
Finland	E-1 / E-2
France	E-1 / E-2
Georgia	E-2
Germany	E-1 / E-2
Greece	E-1
Grenada	E-2
Honduras	E-1 / E-2
Iran	E-1 / E-2
Ireland	E-1 / E-2
Israel	E-1 / E-2
Italy	E-1 / E-2
Jamaica	E-2
Japan	E-1 / E-2
Jordan	E-1 / E-2
Kazakhstan	E-2
Korea (South)	E-1 / E-2
Kosovo	E-1 / E-2
Kyrgyzstan	E-2
Latvia	E-1 / E-2
Liberia	E-1 / E-2

Lithuania	E-2
Luxembourg	E-1 / E-2
Macedonia	E-1 / E-2
Mexico	E-1 / E-2
Moldova	E-2
Mongolia	E-2
Montenegro	E-1 / E-2
Morocco	E-2
Netherlands	E-1 / E-2
New Zealand	E-1 / E-2
Norway	E-1 / E-2
Oman	E-1 / E-2
Pakistan	E-1 / E-2
Panama	E-2
Paraguay	E-1 / E-2
Philippines	E-1 / E-2
Poland	E-1 / E-2
Romania	E-2
Senegal	E-2
Serbia	E-1 / E-2
Singapore	E-1 / E-2
Slovak Republic	E-2
Slovenia	E-1 / E-2
Spain	E-1 / E-2
Sri Lanka	E-2
Suriname	E-1 / E-2
Sweden	E-1 / E-2
Switzerland	E-1 / E-2
Thailand	E-1 / E-2
Togo	E-1 / E-2
Trinidad & Tobago	E-2
Tunisia	E-2
Turkey	E-1 / E-2
Ukraine	E-2
United Kingdom	E-1 / E-2
Yugoslavia	E-1 / E-2

The first step in every E visa case is determining whether the foreign national in need of the visa and the enterprise have the same nationality and whether that nationality is party to the relevant treaty. Nationality of the individual is determined by his or her citizenship. In cases of dual or multiple citizenships, a person may apply under any citizenship he or she holds (the one caveat is that a citizen of the United Kingdom (UK) must also establish that he or she has been domiciled in the UK for the previous year).

The general rule to determine the nationality of the company is to see whether nationals of the treaty country own *at least 50 percent* of the company.[2] If the company is owned by another company, then the analysis must continue up the holding structure to establish that the parent company meets the "Fifty Percent Rule." If the company is owned 50/50 by nationals of two treaty countries, then the company must pick *one* nationality and use that for E visa purposes.[3] A company *cannot act as a dual citizen*, petitioning employees from both countries. If the company is publicly traded on one country's exchange, then that nationality is presumed; but evidence should still be submitted to explain the nationality.

E-1 Treaty Traders

As noted, E-1s are available where there is substantial trade, principally between the United States and the treaty trader's country. To be approved for an E-1, the following must be established:[4]

1. Requisite treaty exists;
2. Individual and/or business possesses the nationality of the treaty country;
3. Activities constitute trade within the meaning of Immigration and Nationality Act (INA) §101(a)(15)(E);
4. Trade is substantial;
5. Trade is principally between the United States and the treaty country;
6. Applicant, if an employee, is destined to an executive/supervisory position or possesses skills essential to the firm's operations in the United States;
7. Applicant intends to depart the United States when the E-1 status terminates.

To constitute trade, there should be an exchange involving goods, moneys, or services. Any service or goods can technically qualify. The flow of the transactions

---

[2] 9 *Foreign Affairs Manual* (FAM) 402.9-4(B)(c).

[3] 9 FAM 402.9-4(B)(d).

[4] 9 FAM 402.9-5(A).

must be traceable between the two countries. Typically, this is done using purchase orders, wire transfers, bills of lading, and the like.

In order to establish that the trade is substantial, the Department of State (DOS) will look to the volume and value of the transactions. DOS will give greater discretion to more valuable, frequent transactions. However, it notes that a smaller business should not be excluded if it can prove that the volume of transactions is sufficient to support the E-1 treaty trader(s) and family. An E-1 cannot be based on one transaction though, even if it was one very large transaction.

DOS again relies on a general 50 percent rule to analyze whether trade is principally between the United States and the treaty country. An application should include documentation of the total trade the company or individual is transacting and proof that at least 50 percent is between the two countries. The other 50 percent or less may be domestic trade or international trade between other countries. If the U.S. enterprise is a subsidiary of a foreign parent company, and the subsidiary meets the 50 percent requirement, it meets the test, even if the parent company abroad does not conduct at least 50 percent of its trade with the United States.

Since the E-1 requires proof of a track record of substantial trade, it can be hard for early stage start-ups to qualify. E-1s are more commonly used by entrepreneurs who have an established company abroad and a U.S. customer base. The entrepreneur will use the E-1 visa to continue the ongoing business or services with U.S. customers. In some cases, foreign companies may be looking to *enter* the U.S. market. They may use the E-1 with a newly established U.S. enterprise and begin trading inventory to the U.S. company for it to sell. In this scenario, all the trade may be between the foreign parent and U.S. subsidiary, easily meeting the 50 percent threshold.

E-2 Treaty Investors

If a startup's founders are from a treaty country that allows for E-2s, it can be a great option, even in very early-stage ventures. As mentioned, E-2s are for entrepreneurs coming to the United States to develop and direct the operations of an enterprise in which he or she has invested, or is actively in the process of investing, a substantial amount of capital.

To qualify for an E-2 visa, the following must be established:[5]

---

[5] 9 FAM 402.9-6(A).

1. Requisite treaty exists;
2. Individual and/or business possesses the nationality of the treaty country;
3. Applicant has invested or is actively in the process of investing;
4. Enterprise is a real and operating commercial enterprise;
5. Applicant's investment is substantial;
6. Investment is more than a marginal one, *i.e.*, solely for earning a living;
7. Applicant is in a position to "develop and direct" the enterprise;
8. Applicant, if an employee, is destined to an executive/supervisory position or possesses skills essential to the firm's operations in the United States; and
9. Applicant intends to depart the United States when the E-2 status terminates.

Determining the Investment

The *Foreign Affairs Manual* (FAM) instructs E visa officers to do the following:

> You must assess the nature of the investment transaction to determine whether a particular financial arrangement may be considered an 'investment' within the meaning of INA §101(a)(15)(E)(ii).[6]

The textbook example of an E-2 investment involves the E-2 investor transferring his or her personal funds from a personal, foreign bank account to the new U.S. enterprise's bank account and thereby documenting the transfer of funds. However, the language in the FAM allows the officer to determine whether any other "arrangement may be considered an 'investment.'"

This is great for startups where the founders are often not personally the ones fully funding the enterprise, meaning many different investment strategies can work in the E-2 context. Those going through more traditional venture capital-based fund raising are not excluded from this broad definition of investment.

For example, a startup using an investment vehicle such as *a convertible note* in its seed round may still be making an E-2 qualifying investment. In this scenario, the founder is from an E-2 country and is exchanging equity (at a certain time) for capital to fund the E-2 enterprise. The E-2 applicant is essentially making his or her qualifying investment through the exchange of his or her equity for the value of the note. Sometimes these investments require further explanation of the investment but

[6] 9 FAM 402.9-6(B)(a).

can still be approvable for E-2 purposes. This is not to say that this exact arrangement will always work, as results tend to vary by consulate and adjudicator.

For those not planning to fund the E-2 enterprise with their *own* capital in total, or in part, then the nationalities of those investors must be taken into consideration to make sure at least 50 percent of the shares in the company are still held by nationals of the E-2 treaty country. For example, one co-founder is American and one co-founder is French; each own 50 percent of the company and put in $30,000 of personal wealth as capital contributions to start the company. In order to raise more capital, they each exchange 5 percent of their equity (10 percent in total) with an angel investor for $100,000. If the angel is also French, then 55 percent of the company is now French; but if the angel is a U.S. citizen, now only 45 percent of the company is French and it no longer qualifies as a French company for E-2 purposes.

This also comes up during future rounds of fundraising, where the founder's equity is being diluted. To make sure the co-founder on an E-2 does not lose his or her visa, dilution must be carefully considered. Specifically, founders need to consider the nationality of the new investors and whether the company is falling below 50 percent foreign-owned by nationals of the treaty country. If this is going to happen, the founder will need to transition to another visa type before the exchange of equity since his or her E-2 will no longer be valid at the time the company loses its treaty nationality.

Determining Source of Funds

A major focus of every E-2 is the "*source of funds*." The E-2 applicant must demonstrate the lawful source of his or her funds and how he or she has obtained possession and is in control of those funds. Classic examples include savings over time in a person's home country that are then invested in an E-2 enterprise, or sale of a property owned in a person's home country from which the funds are then invested into an E-2 enterprise. Documenting the source of the funds, whether through savings account statements and tax returns or proof of the ownership and sale of a property, are essential to the success of an application.

To qualify as an E-2 investment, the funds or assets must be "*at risk*."[7] In other words, if the business were to fail, *the investment would be proportionately lost*. Investment capital can be based on a loan, but the loan cannot be secured by assets of the E-2 enterprise.[8] Only personal loans may be used. Personal loans, though, may

[7] 9 FAM 402.9-6(B)(c).

[8] *Id.*

be secured by personal assets such as a second mortgage, or they may be unsecured loans that are commonly from family, friends, or business partners. In those cases, a promissory note documenting the personal loan is generally included. Low interest loans with future balloon payments are acceptable.

The funds must also be "*irrevocably committed*" to the E-2 enterprise.[9] This term-of-art means that the business is either already using the investment or the company is at least very close to the start of business operations, at which point they will be used. If purchasing a business, the deal can be structured in a way that the assets are held in escrow conditioned on the issuance of the E-2 visa, but the agreement should make clear that the investor cannot receive the visa and then pull out of the investment.

It is also important to note that the investment does not have to be a cash investment. While cash is a typical E-2 arrangement, the investment can be in the form of equipment, inventory, or even intellectual property (IP). Proof of the value of the equipment or inventory should be submitted, as well as evidence of the "investment" or the inventory, such as proof of shipping the inventory to the U.S. company.

If using intellectual property as the means of investment, you will still have to document the value of the IP so the E visa unit can determine that the investment is substantial. If a market value cannot be easily determined, you should submit evidence of its value.[10]

E-2s are not for passive investments or nonprofits. They cannot be "*paper organizations*" or the purchase of land or other assets to simply be held. The E-2 enterprise needs to be a real and active commercial undertaking that is going to produce a service or commodity.[11] That is not to say that the company must have revenues at the time of filing; an early stage startup can qualify. However, the company should be able to document what real service or product it will be actively developing and selling for a profit.

The Required Investment

The most common E-2 question is, "How much do I have to invest?" Well, there is no bright line rule. Instead, DOS uses a *proportionality test* to determine whether

[9] 9 FAM 402.9-6(B)(d).

[10] 9 FAM 402.9-6(B)(h).

[11] 9 FAM 402.9-6(C).

the investment is substantial enough to reasonably expect the company to be successful. "Substantial" for E-2 purposes is:[12]

1. Substantial in a *proportional sense*, as determined through the application of the proportionality test outlined below;

2. Sufficient to *ensure the treaty investor's financial commitment* to the successful operation of the enterprise; and

3. Of a magnitude to support the likelihood that the treaty investor will successfully develop and direct the enterprise.

The *proportionality test* weighs the investment amount versus the cost of the business. DOS explains that if the investment amount and the cost of the business are the same, *i.e.*, the investment pays for 100 percent of the business, then investment is substantial. Since this is often not the case:

> The proportionality test can best be understood as a sort of inverted sliding scale. The lower the cost of the business the higher a percentage of investment is required. On the other hand, a highly expensive business would require a lower percentage of qualifying investment.[13]

The FAM explains that a $100,000 investment in a company that costs $100,000 would qualify, but so would a $10 million investment in a $100 million company based on the size of the investment. However, the FAM makes clear that there is no bright line rule. Many people like to refer to the $100,000 figure in the FAM, but companies with lower startup costs should be able to determine that a lower investment amount is still substantial if proportionate. To determine the cost of the business, the E visa unit will look to the sale price of an existing business. With a startup, the unit will look to the actual costs needed to fund the company to the point that it is operational.

The enterprise must be more than marginal.[14] This means that it should be capable of generating enough income to provide the E-2 applicant and his or her family with more than minimal means of living. Having said that, a startup can demonstrate that it has the potential to reach such income—even though it may not have any immediate revenue. The potential should be realizable *within five years*. A business plan with financial projections showing more than marginal revenues within five years can demonstrate marginality.

---

[12] 9 FAM 402.9-6(D)(b).

[13] 9 FAM 402.9-6(D)(c).

[14] 9 FAM 402.9-6(E).

An initial E-2 application for a start-up should have a formal business plan laying out details such as:

- the business model
- business plan
- market analysis
- marketing plan
- operations details
- hiring projections
- job descriptions for key employees
- five-year financial projections including sales, first year operating budget, and allocation of the invested capital.

In many cases, companies already have business plans that they've developed for internal purposes or a pitch deck for fundraising, which can serve as a great starting point. Many E-2 applicants contract with business plan writers who work specifically with immigration-related business plans since they are familiar with what the consular officers are looking for.

An E-2 investor must be in a position to develop and direct the E-2 enterprise.[15] If the person applying for the E-2 is also the investor, then he or she can use a formal job description in the business plan to demonstrate how he or she will be developing and directing the business. For example, "As CEO, her duties include developing and implementing company policies, setting goals and procedures, and making all financial decisions for the company…" If the E-2 enterprise is owned by foreign nationals other than the applicant (covered in more detail below) or by a foreign company, then the application should explain how that foreign national or foreign corporation, *i.e.*, the "investor," develops and directs the E-2 enterprise in the United States.

Employees of the Company

One of the major benefits to the E-2 is that some employees of the company who share the same nationality as the investor (and enterprise) can also obtain E-2 visas. For example, an E-2 enterprise with Italian nationality can obtain E-2 visas for its Italian employees, so long as a few conditions are met:[16]

1. Prospective employer must meet the nationality requirement, *e.g.*, if an individual, then the nationality of the treaty country; or if a corporation or other

[15] 9 FAM 402.9-6(F).

[16] 9 FAM 402.9-7(A).

business organization, then at least 50 percent of the ownership must have the nationality of the treaty country;

2. Employer and the employee must have the same nationality; and
3. Employer, if not residing outside the United States, must be maintaining "E" status in the United States.

It must be determined whether the employee fits within one of the acceptable categories: Executives, Supervisory Employees (supervisors and managers), and Essential Employees. In some cases, a position obviously qualifies as a company executive or supervisor. In other cases, the consular officer will use the following criteria to make a determination:

1. The *title* of the position for which the applicant is destined, its place in the firm's organizational structure, the duties of the position, the degree to which the applicant will have ultimate control and responsibility for the firm's overall operations or a major component thereof, the number and skill levels of the employees the applicant will supervise, the level of pay, and whether the applicant possesses qualifying executive or supervisory experience;
2. Whether the executive or supervisory element of the position is a *principal and primary function* and not an incidental or collateral function. For example, if the position principally requires management skills or entails key supervisory responsibility for a large portion of a firm's operations and only incidentally involves routine substantive staff work, an E classification would generally be appropriate. Conversely, if the position chiefly involves routine work and secondarily entails supervision of low-level employees, the position would not be termed executive or supervisory; and
3. The *weight to be accorded a given factor*, which may vary from case-to-case. For example, the position title of "vice president" or "manager" might be of use in assessing the supervisory nature of a position if the applicant were coming to a major operation having numerous employees. However, if the applicant were coming to a small two-person office, such a title would be of little significance.[17]

Essential employees, on the other hand, are usually those employees who have specialized skills that company operations depend on. Applicants should include job descriptions that detail how the skills are specialized and how the individual ob-

---

[17] 9 FAM 402.9-7(B).

tained the skills and is therefore qualified for the position. Understanding a foreign language or culture alone does not generally qualify a person as an essential employee, but it can be a factor in the position's essential functions. In cases involving essential employees, the consular officer will consider:

1. The experience and training necessary to achieve such skill(s);
2. The uniqueness of such skills;
3. The availability of U.S. workers with such skills;
4. The salary such special expertise can command;
5. The degree of proven expertise of the alien in the area of specialization; and
6. The function of the job to which the alien is destined.[18]

Essential employees do not have to prove that they have previously worked for the company or an affiliate, merely that they will be filling positions that are important to the success of the company. Beyond that, a person's skill set does not have to be unavailable in the United States; the analysis is based on the significance to the company. Significance to the company, however, can change as well. An early stage start-up may have essential employees tasked with fundraising, training on new technology, or launching a new initiative that may not continue to be in an essential role at a later date. Thus, an essential employee may not continue to be eligible for an E-2 once the position significantly changes.

The Application Process

The process of applying for an E visa has many variables. Investors or employees may apply for an E visa at a U.S. consulate or embassy, or, if they are in the United States in another lawful status, they may file an application for change of status to E-1 or E-2 with U.S. Citizenship and Immigration Services (USCIS). While certain situations may call for a change of status in the United States, most people opt to file at a U.S. consulate because only the Department of State can issue a *visa*. USCIS can only change and extend the person's status while in the United States. It is the physical E visa stamped in an individual's passport, however, that allows him or her to travel in and out of the United States, entering in E status upon each entry on the visa. If granted a change of status to E-1 or E-2 by USCIS, the individual will still need to process a visa at a consulate or embassy once he or she leaves the United

[18] 9 FAM 402.9-7(C).

States in order to obtain an E visa upon which he or she can use to re-enter the United States.

The Initial Application

The process of applying for an E visa with the Department of State also varies by consulate. Many U.S. consulates list on their website instructions on how to apply for an E visa. In some cases, there are separate processes in place for "initial company registrations" (the first time a company applies for an E visa), subsequent applications for employees, and dependent family members.

Some consulates have formal procedures in place for company registration. For example, the consulate may have one investor complete an online DS-160 visa application, pay the MRV (*Machine Readable Visa*) fee, and submit all the documentation to prove eligibility. Then, once the E visa unit gives permission or requests any additional documents needed, the investor is notified to schedule an interview at the consulate. The investor then attends the interview at the consulate. Once the investor and company are approved, some consulates register the company's approval and issue a Notice of E-Visa Company Registration. Future employees can then apply under a more streamlined process using the registration.

When making an initial application, you must review the specific documents required by that consulate and the guidelines for submission. Many consulates even have directions on how they want the application tabbed. For example, the U.S. consulate in Tel Aviv, Israel, requires E-2 applications to be as follows:[19]

Tab A	Cover Letter on company letterhead outlining eligibility
Tab B	Table of Contents
Tab C	Completed Form DS-156E
Tab D	Evidence that the company meets the ownership requirements
Tab E	Evidence of nationality of the treaty country
Tab F	Evidence of investment
Tab G	Evidence that the commercial enterprise is real and operating
Tab H	Evidence that the investment is substantial
Tab I	Evidence that the investment is marginal
Tab J	Employee's visa application
Tab K	Dependents' visa applications

Some consulates also have restrictions on the size of the initial application. For example: Toronto–no more than 70-pages, Dublin–no more than 80-pages, and Frankfurt–no more than 90-pages. Each consulate also has separate rules on what

[19] https://il.usembassy.gov/visas/visas-for-treaty-traders/_Required/.

types of documents are exempt from the page count, such as tabs, forms, and biographic documents in some cases. Some consulates will accept e-mailed versions of the applications (usually capped at 5MB), while others require mailed applications; still others request both. In the case of electronic applications, most consulates will accept multiple e-mails with the attachments broken into acceptable sizes.

These instructions are subject to change, and applicants always should check the consulate's website for updates to guidelines to ensure acceptance and adjudication of the application.

Employee Applications

Employees can often benefit from a more streamlined process that requires less documentation on the company once the company is registered. This usually reduces processing times significantly because the applicant can submit the online DS-160 visa application, pay the MRV fee, and schedule an interview.

Then at the interview, the employee may present (depending on the consulate) the following documents:

- The DS-160 confirmation page
- MRV receipt
- Completed form DS-156E E visa application
- Passport
- Detailed CV or résumé
- Signed letter from the company explaining the beneficiary's qualifications and role with the company in the United States.
- All E visa applicants must bring a 2x2 inch passport style photo for the printing of the E visa in his or her passport.

Family Applications

Spouses and unmarried children under 21 years old are eligible for E-1 and E-2 status. Family members do not have to hold the same nationality as the primary E-1 or E-2 beneficiary to qualify. They can apply at the same time as the primary, or they may apply at a later time and bring proof of the primary's E visa with them. In most cases, dependents will receive the same duration of status or visa validity period as the primary.

Dependents still must complete the online DS-160 visa application, pay the MRV fee, and attend an interview. At some consulates, children under a certain age may be exempt from the interview. At an interview, dependents usually need to present documents such as, the primary's E visa, the DS-160 confirmation page, MRV receipt, passport, and proof of the familial relationship (*i.e.*, marriage or birth certificates) with certified translations. They also must bring a passport-style photo.

E-1 and E-2 spouses are eligible for work authorization, making it a much more conducive visa category compared to others. However, the primary E holder obtains work authorization upon issuance of his or her E visa or change of status. Spouses, on the other hand, must enter the United States and separately apply for work authorization using Form I-765. While this slows down the spouse's work authorization by a few months, it ultimately gives the spouse the ability to work for any employer in the United States—unlike the primary E visa holder who is tied to the E-2 enterprise. Principals, spouses, and unmarried children under 21 may study at U.S. schools and institutions while on E visas.

Length of Eligibility

The Department of State's visa reciprocity schedule will determine how long the visa is issued for. *Five years (60 months) is usually the maximum time.* However, unlike other visa categories, Es are not restricted to a certain number of allowable years spent in the United States in E status; as long as the eligibility remains, you can continue to renew an E visa. Customs and Border Protection will generally admit a person on an E visa for two years. So, a person with one year left on an E visa, for example, may be admitted for up to two years before needing to visit a U.S. consulate and process a visa renewal.

Change of Status

Applying for a change of status to E-1 or E-2 in the United States is quite different and does not vary by nationality since all changes of status are adjudicated by USCIS. For the reasons described earlier, the pros and cons of filing in the United States should be seriously considered. In order to file a change of status to E-1 or E-2 from the United States, a person must already be in the United States in a lawful status.

Like other changes of status to employment-based categories, applicants submit the evidence of their eligibility for E status plus Form I-129 and the I-129 E supplement. When filing with USCIS, there are no specific instructions on tabs or page limits, but all requirements of the E visa must still be explained and documented (*i.e.*, treaty nationality, substantial investment, marginality, etc.).

Changes of Status to E-1 and E-2 can be premium processed with USCIS for an additional government fee ($1,440 as of December 2019)—meaning the case will be adjudicated in 15 days. Since the request is for a change of status, upon approval, USCIS will issue a new I-94 showing the applicant is in E-2 status. USCIS will give an initial grant of up to two years of E-2 status. Afterward, USCIS will continue to extend E status in two-year increments. There is still no cap on time spent in E-2 status, so long as the person complies with his or her status and continues to be eligible for extensions.

Dependent family members who are also in the United States in a lawful status may request a change of status. Form I-539 must be included for dependents. Dependents must similarly submit evidence of their eligibility and the familial relationship to the primary E holder (*i.e.*, marriage or birth certificates) with certified translations.

Nonimmigrant Intent

Whether applying at a U.S. consulate or embassy, or requesting a change of status with USCIS, any applicant for an E visa or E status must demonstrate intent to depart the United States when status expires or is terminated.[20] To do so, an applicant does not have to maintain a foreign residence or establish intent to end E status in a specific duration of time. He or she must, however, *express intent* to depart after the period of authorized stays. DOS states, "The alien's expression of an unequivocal intent to depart the United States upon termination of E status is normally sufficient."[21] Therefore, a signed statement of intent to depart explaining an understanding of this requirement and intent to comply is normally sufficient.

The issue of intent most commonly comes up when people are trying to transition from a nonimmigrant E-1 or E-2 status to permanent residence. Obtaining green cards will be covered much more in depth in Chapter 11, but some E visa holders can encounter challenges worth noting. Many people in the United States apply for their green cards through adjustment of status in the United States (*i.e.*, they apply to change from their nonimmigrant status to permanent resident status in the United States). The FAM, however, states:

> An applicant who is the beneficiary of an immigrant visa petition will need to satisfy that his/her intent is to depart the United States at the end of his/her authorized stay, and not stay in the United States to adjust status or otherwise remain in the United States.[22]

---

[20] 9 FAM 402.9-4(C).

[21] *Id.*

[22] *Id.*

Thus, an immigrant visa petition can make a person ineligible for an extension of his or her E visa. This is not to say that a person cannot transition from an E visa to a green card. The green card process can be completed at a U.S. consulate or embassy through consular processing of the immigrant visa. This is only to note that in some cases the process should be *completed abroad*, and then the person may enter on the immigrant visa and become a lawful permanent resident.

Many E visa holders obtain lawful permanent residence through marriage or sponsorship by other family members. E visa holders also may obtain permanent residence through self-sponsored categories, such as EB-1 Extraordinary Ability, EB-2 National Interest Waiver, and the EB-5 Immigrant Investor Program (all covered within individual chapters in this book). An E visa holder may be sponsored by another company in a prospective position, which he or she will fill upon obtaining permanent residence. Transitioning from an E visa to a green card requires compliance with the E visa intent to depart and should therefore be discussed with an attorney who can help navigate that process.

Conclusion

In general, a treaty trader, investor, or employee may only work for the company that he or she is approved to work with at the time the application is approved. However, he or she may work for the approved company's parent or subsidiary so long as:

1. The enterprise or organization, and any subsidiaries thereof, where the work will be performed; the requisite parent-subsidiary relationship; and that the subsidiary independently qualifies as a treaty organization or enterprise under this paragraph;
2. In the case of an employee of a treaty trader or treaty investor, the work to be performed requires executive, supervisory, or essential skills; and
3. The work is consistent with the terms and conditions of the activity forming the basis of the classification.[23]

Any *substantive* changes to the employment of a treaty trader, investor, or employee must be approved by USCIS:[24]

---

[23] 8 CFR 214.2(e)(8)(ii).

[24] https://bit.ly/USCISE2 based on the regulations at 8 CFR 214.2(e)(8)(iii).

> A 'substantive change' is defined as a fundamental change in the employer's basic characteristics, such as, but not limited to, a merger, acquisition, or major event which affects the treaty investor or employee's previously approved relationship with the organization.

In the case of a substantive change to the terms of employment, a new Form I-129, E supplement, and supporting documents must be filed with USCIS and approval must be granted. When amending an E for substantive changes, a request for an extension can be submitted at the same time.

As with all visa categories, careful analysis must be performed in anticipation of company mergers, acquisitions, or changes in corporate structure. Substantive changes involving company ownership may require an amendment to an E visa. Most notably in the E context, any change in company ownership must still result in the company having at least 50 percent ownership by nationals of the treaty country.

If, for example, an E-2 enterprise is acquired completely by an American-owned company, then it no longer holds the treaty nationality—it is now a 100 percent U.S. company. Therefore, any investors or employees holding E visas tied to that company are no longer eligible for E status. The eligibility ends at the time the company nationality no longer meets the requirements.

6

Entering the United States via Transfer: The L-1 Intracompany Transfer Visa

The L-1 intracompany transfer visa is one of the most common employment-based nonimmigrant visas used by companies in the United States. While it is often thought of as a "go-to" visa for large multinational companies, it is available to startups that can meet the visa requirements. The L-1 visa allows employers to transfer executives, managers, and specialized-knowledge employees from one of the organization's foreign offices to one of its offices in the United States. The transferred employee may also be coming to the United States to establish an office if the company does not yet have U.S. operations.

The L-1 visa is *not* a good option for someone at the very beginning stages of starting a company, particularly if the company is being formed in the United States; but it may be an option for an entrepreneur who, for example, has initially started a business outside the United States that will continue its operations, or if the entrepreneur combines operations with a company abroad at which they have previously worked.

Before outlining the requirements for L-1 visas, it is worth noting the Trump administration's April 18, 2017, Executive Order (EO 13788) titled "Buy American Hire American." The measure is intended to "create higher wages and employment rates for workers in the United States, and to protect their economic interests." Adjudicators have been ordered to scrutinize applications more closely, presumably looking to prevent fraud and abuse. That has translated into greater scrutiny of L-1 cases, just as it has for other nonimmigrant categories.

Furthermore, the L-1 category, like the H-1B, H-2B, and J-1 visa, is subject to the White House's Proclamation 10052, which bars the issuance of visas in the covered nonimmigrant categories as a response to rising unemployment in the United States. The order is set to expire December 31, 2020, though Trump could extend it, and it is also likely to face a serious challenge in the courts.

The Employer Requirements

Qualifying Relationship

For an employer to meet the L-1 visa requirements, there must be a *qualifying relationship* between a foreign company and an employer that is currently, or will be, doing business in the United States. The U.S. and foreign businesses need not be in the same field. That relationship can be a parent/subsidiary relationship (the U.S. entity can either be the parent or subsidiary), a branch office relationship, or an affiliate relationship. The qualifying relationship need not have existed during the one-year period that the L-1 nonimmigrant worked abroad for the company. Also, the entity abroad that employed the L-1 nonimmigrant can cease operating or no longer be a part of the sponsoring company (often the case after a merger or acquisition) while the L-1 is in the United States, so long as the company maintains a related foreign entity for the duration of the L-1 period in the United States.

For an entity to have a qualifying parent/subsidiary relationship, the following must exist:

- One of the entities *must own at least 50 percent of the other entity*;
- One of the entities must have *a 50 percent stake in a joint venture* as long as the entity seeking the L-1 visa has veto control over decision-making in the venture; or
- The entity seeking the L-1 *has de facto control over the other entity* even if it owns less than half.

To show control, U.S. Citizenship and Immigration Services (USCIS) requires showing "the right and authority to direct the management and operations of the business entity."[1]

Normally, showing control over the majority of shares will demonstrate that the amount of control necessary for complying with the L-1 qualifying relationship has been obtained by the entity. However, USCIS could look at additional factors, such as a voting rights agreement or a franchise agreement, which can open the door for further scrutiny. An entrepreneur will want to provide additional documentation to prove that the necessary control does, in fact, exist.

With respect to joint ventures, because there is a 50-50 shareholder relationship, control is demonstrated by showing "*negative control*." That is, either party can pre-

---

[1] USCIS *Adjudicator's Field Manual* (AFM) §32.6(b).

vent an action by not voting in favor of it. That is sufficient for L-1 purposes unless a voting agreement between the two entities states otherwise.

In instances where control is to be demonstrated by "de facto" control rather than an outright ownership of a majority of the equity, the petitioner must show that there are a number of other influential shareholders, and that, despite this, the petitioner has a *large enough share* to be able to force decisions. For example, having enough shares to appoint a board of directors or having a voting agreement with other shareholders may be enough.

A branch office is a fairly easy relationship for L-1 purposes because there is only one company, which is either based in the United States or abroad. If the U.S. entity is the branch, USCIS will want to see documentation that the U.S. entity is registered as a foreign corporation operating in the United States. A recent USCIS appeals case suggested the following documentation could be provided:

- The business license in the state where the branch is operating
- IRS Form 1120-F (the foreign corporation's tax return)
- IRS Form 941 (Employer's Quarterly Federal Tax Return)
- State tax returns showing the entity is a branch of a foreign company

If the situation is reversed and the foreign office is the branch, USCIS will seek similar evidence regarding the foreign office.

For two entities to be considered affiliates, both entities must be controlled by the same parent company as its subsidiaries or be under control of the same individual. Also, if two companies are controlled by a group of individuals, they can be considered affiliates so long as each owner controls about the same amount of stock of each company.

Note: A common mistake is failing to understand that two entities controlled by the same group of individuals will qualify if the ownership breakdown of each entity is the same. If additional investors are added or one entity loses an investor, such that the ownership breakdown of each entity is no longer about the same, the qualifying relationship will be lost. There are special rules for accounting and management consulting firms that are somewhat relaxed; if a startup in the United States is one of those two industries, discuss with immigration counsel how these rules may apply.

Employment Abroad

Within the three years preceding the time of filing an L-1 petition, an L-1 nonimmigrant must have been employed abroad continuously for one year by a qualifying organization. The job abroad being used as the basis for the L-1 does not need to be in existence *immediately* before seeking an L-1 visa, so long as it is *within the three years prior* to filing for the L-1 visa and the applicant can be working for another company at the time of filing for the L-1.

Brief trips to the United States for business will not break the one-year continuous employment requirement, but days in the United States will not count *toward* the one-year requirement either. For example, someone who has traveled to the United States for 10 days during the employee's first year of employment abroad for a company will not be eligible for an L-1 until one year *and 10 days* after beginning work with the employer. It is still possible to qualify for an L-1 if one has come to the United States for more than a few weeks, so long as he or she continues to work for the foreign employer. If the foreign employer sends the worker to participate in a training program in the United States on an H-3 visa that lasts for more than a year, for example, the training would still count toward maintaining continuous employment. However, the employee would still need to show that he or she had been working at least 365 days for the employer outside the United States.

Full– and part-time employment may not be aggregated in order to satisfy the 365 days of qualifying overseas employment. However, there is an exception if the work is divided among *affiliate* companies—each using the employee on a part-time basis—that can constitute full-time employment if the aggregate time meets or exceeds the hours of a full-time job.

The job abroad can differ from the job to be performed in the United States. An example of this could be when a person who works as a manager in the foreign operations of the company is sent to the United States as a specialized-knowledge worker. Additionally, someone who worked in a specialist position can be sent to the United States as a manager even if he or she had not previously worked as a manager abroad. In cases where the position differs from the one held abroad, a petitioner should still demonstrate how the work performed abroad will apply to the work to be done in the United States. *Note*: The exception to this is in a new office situation, when a person who is coming to work as a manager or executive in the United States must have worked in the same category abroad.

Executive, Managerial, or Specialized Knowledge Capacity

Executives and Managers

The nonimmigrant must be coming to serve in a capacity that is managerial, executive, or involves specialized knowledge. Managers and executives use the L-1A visa. Specialized knowledge employees use the L-1B visa. L-1A visa holders can remain in L-1A status for *up to seven years*. L-1B visa holders can hold L-1B status for *up to five years*. Time spent abroad during the L-1 period may be recaptured if documentation of the time abroad can be presented.

According to the USCIS *Adjudicator's Field Manual* (AFM):

> An executive or managerial capacity requires a certain level of authority and an appropriate mix of job duties. Managers and executives plan, organize, direct and control an organization's major functions and work through other employees to achieve the organization's goals. Front-line supervisors, such as those who plan, schedule, and supervise the day to day work of nonprofessional employees, are not employed in an executive or managerial capacity, even though they may be referred to as managers in their particular organization. In addition, individuals who primarily perform the tasks necessary to produce the produce the product(s) or provide the service(s) of an organization are not employed in an executive or managerial capacity.[2]

USCIS regulations define "managerial capacity" as an assignment within an organization in which the employee primarily:

1. Manages the organization, or a department, subdivision, function, or component of the organization;
2. Supervises and controls the work of other supervisory, professional, or managerial employees, or manages an essential function within the organization, or a department or subdivision of the organization;
3. Has the authority to hire and fire or recommend those as well as other personnel actions (such as promotion and leave authorization) if another employee or other employees are directly supervised; if no other employee is directly supervised, functions at a senior level within the organizational hierarchy or with respect to the function managed; and

[2] USCIS *Adjudicator's Field Manual*, Chapter 32, Section 32.6(d).

4. Exercises discretion over the day-to-day operations of the activity or function for which the employee has authority. A first-line supervisor is not considered to be acting in a managerial capacity merely by virtue of the supervisor's supervisory duties unless the employees supervised are professional.[3]

The notion that one cannot be supervising day-to-day work of nonprofessional employees can be a challenge for startups where entrepreneurs in the early days may take on multiple roles until the operation has grown enough to make this unnecessary. However, USCIS does note in the AFM:

> This does not mean that the executive or manager cannot regularly apply his or her technical or professional expertise to a particular problem. Certain positions necessarily require a manager or executive's application of his technical or professional expertise.[4]

Also, as discussed later in this chapter, a more relaxed view is applied during the one-year period immediately following the establishment of a new office in the United States.

For several decades of the L-1 visa's history, managers had to supervise people. The Immigration Act of 1990 changed the definition of manager to include "*functional managers.*" This applies to executives or managers who direct a function within the organization. That may include supervising non-employees like contractors or supervising employees of the company abroad. The particular function may not be directly performed by the manager or executive. Performing the function directly likely means the nonimmigrant is more suitable for the "specialized knowledge" category.

With respect to executives, USCIS regulations define "executive capacity" as an assignment within an organization in which the employee primarily:

1. Directs the management of the organization or a major component or function of the organization;
2. Establishes the goals and policies of the organization, component, or function;
3. Exercises wide latitude in discretionary decision-making; and
4. Receives only general supervision or direction from higher level executives, the board of directors, or stockholders of the organization.[5]

---

[3] 8 Code of Federal Regulations (CFR) §214.2(l)(ii)(B).

[4] *Id.*

[5] 8 CFR §214.2(*l*)(1)(ii)(C).

Specialized Knowledge Capacity

The Immigration and Nationality Act states that an L-1 petitioner can demonstrate a beneficiary employee has "specialized knowledge" if he or she has

1. a "special" knowledge of the company product and its application in international markets; or
2. an "advanced" level of knowledge of the processes and procedures of the company.[6]

The USCIS regulation states:

> Specialized knowledge possessed by an individual of the petitioning organization's product, service, research, equipment, techniques, management, or other interests and its application in international markets, or an advanced level of knowledge or expertise in the organization's processes and procedures.[7]

Specialized knowledge cases have long been a challenge to win because this language can be read broadly or restrictively, depending on the examiner. In 2015, USCIS issued a memorandum[8] that attempted to provide more guidance on what is and is not "specialized knowledge," though many believe it is still largely at the discretion of the examiner.

The 2015 guidance looked initially to the common dictionary to define "*special*" as "surpassing the usual," "distinct among others of a kind," "distinguished by some unusual quality," "uncommon," or "noteworthy."

"*Advanced*" is defined in the common dictionary as "greatly developed beyond and initial stage," or "ahead or far or further along in progress, complexity, knowledge, skill, etc."

Taken together, USCIS now uses the following definitions[9]:

- ***special knowledge*** is knowledge of the petitioning employer's product, service, research, equipment, techniques, management, or other interests and its applications in international markets that is demonstrably distinct or uncommon in comparison to that generally found in the particular industry or within the petitioning employer; or

---

[6] Immigration and Nationality Act (INA) §214(c)(2)(B).

[7] 8 CFR §214.2(*l*)(1)(ii)(D).

[8] USCIS Policy Memorandum, Subject: L-1B Adjudications Policy, Aug. 17, 2005 (AILA Doc. No. 15081801).

[9] USCIS *Adjudicator's Field Manual*, Chapter 32, Section 32.6(e)(1).

- ***advanced knowledge*** is knowledge or expertise in the organization's specific processes and procedures that is not commonly found in the relevant industry and is greatly developed or further along in progress, complexity and understanding than that generally found within the petitioning employer.

An L-1 applicant can be considered to meet the "specialized knowledge" test if he or she can demonstrate either possession of special knowledge or advanced knowledge.

The 2015 memorandum did ease one requirement regarding the possession of proprietary knowledge about the company's operations that had previously worried many disqualified applicants:

> With respect to either special or advanced knowledge, the petitioner ordinarily must demonstrate that the beneficiary's knowledge is not commonly held throughout the particular industry or within the petitioning employer … However, such knowledge need **not** be proprietary in nature or narrowly held within the employer's organization …"[10]

The memorandum contains a list of some factors USCIS may consider when determining specialized knowledge:

- The beneficiary is qualified to contribute to the U.S. operation's knowledge of the foreign operation's conditions as a result of having knowledge not usually found in the industry or the organization's U.S. operations.
- The beneficiary has knowledge that is particularly beneficial to the employer's competitiveness in the marketplace.
- The beneficiary has been employed abroad in a capacity involving assignments that have significantly enhanced the employer's productivity, competitiveness, image, or financial position.
- The beneficiary's claimed specialized knowledge normally can be gained only through prior experience with that employer.
- The beneficiary possesses knowledge of a product or process that cannot be easily taught to another individual without significant economic cost or inconvenience.
- The beneficiary has knowledge of a process or product that either is sophisticated or complex, or of a highly technical nature, although not necessarily unique to the firm.

The 2015 memorandum also provided a detailed list of potential forms of evidence that can be submitted to demonstrate specialized or advanced knowledge. Petitioners

---

[10] USCIS Policy Memorandum, Subject: L-1B Adjudications Policy, Aug. 17, 2005 (AILA Doc. No. 15081801).

should first submit a detailed description of the services to be performed, as well as evidence of the beneficiary's prior education, training, and employment qualifying him or her for the position.

Other documentation that will show specialized or advanced knowledge includes:

- Evidence of training, work experience, or education establishing the number of years the individual has been using the specialized knowledge at the employer;
- Evidence of how the transfer of the beneficiary will help the organization's U.S. operations;
- Proof the beneficiary is able to contribute to the U.S. operation's knowledge of foreign operating conditions because he or she has knowledge not generally found in the industry or the organization's U.S. operations;
- Contracts, statements of work, or other documentation showing the beneficiary's background would be particularly beneficial to the organization's competitiveness in the marketplace;
- Evidence, such as correspondence or reports, showing the beneficiary has had assignments that have significantly enhanced the organization's productivity, competitiveness, image, or financial position;
- Personnel or in-house training showing the beneficiary's knowledge can only be gained through prior experience or training with that employer;
- Curricula and training manuals for internal training courses, financial documents, or other evidence showing knowledge of a product or process that cannot be transferred or taught to another individual without significant economic cost or inconvenience;
- Evidence of patents, trademarks, licenses, or contracts awarded to the organization based on the beneficiary's work, or similar showing beneficiary's knowledge is sophisticated or complex, or of a highly technical nature, although not necessarily proprietary or unique to the petitioning organization; and
- Payroll documents, federal or state wage statements, résumés, organizational charts, or similar evidence showing the positions held and the wages paid to the beneficiary and parallel employees in the organization.

The memorandum made it clear that the specialized knowledge analysis *does not* involve a test of the U.S. labor market and a petitioner *does not* need to show a lack of readily available workers to perform the relevant duties in the United States. The test is not whether workers in the United States are available, but whether there are "so many such workers that the knowledge is generally or commonly held in the relevant industry, and thus not specialized." If there are a lot of workers in the United States with similar knowledge to the beneficiary's, the petitioning employer must show the beneficiary's knowledge is truly specialized.

Of course, with the "Buy American Hire American" Executive Order, petitioners would still be wise to address this subject and demonstrate that U.S. workers are not readily available, rather than relying on this memorandum alone.

If there are other workers in the U.S. operation with the same specialized knowledge, the following factors will be considered by a USCIS examiner:

- How the duties to be performed by the beneficiary that require his or her specialized knowledge may or may not differ from those already employed in the U.S. operations;
- The extent to which the petitioner would suffer economic inconvenience or disruption to its U.S. or foreign-based operations if it were unable to transfer the beneficiary;
- Whether the salary to be paid to the beneficiary is comparable to similarly situated peers in the U.S. operations.

Being paid much less than U.S. peers may indicate a lack of specialized knowledge and the employer will need to show valid business reasons to explain the discrepancy.

A "specialized knowledge" worker does not need to occupy a managerial or similar position or command a high salary compared to his or her peers. Rank and salary might be factors considered when analyzing whether a beneficiary has specialized knowledge, but there is no requirement that a beneficiary be of a certain rank or have a salary "elevated" compared to his or her peers. The memorandum notes that this is especially applicable to startups.

Specialized knowledge L-1s who are later promoted to managers or executives can change from an L-1B status to L-1A status upon approval by USCIS. However, the employee must have been employed *at least six months* in the managerial or executive position in order to be eligible for a stay of seven years, or the change and extension of status must be requested before the L-1B has been in that status for *four and one-half years.*

Owners of Businesses

An owner or shareholder of a business may qualify as an L-1 if the petition is accompanied by evidence that the beneficiary's services are to be used for a *temporary* period and evidence that the beneficiary will be transferred to an assignment abroad upon the completion of the temporary services in the United States.[11]

The petitioner must establish that the foreign qualifying company will be doing business the entire time the owner or shareholder is in the United States as an L-1.

New Offices and Small Businesses

L-1s transferring to offices in the United States doing business for less than a year and L-1s petitioned by small businesses—likely the case for many entrepreneurs—are subject to additional requirements. USCIS, not surprisingly, tends to apply greater scrutiny to these petitions.

New Office L-1s

Ideally, a company will try to have its U.S. office running for a year before attempting an L-1 visa in order to reduce the likelihood of a denial. But if a company needs the executive, manager or "specialized knowledge" employee sooner than that, then the petitioner will need to be prepared to address several issues.

The main consequence of being considered a new office is the length of time for which the L-1 petition will be approved. An initial L-1 for a new office will be approved for *only one year* versus up to three years for other L-1s. Also, only those who worked as executives or managers abroad may seek L-1A visas for new offices.

One must address the question of whether a business is considered to be doing business for a year. If a business is merely incorporated, for example, that will not be enough. The L-1 rules define "doing business" as something that requires:

> [T]he regular, systematic, and continuous provision of goods and/or services by a qualifying organization and does not include the mere presence of an agent or office of the qualifying organization in the United States and abroad."[12]

A business that has been dormant for an extended period of time and has resumed operations also will be treated as a new business.

The rules are somewhat less clear when it comes to the acquisition of a business that has been operating more than a year. According to USCIS L-1 Training Materials

---

[11] 8 CFR §214.(*l*)(3)(vii).

[12] 8 CFR §214.2(*l*)(1)(ii)(H).

obtained by the American Immigration Lawyers Association, if the petitioner purchases and takes over the management of an established business that is already staffed and capable of supporting an executive or managerial employee, the petition *should not* be treated as that for a "new office" and a "new employee."[13]

Aside from demonstrating the basic L-1 requirements—that there is a United States and a related foreign entity and that the beneficiary has the qualifying employment with the petitioner outside the United States—new office petitioners are not required to demonstrate that the new office is currently doing business. However, for executive and managerial transfers, evidence must be submitted showing that:

1. Sufficient physical premises to house the new office have been secured;
2. The beneficiary has been employed for *one continuous year* in the three-year period preceding the filing of the petition in an executive or managerial capacity and that the proposed employment involved executive or managerial authority over the new operation; and
3. The intended U.S. operation, within one year of the approval of the petition, will support an executive or managerial position supported by information regarding:
   a. The proposed nature of the office describing the scope of the entity, its organizational structure, and its financial goals;
   b. The size of the U.S. investment and the financial ability of the foreign entity to pay the beneficiary and to start doing business in the United States; and
   c. The organizational structure of the foreign entity.[14]

Note that the normal requirements stating that managers and executives not be involved in the day-to-day operations of a business are relaxed for new office L-1s.[15] However, according to the Department of State's *Foreign Affairs Manual* (FAM):

> [W]hile it is expected that a manager or executive in a new office will be more than normally involved in day-to-day operations during the initial phases of the business, he or she must also have authority and plans to hire staff

[13] "I-129 L-1 Adjudication" L-1 Training Materials obtained by the American Immigration Lawyers Association via FOIA requested (*undated, posted* Apr. 26, 2013), AILA Doc. No. 13042663, p. 158.

[14] 8 CFR §214.2(*l*)(3)(5).

[15] The authors have received anecdotal reports in the period since President Trump was elected regarding USCIS issuing Requests for Evidence and denials on this issue; petitioners should proceed cautiously.

and have wide latitude in making decisions about the goals and management of the organization.[16]

For "specialized knowledge" employee transfers, the petitioner must show that:

1. Sufficient physical premises to house the new office have been secured;
2. The business entity in the United States is or will be a qualifying organization (*i.e.*, sufficiently related to the foreign entity); and
3. The petitioner has the financial ability to pay the beneficiary and to begin doing business in the United States.

With respect to the third requirement, demonstrating the new office has the financial ability to pay the employee for the duration of the one-year initial L-1 period will obviously be more persuasive than depending on cash flow to cover the beneficiary's payroll.

The specific evidence that can be submitted to meet the above requirements for both manager/executive new office transfers and "specialized knowledge" employee new office transfers can include:

- Purchase or leasing documents related to the premises (*note that home offices are likely to be frowned upon in new office petitions*);
- A detailed business plan showing the proposed nature and scope of the business, its organizational structure and its financing goals including strategies, targets, and growth projections;
- Financial records such as tax returns, audited financial statements and bank records showing the amount of the U.S. investment, source of funds and the ability of the foreign entity to pay the U.S. entity's bills;
- An organizational chart of the foreign entity;
- Contracts, invoices, letters of credit and letters of intent documenting the business will be providing goods and services in the near future;
- Evidence the business has begun hiring such as payroll records; and
- Letters of support from local chambers of commerce or bilateral investment organizations.

With respect to the business plan and general projections regarding the business, petitioners should be careful not to promise much more than can be delivered. At the time of the extension, the petitioner will be expected to demonstrate that the plan was followed and, if necessary, have very good reasons to explain why the performance of the company did not match expectations.

---

[16] 9 *Foreign Affairs Manual* (FAM) 402.12-11(B).

The extension of the new office L-1 petition after a year requires petitioners to present the following documents:

1. Evidence that the U.S. and foreign entities are still qualifying, related organizations;
2. Evidence that the U.S. entity has been doing business for the previous year by providing goods and/or services on a regular basis;
3. A statement of the duties performed by the beneficiary for the previous year and the duties the beneficiary will perform under the extended petition;
4. A statement describing the staffing of the new operation, including the number of employees and types of positions held accompanied by evidence of wages paid to employees when the beneficiary will be employed in a managerial or executive capacity; and
5. Evidence of the financial status of the U.S. operation.

With respect to managers and executives, the relaxed rule on performing operational and administrative tasks will no longer apply and the petitioner must demonstrate that there is adequate staff to perform those duties. Nevertheless, USCIS may choose to extend in cases where a business struggled initially but has shown recent progress. USCIS will sometimes approve a *second* new office L-1 recipient to set up a second new office if or when the first venture has failed. Obviously, a petitioner cannot count on either of these results. Additionally, changes in plans are more likely to be approved when new capital is available to demonstrate ability to continue paying employees.

Small Businesses

If a small– or medium-sized business supports a position wherein the duties are primarily executive or managerial, the position may qualify under the L category. However, neither the title of a position nor ownership of the business are, by themselves, indicators of managerial or executive capacity.[17] The USCIS *Adjudicators Field Manual* advises on the type of evidence that should be submitted by small businesses:

> "In addition to a statement of an authorized official regarding ownership and control of each qualifying organization, other evidence of ownership and control should be submitted, such as records of stock ownership, profit and loss

[17] AFM §32.6(d).

statements or other accountant's reports, tax returns, or articles of incorporation, by-laws, and minutes of board meetings."[18]

Petition Processing

The L-1 visa requires initial approval of an I-129 petition with USCIS. The Immigration and Nationality Act mandates that USCIS must adjudicate an initial L-1 petition within 30 days and the agency is also required to adjudicate the case within 30 days of a Request for Evidence response being received.[19] I-129 petitions are filed with a USCIS service center having jurisdiction over the state where the U.S. office is located.

Spouses and children under the age of 21 can accompany an L-1 by using the L-2 visa. The period of stay for the L-2 corresponds to the L-1. If an L-2 applies for the visa at a consulate[20] after the L-1 is already in the United States, then the applicant only needs to document the relationship to the L-1 and that the L-1 is in valid L-1 status in the United States. L-2 applications are filed using Form I-539. L-2 spouses may apply for employment authorization using Form I-765.

Canadian L-1 applicants file a Form I-129 with Customs and Border Protection (CBP) at a port of entry on the Canadian-U.S. land border or at Pre-Clearance/Pre-Flight Inspection facilities in Canada.[21] Canadians can file an I-129 with a USCIS service center and, if approved, may seek admission to the United States without a visa by use of the approval notice. If the CBP officer approves the application, he or she will issue an I-94 and then forward the approved I-129 to USCIS where a Form I-797 approval notice is issued.

---

[18] AFM §32.6(d).

[19] INA §214(c)(2)(C). Note that USCIS appears to be routinely ignoring this statutory requirement.

[20] As noted earlier in this chapter, the Trump Administration has temporarily suspended the issuance of L-1 and L-2 visas under Proclamation 10052, which was signed June 22, 2020. The measure, set to expire December 31, 2020, is being challenged in court. With respect to the L-1 travel ban implemented by the Trump administration on June 22, 2020, U.S. Customs and Border Protection has confirmed that Canadian L-1s are not subject to the Proclamation.

[21] In early 2019, the American Immigration Lawyers Association reported that at least two ports of entry on the U.S.-Canadian border stopped processing L-1s for Canadians without prior USCIS approval of an I-129 petition.

7

Foreign Nationals with Extraordinary Ability: The O-1 Visa

People applying for O-1 visas are trying to establish that they are at the top of their given field—by either presenting evidence of a major international award or satisfying at least three U.S. Citizenship and Immigration Services (USCIS) criteria.

O-1A visas are for foreign nationals of extraordinary ability in business, science, arts, education, and athletics. O-1B visas are available for aliens of extraordinary achievement in the arts, television, and film.

In the O-1A context, evidence is required of an award, such as a Nobel Prize, or at least three of the following eight possibilities[1]:

1. Receipt of nationally or internationally recognized prizes or awards for excellence in the field of endeavor;
2. Membership in associations in the field for which classification is sought, which require outstanding achievements, as judged by recognized national or international experts in the field;
3. Published material in professional or major trade publications, newspapers or other major media about the beneficiary and the beneficiary's work in the field for which classification is sought;
4. Original scientific, scholarly, or business-related contributions of major significance in the field;
5. Authorship of scholarly articles in professional journals or other major media in the field for which classification is sought;

[1] 8 Code of Federal Regulations (CFR) §214.2(o)(3)(iii)(B).

6. A high salary or other remuneration for services as evidenced by contracts or other reliable evidence;
7. Participation on a panel, or individually, as a judge of the work of others in the same or in a field of specialization allied to that field for which classification is sought; and
8. Employment in a critical or essential capacity for organizations and establishments that have a distinguished reputation.

For those applying under the O-1B category, the applicants either present evidence of major awards, such as Academy Award, Emmy, Grammy or Director's Guild Award, or alternatively establish at least three of the following six criteria[2]:

1. Performed and will perform services as a lead or starring participant in productions or events which have a distinguished reputation as evidenced by critical reviews, advertisements, publicity releases, publications, contracts or endorsements;
2. Achieved national or international recognition for achievements, as shown by critical reviews or other published materials by or about the beneficiary in major newspapers, trade journals, magazines, or other publications;
3. Performed and will perform in a lead, starring, or critical role for organizations and establishments that have a distinguished reputation as evidenced by articles in newspapers, trade journals, publications, or testimonials;
4. A record of major commercial or critically acclaimed successes, as shown by such indicators as title, rating or standing in the field, box office receipts, motion picture or television ratings, and other occupational achievements reported in trade journals, major newspapers, or other publications;
5. Received significant recognition for achievements from organizations, critics, government agencies, or other recognized experts in the field in which the beneficiary is engaged, with the testimonials clearly indicating the author's authority, expertise, and knowledge of the beneficiary's achievements;
6. A high salary or other substantial remuneration for services in relation to others in the field, as shown by contracts or other reliable evidence.

The USCIS criteria will generally lend themselves more to some fields than others. Therefore, if the criteria do not "readily apply" to a certain field, he or she may

[2] 8 CFR §214.2(o)(3)(iii)(B).

submit *comparable evidence* to prove eligibility. Certain industries and occupations fit the O-1 framework more naturally. Startup founders and some key employees are often well-suited for O-1A, and the O-1 rules are often conducive to startup needs, such as equity ownership, bootstrapping, and entrepreneurs wearing many hats for their young company.

An O-1 application requires a petitioner who is either an employer or an agent. Unlike the H-1B, there is far less issue with the beneficiary owning equity in the petitioning company because there is not an emphasis on employer-employee control. Thus, while an entrepreneur cannot purely "self-petition," the company he or she co-founds can file the petition on his or her behalf. The ownership of the company should be disclosed on the I-129, and an employment contract should be included in the petition.

Another positive aspect of the O-1 compared to the H-1B is that there is no prevailing wage requirement. O-1s do not require a particular wage structure or wage minimum as set by the Department of Labor. Instead, the petition should include a description of the wage and benefits the beneficiary will receive. Companies that are bootstrapping generally prefer this to the prevailing wage requirement of the H-1B, particularly for the company's founders who may be in roles, such as chief executive officer, to which the Department of Labor would assign extremely high prevailing wages.

In trying to establish that the beneficiary is at the top of his or her field, the first step is defining the field. The field should be defined specifically, because arguing extraordinary ability in "business" would cast such a wide net that the person could accidentally end up comparing him- or herself to a Warren Buffet or a Jeff Bezos of the world. A more appropriate defined field may be something along the lines of extraordinary ability in the field of *financial technology entrepreneurship.*

Once the field is defined, the questions then become: Are three of the criteria satisfied? If not, what can be done to build the O-1 beneficiary's résumé?

Receipt of Nationally or Internationally Recognized Prizes or Awards for Excellence in the Field of Endeavor

Assuming the beneficiary has not won a Nobel Prize or similar award, the focus should be on any awards he or she has won within the industry. USCIS will not be persuaded by purely academic awards, such as scholarships to college or graduate school. USCIS will also push back against awards that are not open to the field, such as awards for which alumni of a particular university are the only eligible winners.

Proving that an award is of national or international significance is best handled by providing evidence of the distinguished nature of the organization granting the prize, evidence of other successful winners, or media coverage documenting the importance of the award. This is particularly true when the award is nationally recognized in a country other than the United States. Applicants should submit evidence of the specific criteria used by the organization granting the prize or award. If the criteria are not clearly defined and publicly available, the organization or individual issuing the award should provide a detailed letter explaining who is eligible, how many people were considered or applied for the award, and what criteria was used to choose the winner.

An advantage for startup founders is that raising significant venture capital can be argued as an award (of capital) for excellence. Under the Obama administration, USCIS went so far as to explain this on its website:

> Note: If you have received venture capital funding or have been awarded a grant, you may submit evidence of the funding or grant awarded, including the amount of the funding or grant and the criteria used in awarding the funding or grant. Evidence of other investments, such as those from an accredited angel investor, may also be submitted.[3]

Under the Trump administration, this information was notably *taken off* the USCIS website. However, the argument can still be made. If the beneficiary has raised significant venture capital for the startup, the investor (or investors) likely passed over hundreds of other possible investments that did not satisfy the criteria for investment. Having the venture capitalist sign a *detailed letter of support* explaining his or her investment criteria and how the beneficiary's extraordinary ability led to the investment can still establish an award for O-1 purposes. USCIS may request additional evidence such as:

- Criteria used to nominate and judge the participants and award winners;
- Evidence that the beneficiary or his or her organization received venture capital funding and, if applicable, the criteria used to award the funding;
- Evidence that the beneficiary was awarded a grant and, if available, the criteria used in electing grant recipients and the number of individuals who have received the grant;
- The origination, purpose, significance, and scope of each award. This includes:
    - The reputation of the organization or panel granting the prizes or awards;

[3] See Appendix for the USCIS document, "Understanding O-1A Requirements."

- How many prizes or awards are awarded each year; and
- Previous winners of each award.

Membership in Associations in the Field for Which Classification Is Sought Which Require Outstanding Achievements, as Judged by Recognized National or International Experts in the Field

As with other criteria, certain fields are more likely than others to meet membership requirements for relevant associations. Entrepreneurs, again, are generally in luck compared to others in the business world. The key to establishing this criterion is defining how an association determines "outstanding achievement" and how the entrepreneurs are judged for admission. Professional organizations that only require a licensure and/or the payment of dues will not rise to the level of requiring outstanding achievement of its members. Organizations like prestigious alumni organizations will also face scrutiny, unless there are other defining requirements for membership, because they are not open to the entirety of your field (only open to alumni of the given university).

A number of distinguished organizations exist specifically for entrepreneurs. Many of these organizations have defined criteria for membership, such as being a co-founder of the company, having raised a certain amount of venture capital, or having made an "exit" of at least a particular value. Furthermore, organizations like this often have interview processes in which other distinguished members ultimately judge whether a new member should be accepted. USCIS will accept formal evidence of membership criteria or a letter of support from the organization explaining the criteria and interview process.

Startups who have participated in well-known accelerator programs can submit evidence of this distinguished membership. Similar to the raising of venture capital, the founder of a startup should be attributed with the startup's success, and this includes membership in distinguished organizations. Most notable accelerators have application processes and defined criteria for admissions. Also, the accelerator itself may have lots of media coverage on its own accomplishments, which can provide great evidence of its acclaim. Again, letters of support from the accelerator explaining the criteria carry weight. It is particularly useful for the letters to include the number of applicants per year (or cycle), acceptance rate, prominent alumni, and other data points that explain how its membership is highly selective.

When submitting evidence that the beneficiary is a member of an association that requires outstanding achievements of its member, USCIS may request additional evidence such as:

- The minimum requirements and criteria used to accept a person for membership;
- The number of members and beneficiary's rankings among the members, if any;
- The status of the association within the national or international community in the field of endeavor;
- Evidence of recognized national or international experts who make determinations about membership; and
- Other relevant requirements for membership.

Published Material in Professional or Major Trade Publications, Newspapers or Other Major Media About the Beneficiary and the Beneficiary's Work in the Field for Which Classification Is Sought

When entrepreneurs ask which criteria is most deserving of further time and resource investment, the reply is *media*. Media coverage contributes to the overarching narrative that the beneficiary is at the top of his or her field and provides other benefits such as simply showing up in search engine results. If the beneficiary were to rise to the level of major media attention, USCIS would still focus on the notoriety of the publication, and, of course, the coverage of the beneficiary.

The best way to address concerns about the publication is to include data on the readership or viewership of the media outlet. Circulation numbers, monthly site visits, or web rankings among media outlets in the field are great ways of proving to USCIS that the source publishing the article or video is major. For example: "Entrepreneur Magazine is a major print and online magazine published in the United States and distributed internationally. Even as of 2012, its readership was over 3,100,000 in print. Its online format, Entrepreneur.com has received over 18 million views."[4]

In regard to the coverage of the beneficiary, it is most valuable for a story to feature the beneficiary, mention his or her title, and his or her extraordinary contributions. However, if the article is more focused on the company's accomplishments, it is still advantageous if there is a quote from the beneficiary or at least a connection made. The media coverage can be both about the beneficiary or his or her work. Cofounders of a company should be attributed with the success and media attention of the company since that is their work. Therefore, if the company is receiving media

[4] Entrepreneur.com.

attention, a simple connection should be made with the entrepreneur, even if the article or story does not spend much time on the person's individual role.

A typical Request for Evidence from USCIS on major media will ask for documentation that:

- Establishes the source and significance of the published material;
- Identifies the beneficiary as a person who has risen to the very top of the field of endeavor; and
- Established that the published material has national or international circulation.

Note: Circulation information should be specific to the media format in which it was published. For example, if the article was published online, the evidence must relate to the website. If it was published in print, the evidence must be related to the printed publication.

Original Scientific, Scholarly, or Business-Related Contributions of Major Significance in the Field

There are many ways to establish that an entrepreneur has made significant contributions to his or her field. The petition should include information on the specific contribution(s) and how it is significant to the field. The petitioning startup should be an original, innovative contribution, which is why it is exciting and potentially receiving venture capital and media attention. The same major media previously used or coverage in trade journals in the given field can provide excellent background on how the contribution or approach is being received by other experts in the field. Letters of support from investors and other industry experts explaining the influence the contribution is having or has had on the industry can be used.

A patent on any of the unique technology a co-founder or his or her company has created is strong evidence of an original contribution. The receipt of a prestigious grant can address the significance of the startup's work. Many early-stage companies avoid seeking grants or filing for patents due to the high costs involved but may have persuasive evidence, such as acceptance to prestigious accelerator programs, as with a detailed letter of support to explain the original contribution at hand. If the contribution can be measured in website traffic or downloads, then this is also persuasive evidence of the contribution and its impact.

If the company is already further along in client acquisition, then the petitioner can submit evidence of contracts with clients already using its product, or commitments to use its product once viable. If the beneficiary, or company, has published articles about his or her work, those publications can be submitted as evidence of the innovation. Speaking about the product or approach at prestigious conferences also can be put forth as evidence of how it is being received by the industry.

The most common form of original contribution evidence will likely come in letters of support from other industry experts. The letters should include details on how the writer is qualified to give expert testimony and his or her individual analysis on how the contribution is significant to the field. The more detailed, the better.

A Request for Evidence from USCIS on whether the beneficiary has made an original contribution to the field will ask for evidence similar to the following:

- Copies of patents (showing the beneficiary as the author or coauthor);
- Objective documentary evidence of the significance of the beneficiary's contributions to the field;
- Documentary evidence indicating that people in the field of endeavor consider the beneficiary's work important;
- Testimony or support letters from experts, which discuss the beneficiary's contributions of major significance, such as:
  - Letters of recommendation from venture capitalists, which describe, in detail, the beneficiary's achievements and how they are of major significance in the field; or
  - Letters from CEOs or founders of distinguished organization, which detail the beneficiary's achievements and how they are of major significance in the field;
- Evidence that the beneficiary's major significant contributions provoked widespread public commentary in the field of endeavor and have been widely cited;
- Evidence of visitor traffic to the beneficiary's website, if the beneficiary's business is primarily based online. Evidence should include:
  - The number of individuals who purchased or downloaded the beneficiary's products or applications;
  - Evidence showing that the product or application made original contributions of major significance to the beneficiary's field;
  - Contracts with companies using the beneficiary's products;
  - The beneficiary's licensed technology being used by others; and
  - The beneficiary's patents being utilized and shown to be significant to the field.

- Evidence of the beneficiary's work being implemented by others. This may include, but is not limited to:
  - Contracts with companies using the beneficiary's products;
  - The beneficiary's licensed technology being used by others; and
  - The beneficiary's patents being utilized and shown to be significant to the field.

Note: If letters and testimonies are submitted, they should provide as much detail as possible about the beneficiary's contribution. They should explain, in detail, how the contribution was "original" (not merely replicating the work of others) and how it was of "major" significance. General statements regarding the importance of the endeavors may be insufficient.

Authorship of Scholarly Articles in Professional Journals or Other Major Media in the Field for Which Classification Is Sought

Authorship of scholarly articles is another example that will lend itself much better to certain industries (*i.e.*, academia and research-driven occupations). It is also, however, something that a beneficiary can seek out to build his or her O-1 résumé. Similar to major media about the beneficiary, USCIS will be most focused on the significance of the scholarly journal or media source where the beneficiary is publishing. This can be established using circulation or traffic numbers. In the case of scholarly journals, it may be more beneficial to provide information on why the journals are important in the context of the industry, since its circulation data cannot be expected to rival major media outlets. This can be established by providing evidence of a journal's impact factor when available.

If the beneficiary has *curriculum vitae* full of publications, then something like a Google Scholar profile page is a helpful way to demonstrate the number of publications, citations, and other data points—such as an *H index*. H index is a metric that measures the number of publications an author has (H) that have been cited at least H times. For example, five publications with at least five citations would produce and H index of five. While an H index is in no way needed to establish this O-1 criterion, it is persuasive evidence if the beneficiary comes from a research and writing-driven background and has an impressive H index.

Startup founders also may satisfy this criterion by writing articles for media sources that deal with entrepreneurship, technology, or their specific field. Many large publications, such as *Forbes* or *TechCrunch*, allow contributing writers to submit content and articles in their field of expertise. Major media sources in the

United States or abroad that are publishing your articles provides great evidence for this O-1 criterion, just like more scholarly articles in trade journals.

A Request for Evidence from USCIS on whether the beneficiary has authored scholarly articles in professional journals or other major media in his or her field will ask for evidence similar to the following:

- The significance and importance of the articles with the beneficiary's field of expertise;
- The significance and importance of the professional or major trade publications or other major media within the beneficiary's field of expertise that published the beneficiary's scholarly articles;
- The publication's circulation (local, national, or international):
- How often the publication is printed;
- The number of copies printed for circulation; and
- The number of citations to the beneficiary's written work.

Note: Circulation information should be specific to the media format in which it was published. For example, if the article was published online, the evidence must relate to the website. If it was published in print, the evidence must relate to the printed publication.

A High Salary or Other Remuneration for Services as Evidenced by Contracts or Other Reliable Evidence

Under this criterion, the beneficiary can argue that the compensation being offered or past compensation he or she has earned is highly relative to others working in the same industry, thereby demonstrating he or she is at the top of that field.

The beneficiary's compensation can be proven with employment contracts, paystubs, and proof of equity compensation. Startup founders are generally most focused on the equity compensation argument since many are taking lower salaries while bootstrapping. Evidence of equity compensation can be submitted as proof of high renumeration; however, it needs to be fully documented and explained. This can include submitting the investment instruments needed to establish the value of the equity the co-founder has received or will receive.

Co-founders may need to submit the actual convertible notes or a Simple Agreement for Future Equity (SAFE) documenting the pre-money valuation of the equity, the awards of venture capital, and the post-money value of the shares. The value of the individual shares can be explained to USCIS along with the overall value of the equity owned by the entrepreneur. The total value of the remuneration being offered to a co-founder may better correspond with the deservingly extraordinary compensation than the strategically lower salary being taken at this time.

Once the amount of remuneration has been documented for USCIS, the next challenge is documenting what is high *for the field.* The first step is establishing the occupation. If the beneficiary is a co-founder and executive, he or she will be compared to other executives in the area. If the person is a developer, he or she should be compared to other developers, and so on and so forth.

USCIS will generally push back against online resources such as Glassdoor, because USCIS considers it unreliable, as any individual can contribute the content to the website. The most persuasive evidence to submit is government data. Once the occupation has been identified, research can be conducted through the Bureau of Labor Statistics,[5] the Department of Labor's Career One Stop website,[6] and the Department of Labor's Office of Foreign Labor Certification Online Wage Library[7]—which was referenced in Chapter 4 for determining prevailing wage on the labor condition application. Evidence of the government-reported wages in comparison to the beneficiary's offered or previously earned remuneration will establish this O-1 criterion.

Some beneficiaries will want to submit evidence of high remuneration earned while serving in roles *outside* of the United States. These arguments are permissible, but they can be harder to document since U.S. government data will not be available. In order to successfully make these arguments, the petition will need to include reputable wage sources from the given country. Again, sources that allow for public contribution of data should be avoided.

Participation on a Panel, or Individually, as a Judge of the Work of Others in the Same or in a Field of Specialization Allied to that Field for Which Classification Is Sought

There are myriad ways to establish that a person has judged the work of others in his or her field. Those with research-driven backgrounds may submit evidence of peer reviews they have performed. Peer review is a great example of the type of work that will establish this criterion since people are required to be experts in the field to participate in peer review and the process at its core is a process of judging and reviewing other industry contributors.

---

[5] www.bls.gov.

[6] www.careeronestop.org.

[7] www.flcdatacenter.com/oeswizardstart.aspx.

Those with startup and entrepreneurial backgrounds often have, or can obtain, experience judging industry-related competitions. Judging business plan competitions or hackathons are some examples. It is beneficial to include information on who is holding the event, how the judges have been chosen, who else has been chosen as a judge, who is participating in the competition, any notable winners or past winners of the competition, prizes and awards for the winners, and any specific criteria used by the judges to determine winners of the competition.

Those with backgrounds in venture capital may submit information on roles they played where they judged companies looking for investments. Many co-founders spent time working at venture capital funds analyzing companies for possible investment. It is particularly useful if they were analyzing companies within their specific field of extraordinary ability. A letter of support from the venture capitalist the beneficiary worked with explaining the number of applicants that he or she judged and the criteria he or she used can be convincing. The letter of support can also contain success stories of companies that the beneficiary endorsed, which received funding, and then went on to notable success.

Beneficiaries with more corporate backgrounds can submit evidence of roles they had within organizations that involved judging and reviewing others. Examples include positions that made a significant amount of hiring decisions or that oversaw programs within the company that co-workers would apply for, and the beneficiary ultimately judged. Choosing co-workers for prestigious memberships within an organization, or grants and awards for entrepreneurship or other projects/significant skills, can also establish this criterion.

Employment in a Critical or Essential Capacity for Organizations and Establishments that Have a Distinguished Reputation

Co-founders should be able to make the argument that they have played a critical role for an organization with a distinguished reputation—such as their own company. Just as with the original contribution argument, the petitioning company should put forth evidence that it is distinguished due to its innovative product, service, or approach to the industry. Further, the evidence of venture capital being submitted should demonstrate how expert venture capitalists have found the company notable and worthy of substantial investment. If the company has garnered media attention, this is another opportunity to use it as evidence to show the company is a distinguished organization.

The entrepreneur's role in the company can best be explained through strong letters of support from a co-founder, which details the beneficiary's duties and responsibilities that are usually plentiful and critical. Letters from members of the board of directors who are *not* company employees and from the venture capitalists who have invested can also give great insight on the role the beneficiary has played in getting the company to where it is, and how he or she is needed to get the company where it is trying to go.

If, before working on this startup the beneficiary held critical positions at other companies, this information should be presented as well. Evidence can come in the form of media coverage or letters of support from previous employers and direct supervisors detailing the impact the beneficiary had on the company. Those who worked at very large corporations will have an easier time proving that the company is distinguished but may need additional details to explain how *their own* role was critical among their hundreds or thousands of co-workers. Meanwhile, those who worked at smaller companies will want to use their energy proving those companies were distinguished as well.

USCIS requires that an O-1 beneficiary provide consultation in the form of a written advisory opinion letter from a peer group, labor organization, or person with expertise in the field. This opinion letter can either state simply that the group has no objection to issuing the visa, or it can detail the applicant's achievements. If the achievements are detailed, the letter should address the applicant's ability, the nature of the position offered, and whether the position requires a person of extraordinary ability. If the consultation is with an organization other than a labor union, USCIS will forward the application to the union it deems appropriate within five days of receiving the petition. The union must issue an opinion on the petition *within 15 days*, and then USCIS will rule on the application.

In most cases, there is not an appropriate labor union or peer group for startups. In these cases, the petitioner needs to explain that a labor organization does not exist, at which point USCIS will waive the consultation requirement, and make its decision on the evidence in the record. By providing letters of support from industry experts who speak to the beneficiary's extraordinary ability, USCIS will determine that the startup has submitted sufficient consultation from a person with expertise, and that further consultation is not required. Obviously, some startups in certain industries will have an appropriate labor organization they need to consult with, but this should be determined on a case-by-case basis.

The Application Process

Similarly, to the discussion in the H-1B chapter (Chapter 4), O-1s are applied for through USCIS using Form I-129 and an additional O supplement. The petition can be submitted as a *change of status* from the beneficiary's current status in the United States, or through *consular processing* so that once approved with USCIS the beneficiary will complete the process abroad through a U.S. consulate issuing the O visa.

O-1 petitions are generally eligible for premium processing through USCIS for an additional fee. USCIS will approve O-1 petitions for a maximum of *three years*. However, unlike other visa categories, there is not a cap on the number of years a person may spend in O-1 status. Therefore, if the work continues to exist, the beneficiary of an O-1 can continue to apply for extensions in one-year increments. Form I-129 is also used to file for an extension. The application for an extension does not need to include a consultation and requires only a statement of *why* the extension is sought and the beneficiary's most recent I-94.

However, under the Trump administration where deference is not given to previous approvals, petitioners should document the beneficiary's qualifications for continued O-1 status. If there is a material change in the terms and conditions of employment for the O-1 holder, then an amendment must be filed with USCIS. The amendment must simply explain the changes in employment and how the criteria are still met. Whether a change is material should be discussed with legal counsel, but some material changes include: changing worksite location, promotions, or substantive changes in job duties or responsibilities.

An O-1 may be transferred to another employer by filing a Form I-129 and accompanying petition. Again, under the Trump administration's no deference policy, the petition should document how the person is an alien of extraordinary ability, include details on the new employer, and the new position the beneficiary will fill. The change of employer can be premium processed, and the beneficiary is eligible to work for the new employer once the I-129 is approved.

If the company petitioning an O-1 goes out of business then the O-1 beneficiaries, including co-founders (with O-1s), will lose their O-1 status. If a startup is acquired or merges with another company, *due diligence* must be performed to analyze the specifics of the corporate transaction. In some cases, the change may not require a filing with USCIS for the O-1 beneficiary. However, in other cases an amendment must be filed to reflect the change in ownership. If necessary, the amendment can be filed via Form I-129 and premium processed in 15 days.

Spouses and children (under 21) of the O-1 holders are eligible for O-3 visas. O-3 visas should be issued for the same period as the O-1. Unfortunately, O-3s are not entitled to work authorization. However, they *are* entitled to study at schools or universities in the United States.

O-2s rarely come up in the start-up context because they are for individuals accompanying and assisting the O-1 alien of extraordinary ability. O-2s are available in O-1A cases dealing with athletes if they are an "integral part" of the O-1A's activity. They are available in O-1B cases where the O-2 applicant is "essential" and has a "critical skill" for the production. Evidence must be presented of the O-2 beneficiary's skills and experience and how it is essential or critical to the O-1's work. O-2's status and work authorization may be granted for the full duration of the O-1's status.

O-1 holders may be interested in pursuing permanent residence (*i.e.*, a green card). Options for O-1 holders will be covered in more detail in the chapters dealing specifically with the different green card processes. It should be noted that *dual intent* is permissible on an O-1. This means a beneficiary can be completing the green card process while in O-1 status. An O-1 is a temporary, nonimmigrant visa, meaning the beneficiary may have to establish (at the consulate) that he or she understands the O-1 is merely temporary and should his or her green card petition be denied, he or she will have to leave the United States at the conclusion or termination of O-1 status. Beneficiaries are not required to maintain a foreign home residence while in the United States on an O-1 to establish this understanding.

The chapter on EB-1A green cards, Chapter 15, will explain that there is a green card category for aliens of extraordinary ability that is very similar to the evidentiary requirements for O-1A. Therefore, those qualified for the O-1 and interested in pursuing permanent residence may be able to apply under this similar category.

Appendix: Understanding O-1A Requirements

U.S. Citizenship and Immigration Services

Home | Contact Us | E-Mail Updates

Search SEARCH

HOME ABOUT US GETTING STARTED RESOURCES VISA GUIDE

Home > Visa Guide > O-1A Extraordinary Ability and Achievement

Print This Page

Understanding O-1A Requirements

Below are some key requirements you must fulfill to apply for an O-1A Visa. For each requirement, we have included forms of evidence that you may submit to meet the requirement and other tips to help you prepare your petition.

Collapse all | Expand all

Requirement 1 - You must be able to establish that you have extraordinary ability in your field.

The O-1A visa is for people who are recognized as being at the very top of their field and who are coming to the United States to continue work in that field. To establish eligibility for an O-1A visa you must either have received a major, internationally recognized award, similar to a Nobel Prize, or submit evidence that affirmatively answers at least 3 of the 8 questions below:

- Have you received a lesser nationally or internationally recognized prize or award for excellence in the field of endeavor?
- Are you a member of any associations which require outstanding achievements of their members as judged by recognized national or international experts?
- Is there published material in professional or major trade publications or major media about you which relates to your work in the field?
- Have you participated on a panel or individually as a judge of the work of others in the same or in an allied field of specialization?
- Have you made original scientific, scholarly or business-related contributions of major significance?
- Have you authored scholarly articles in professional journals or other major media?
- Have you been employed in a critical or essential capacity for organizations and establishments that have a distinguished reputation?
- Have you or will you command a high salary or other remuneration for your services?

Note: If the criteria discussed in this section do not readily apply to your occupation, you may submit comparable evidence in order to establish your eligibility.

+ How do I demonstrate that I have received a major, internationally recognized prize or award?

+ 1) How do I show that I have received a nationally or internationally recognized award for excellence in my field?

Some of the evidence you may submit to demonstrate that the award is a national or internationally recognized award includes:

- Documentation verifying the origination, purpose, significance and scope of each award
- Criteria used to nominate and judge the participants and award winners
- The reputation of the organization or panel granting the prizes or awards
- How many prizes or awards are awarded each year
- Previous winners of each award

Understanding O-1A Requirements | USCIS

Note: If you have received venture capital funding or have been awarded a grant, you may submit evidence of the funding or grant awarded, including the amount of the funding or grant and the criteria used in awarding the funding or grant. Evidence of other investments, such as those from an accredited angel investor, may also be submitted.

+ 2) What evidence can I provide that establishes that I am a member of an association which requires outstanding achievements of its members?

Some of the evidence you may submit to demonstrate that you are a member of an association which requires outstanding achievements of its members includes:

- The minimum requirements and criteria used to apply for membership
- The number of members in the association
- The status of the association within the national or international community in the field of endeavor
- Evidence of national or international experts who make determinations about membership
- Other relevant requirements for membership

+ 3) How do I demonstrate that material has been published about me, and my work in the field,in professional or major trade publications or major media?

Some of the evidence you may submit to demonstrate that material has been published about you, and your work in the field, in professional or major trade publications or major media includes:

- The name of the publication and a description of the significance of the published material
- The circulation information of the published material (e.g. local, national or international circulation) and the number of copies provided for circulation
- The frequency of the publication

+ 4) How do I demonstrate that I have participated on a panel or was a judge of the works of others?

Some of the evidence you may submit to demonstrate that you have participated on a panel or was a judge of the works of others includes:

- Evidence showing the significance of the work you judged
- Information identifying the criteria used to select the judges
- An explanation describing how and why you received an invitation to be a judge

+ 5) How do I demonstrate that I have made an original scientific, scholarly or business-related contribution of major significance?

Some of the evidence you may submit to demonstrate that you have made an original scientific, scholarly or business-related contribution of major significance includes:

- Objective documentary evidence of the significance of your contribution to the field (e.g. patents, pioneering new technology, etc.)
- Documentary evidence that people in the field of endeavor currently consider your work important
- Testimony or support letters from experts that discuss your contributions of major significance, which could include:
    - Letters of recommendation from prominent investors which describe, in detail, your achievements in and how such achievements are of a major significance in the field;
    - Letters from CEO's/founders of distinguished organizations that detail your achievements and how they are of a major significance in the field.
- Evidence that your major significant contributions have provoked widespread public commentary in the field of endeavor and have been widely cited;
- Evidence of your work being implemented by others such as:
    - Contracts with companies using the beneficiary's products;
    - Licensed technology being used by others; and
    - Patents currently being used and shown to be significant to the field.
- If your business successes are primarily based on-line, evidence of website usage/visitor traffic to your website, including the number of individuals that have purchased and/or downloaded your product(s) or applications

Note: When submitting letters or testimonies, it is best to provide as much detail as possible about your contribution. They should explain, in detail, how the contribution was "original" (not merely replicating the work of others) and how they were of "major" significance. General statements regarding the importance of the endeavors are normally insufficient.

+ 6) How do I demonstrate authorship of scholarly articles in professional journals or other major media?

Some of the evidence you may submit, in addition to a copy of the articles, to demonstrate that you have authored articles in professional journals or other major media includes:

- Other articles or documentary evidence (e.g. letters, affidavits) that show the significance and importance of the articles in your field
- Evidence that demonstrates the work was primarily created by you
- The significance and importance of the professional or major trade publications or other major media in which your scholarly article was published, which may be shown by submitting evidence of:
    - The publication's circulation (e.g. local, national or international)
    - How often the publication is produced
    - The number of citations to your written work

+ 7) How do I demonstrate that I have been employed in a critical or essential capacity for an organization that has a distinguished reputation?

Some of the evidence you may submit to demonstrate that you have been employed in a critical or essential capacity for an organization that has a distinguished reputation includes:

- A letter from the employer which establishes your employment in a critical capacity with the organization or establishment
- Publications written about your employment in a critical or essential capacity
- Publications recognizing the organization or establishment where you worked in the critical or essential capacity as having a distinguished reputation

+ 8) How do I demonstrate that I command or have commanded a high salary or other remuneration for my services?

Some of the evidence you may submit to demonstrate that you command or have commanded a high salary or other remuneration for your services includes:

- Copies of employment contracts detailing the salary you were paid or will be paid
- Copies of payroll documents or tax returns detailing the wage you were paid
- Evidence establishing that you have received other significant forms of compensation for your services, which may include, but is not limited to, equity in-lieu of cash remuneration, deferred compensation, profits from the sale of a business you started, or other forms of remuneration in addition to salary
- A statistical comparison of the salaries in the field in which you are starting your business from a government or private institution or a similar organization. The comparison should show that the salary or other remuneration you commanded, or will command, is significantly higher than that commanded by others in the field

Requirement 2 - The petition must be filed by a United States employer, a United States agent, or a foreign employer through a United States agent.

While the regulations prohibit an O-1A beneficiary from petitioning for himself or herself, an entity owned by the beneficiary may be eligible to file the petition on behalf of the O-1A owner.

Requirement 3 - You must obtain a consultation letter from an appropriate peer group.

A consultation is an advisory opinion written by an individual or group with expertise in your field, which in some instances may be a labor and/or management organization, regarding the nature of your work and your qualifications. The consultation should describe your ability and achievements in your field.

I'm ready to apply, what's next?

Once you have determined that the O-1A visa classification is the best pathway for you and you are ready to apply, you can find the full application process and legal requirements outlined on USCIS's website.

Note: When submitting evidence to USCIS, it is important to fully and clearly explain how the submitted evidence establishes eligibility for petition approval. The more clearly the petitioner can articulate his or her eligibility, the more efficiently and consistently USCIS can review and process the petition and determine eligibility for the benefit sought.

BACK

8

THE J-1 EXCHANGE VISITOR VISA

The J-1 exchange visitor visa is a nonimmigrant category for work– and study-based exchange visitors. The J-1 category was created by U.S. Congress in 1961 and is actually a conglomeration of 15 different programs in both the private and government sectors. More than 300,000 people enter the United States each year in various J-1 programs. The categories are[1]:

- Professors
- Research scholars
- Short-term scholars
- Trainees
- Interns
- College and university students
- Teachers
- Secondary school students
- Specialists
- Physicians
- Camp Counselors
- Au Pairs
- Summer work travel
- Government visitors
- International visitors

Some rules are common to all the programs, but each program has its own restrictions. For each category, the Department of State designates exchange program sponsor organizations that are charged with administering these programs. In some categories where work is authorized, the exchange program is not the employer and

[1] On June 22, 2020, President Trump signed Proclamation 10052, which bars the issuance of certain types of nonimmigrant visas. The travel ban covers J-1 visas for trainees, interns, teachers, au pairs, camp counselors, and summer workers. The order is set to expire on December 31, 2020, and is being challenged in court.

instead is charged with ensuring that the employers and exchange visitors are meeting the program requirements. For example, the Educational Commission on Foreign Medical Graduates is the sole organization charged with administering the physician J-1 program. However, hundreds of teaching hospitals around the country are approved worksites for J-1 physicians.

The Home Residency Requirement

Before getting into the details of the various J-1 programs that may be available to entrepreneurs and those hoping to eventually start businesses, a key restriction on the J-1 visa needs to be explained. Under Section 212(e) of the Immigration and Nationality Act, certain J-1 visa recipients are required to return to their home country for two years or face various restrictions on their immigration abilities in the United States. The J-1 home residency requirement applies in three circumstances:[2]

- The J-1 visitor's participation in the program was "financed in whole or in part, directly or indirectly, by an agency of the government of the United States or by the government of his nationality or last residence";
- The J-1 was at the time of admission or acquisition of J-1 status engaged in a field on the State Department's Exchange Visitor Skill List; or
- The J-1 is coming to the United States to receive graduate medical education or training.

If the J-1 is subject to the home residency requirement, then the following restrictions apply until the two-year requirement has been satisfied[3]:

- The J-1 may not receive an immigrant visa;
- The J-1 may not change nonimmigrant status from J-1 to another nonimmigrant category in the United States; and
- The J-1 may not receive an H-1B or an L-1 visa.

Waivers of the two-year home residency requirement are available based on the following four reasons:[4]

- Possible persecution;
- Exceptional hardship;
- A no-objection letter issued by the country where the home residency requirement must be satisfied; and

---

[2] Immigration and Nationality Act (INA) §212(e), 8 U.S. Code (USC) §1182(e).

[3] *Id.* Also see 22 Code of Federal Regulations (CFR) §62.2 defining the home-country physical presence requirement.

[4] 8 CFR §§212.7(c), 1212.7(c); 22 CFR §41.63(a)(2)–(g).

– Requested by a U.S. government agency (or, in some instances, physicians can get waivers sponsored by state health agencies).

Note that when U.S. government funds are received, a no-objection letter from the home country is not enough. In addition, if a J-1 received funding from certain U.S. government agencies, such as a Fulbright scholarship, a waiver is granted in only a small percentage of cases.

Someone considering the J-1 category will need to carefully analyze these issues. Does the J-1 home residency requirement apply? If it does, how hard would it be to get a waiver, or is leaving the United States for two years following the program something the person can tolerate? Note that some countries routinely grant no-objection letters while others rarely do.

Assuming the home residency requirement is not a problem, various J-1 programs may be of interest to entrepreneurs.[5] More than half the J-1s entering the United States are coming in the student category. There is a key difference, however, that may make the F-1 student visa the more attractive option for a would-be student. See Chapter 3 for more on F-1s.

The Student Category

The J-1 student category is open to those pursuing degrees from the associate level up to the PhD. And certain non-degree programs are eligible. However, it is how the programs are funded that presents the issue for those thinking about starting up companies. Students are eligible for J-1 visas if the program is:

1. Financed directly or indirectly by the U.S. government, the home country government or an international organization of which the United States is a member by treaty or statute,

2. If the program is carried out pursuant to an agreement by the United States (or state and local governments) and the home country governments,

3. The program is carried out pursuant to written agreements between the United States and foreign academic institutions or the U.S. institution and the foreign government, or

[5] Spouses of J-1 holders are eligible for J-2 visas. One important benefit of the J-1 visa that is worth noting is that J-2 spouses can apply for employment authorization.

4. The student is primarily funded by sources other than personal or family funds. [6]

There is a high probability the home residency requirement will be triggered by most of these routes.

The J-1 student category permits employment including on-campus work and 18 months of post-graduate training (36 months for post-doctoral training). Also, the J-1 procedures are generally seen as less complex and cumbersome than the F-1 (for example, fewer times an application needs to be made to U.S. Citizenship and Immigration Services).

Internships and Training

Two other categories that might be of interest to startup founders are the J-1 internship and trainee programs.

J-1 internship opportunities exist for those either enrolled in and pursuing studies at a degree or certificate-granting, post-secondary institution outside the United States or for those who have graduated from such an institution within the 12 months prior to the start date of the exchange program. Also, the applicant needs to have the English skills necessary to do the internship on a day-to-day basis. Finally, the internship must be in the intern's field of study. Internships can be granted for up to 12 months.

The J-1 trainee program has slightly different rules. J-1 trainees must have either a degree or a professional certificate from a foreign post-secondary academic institution *and* one year of prior work experience in their field outside the United States *or* five years of work experience outside the United States in their fields. Trainees can be generally granted trainee opportunities of up to 18 months (hotel and tourism opportunities are limited to 12 months and agriculture is limited to 12 months unless there is six months of classroom training).

Internship and training opportunities are limited to the following categories:

- Agriculture, forestry and fishing,
- Arts and culture,
- Construction and building trades,
- Education, social sciences, library science, counseling and social services,
- Health related occupations,

[6] 22 CFR §62.23.

- Hospitality and tourism,
- Information media and communications,
- Management, business, commerce and finance,
- Public administration and law, and
- The sciences, engineering, architecture, mathematics and industrial occupations.

The internship and trainee categories are not generally going to be appropriate for starting a business, but the category can be useful for startups looking for international talent or who are interested in training people to run overseas operations. Employers must work through a designated J-1 internship or trainee program[7].

Employers sponsoring an intern or a trainee are required to work from a training plan, provide continuous supervision, provide mentoring by experienced staff, and ensure that the J-1 visitors are provided educational opportunities through activities like classroom training and attending conferences.

Like the student category, the applicability of the two-year home residency requirement can impact a would-be startup founder's plans, as well as those of the startup looking to continue the employment of an intern or trainee.

---

[7] Approved programs can be found at https://j1visa.state.gov/participants/how-to-apply/sponsor-search/.

9

Visas for Nationals of Certain Countries Through Specific Trade Agreements and Treaties

The previous chapters have dealt with the common nonimmigrant visas that a startup may consider for its founders and as it scales and inevitably hires foreign-national talent. This chapter will address a few remaining nonimmigrant visa categories only available to nationals of certain countries mostly through trade agreements and specific treaties with the United States, such as TN NAFTA Professionals from Mexico and Canada; E-3 Certain Specialty Occupation Professional from Australia; and H-1B1 Specialty Occupation Professional from Singapore and Chile.[1]

TN NAFTA Professionals from Mexico and Canada

The North American Free Trade Agreement (NAFTA) was signed by the United States, Canada, and Mexico in 1992 and went into effect January 1, 1994. The trade agreement created a free-trade zone among the three countries, removing tariffs on most goods produced and sold within the continent. NAFTA covers many issues including intellectual property, agriculture, trade in services, dispute resolution, and much more. For our purpose, it most notably covers some categories of visas Canadian and Mexican nationals can obtain for employment in the United States (B-1, E-1, E-2, L-1, and TN). In the context of some visas like L-1 intracompany transfers, special procedural steps not available to citizens of other countries exist under NAFTA for the adjudication of these types of cases for Canadians. Entrepreneurs

[1] While H-1Bs are subject to the travel ban stated in President Trump's Proclamation 10052 (signed June 22, 2020), the Department of State has indicated that the H-1B1 category for Chile and Singapore nationals is not included.

will most often see the effects of NAFTA on U.S. immigration through the TN NAFTA Professional nonimmigrant classification.

To be eligible to come to the United States temporarily to engage in business activities in TN status, the applicant:

1. Must be a citizen of Canada or Mexico;
2. Must be in a profession that qualifies under the regulations;
3. Must have a position in the United States that requires a NAFTA professional;
4. Must have a prearranged full-time or part-time job with a U.S. employer (but not self-employment); and
5. Must meet the qualifications to practice in the profession in question.

Entrepreneurs and founders will quickly notice point four regarding self-employment. The regulations state, "It [NAFTA] does not authorize the establishment of a business or practice in the United States in which the professional will be, in substance, self-employed."[2] The U.S. Customs and Border Protection (CBP) *Inspector's Field Manual* goes on to explain, "Self-employment also clearly conflicts with the intent of the NAFTA Implementation Act and its accompanying Statement of Administrative Action," because the section for "traders and investors" (E-1 and E-2) is in place for those operations.

However, self-employment in the TN context speaks to arrangements where the foreign national "is the sole or controlling shareholder or owner or over which he or she holds de facto control."[3] The regulation explains: "A professional will be deemed to be self-employed if he or she will be rendering services to a corporation or entity of which the professional is the sole or controlling shareholder or owner."[4]

For situations in which a co-founder or equity owner clearly is not a sole proprietor, controlling shareholder, or holding control over the company, the CBP *Inspector's Field Manual* provides further guidance:

> (E) Substantial Control. Whether the businessperson "substantially controls" the U.S. enterprise will depend on the specific facts of each case. The following factors, among others, are relevant in determining what constitutes substantial control:
>
> - whether the applicant has established the receiving enterprise;

[2] 8 Code of Federal Regulations (CFR) §214.6.

[3] *Inspector's Field Manual* §15.5(f)(1)(A).

[4] 8 CFR §214.6.

- whether, as a matter of fact, the applicant has sole or primary control of the U.S. enterprise (regardless of the applicant's actual percentage of share ownership);
- whether the applicant is the sole or primary owner of the business; or
- whether the applicant is the sole or primary recipient of income of the business.

(F) Establishment of a Business in Which the Professional Will be Self-Employed in the United States. The following factors, among others are relevant in determining whether the businessperson will be self-employed in the United States:

- incorporation of a company in which the businessperson will be self-employed;
- initiation of communications (*e.g.*, by direct mail or by advertising) for the purpose of obtaining employment or entering into contracts for an enterprise in the United States; or
- responding to advertisements for the purpose of obtaining employment or entering into contracts.

On the other hand, the following activities do not constitute the establishment of a business in which the businessperson will be self-employed in the United States:

- responding to unsolicited inquiries about service(s) which the professional may be able to perform; or
- establishing business premises from which to deliver pre-arranged service to clients.[5]

TN applications involving co-founders and equity owners are not barred outright unless the arrangement is self-employment as defined above. An example of an approvable TN arrangement would be one in which a company with a few co-founders is petitioning one of its entrepreneurs who has a less-than-controlling share in the company. Demonstrating that the board of directors of the company is arranged in such a way that the TN applicant cannot exercise control over the company perhaps because the applicant is not on the board or can be simply outvoted is beneficial.

Despite the limitations on self-employment, U.S. companies often find excellent candidates for hire in Canada and Mexico and in many cases can employ them in the United States in TN status. Generally, the first question in TN analysis of a potential hire is whether the proffered position is within the NAFTA list of professions. The

---

[5] *Inspector's Field Manual* §15.5(f)(1)(E)–(F).

next question is whether the individual meets the qualifications for that occupation under NAFTA. For *most* categories, the requirements are merely a bachelor's degree or *licenciatura degree* (a degree common in Mexico that usually requires three–five years of study and is generally equivalent to a U.S. bachelor's degree) related to the field. Some categories allow for the person to qualify based on federal/state/provincial licensure in the given occupation. Then some other categories allow for qualification based on a post-secondary diploma or post-secondary certificate. A post-secondary diploma is generally based on two or more years of study as an accredited U.S. or Canadian institution of higher education. A post-secondary certificate is comparable to the diploma but from an institution accredited by the Mexican federal government of a Mexican state government. The full list of occupations and their requirements, which can be found at Appendix 1603.D.1 to Annex 1603 of the NAFTA, includes:

- Accountant
- Architect
- Computer Systems Analyst
- Economist
- Engineer
- Forester
- Graphic Designer
- Hotel Manager
- Industrial Designer
- Interior Designer
- Land Surveyor
- Landscape Architect
- Lawyer
- Librarian
- Management Consultant
- Mathematician
- Range Manager
- Research Assistant
- Scientific Technician
- Social Worker
- Technical Publications Writer
- Urban Planner
- Vocational Counselor
- Dentist
- Dietitian
- Medical Laboratory Technologist
- Nutritionist
- Occupational Therapist
- Pharmacist
- Physician
- Physiotherapist
- Psychologist
- Recreational Therapist
- Registered Nurse
- Veterinarian
- Agriculturist
- Animal Breeder/Scientist
- Apiculturist
- Astronomer
- Biochemist
- Biologist
- Chemist
- Dairy Scientist
- Entomologist
- Epidemiologist
- Geneticist
- Geochemist
- Geologist
- Geophysicist
- Horticulturist
- Meteorologist
- Pharmacologist
- Physicist
- Plant Breeder
- Poultry Scientist
- Soil Scientist
- Zoologist
- College Professor
- Seminary Professor
- University Professor

For example, if your startup is trying to fill a position for a graphic designer and identifies a Mexican or Canadian national with a bachelor's degree in graphic design or closely related field, this individual and position would likely qualify for a TN under NAFTA (of course, other general visa eligibility and admissibility need to be considered).

However, unlike in the H-1B context, the person's degree must actually be in the field closely related to graphic design, because TNs cannot use combined academic and work experience evaluations to qualify for the position. If the occupation at hand is one that typically requires licensure in Mexico or Canada but not in the United States, it is not required to have such licensure to fill the position in the United States—but the consular officer, CBP officer, or USCIS examiner may wish to see such licensure in support of your application.

Unfortunately, while some NAFTA occupations and degree titles match very closely to job titles (*i.e.*, mechanical engineer with a bachelor's degree in mechanical engineering) that is not always the case. Thus, below are some of the less straightforward occupations, which are most commonly used by startups.

Software Engineers. Startups commonly need to add Software Engineers and look to Canada and Mexico to fill this highly sought-after position. Although this occupation logically fits under the broader NAFTA occupation category of *Engineer*, most software engineers do not hold degrees with engineering titles (*i.e.*, bachelor of software engineering). These candidates more commonly hold computer science degrees. Fortunately, the U.S. Department of Labor's (DOL) *Occupational Outlook Handbook* (OOH) shows that software developers and software engineers are synonymous. We look for further guidance in the OOH, which explains:

> Software developers usually have a bachelor's degree, typically in computer science, software engineering, or a related field.

It can be shown that a candidate with a degree in Computer Science does "have the qualifications to practice in the profession in question."

Computer Systems Analysts. Similar to software engineers, many companies look to Mexico and Canada for additional candidates to fill systems analyst positions. In the same spirit, many candidates will hold degrees in computer science. Though not a perfect match, it is still the typical degree held by such professionals, and a candidate with a degree in computer science does "have the qualifications to practice in the profession in question."

Management Consultants. Unlike the other TN occupations, the management consultants are one of the two occupations that do not necessarily require a degree or licensure for a candidate to receive a TN. Instead, NAFTA requires either

> [1] Baccalaureate or *Licenciatura* Degree; or [2] equivalent professional experience as established by statement or professional credential attesting to five years' experience as a management consultant, or [3] five years' experience in a field of specialty related to the consulting agreement.

Because applicants can use work experience instead of a degree to qualify, many people without degrees or in occupations that are not on the NAFTA list try to force themselves into this category by arguing that they are management consultants. This has led to increased scrutiny of applications under this category.

The OOH explains that management consultants (or management analysts) "advise managers on how to make organizations more profitable through reduced costs and increased revenues." No matter the department the candidate may be joining, he or she should be filling a role to consult company or department management on specific initiatives that will affect the company's bottom line.

Scientific Technician/Technologist (ST/T). *Scientific Technicians* is the second category that does not necessarily require a degree or licensure in the field to qualify. NAFTA requires a ST/T have:

> Possession of (a) theoretical knowledge of any of the following disciplines: agricultural sciences, astronomy, biology, chemistry, engineering, forestry, geology, geophysics, meteorology, or physics; and (b) the ability to solve practical problems in any of those disciplines, or the ability to apply principles of any of those disciplines to basic or applied research.

An application for a ST/T should clearly demonstrate how the individual is supporting another individual who is working in one of those disciplines (such as the chief technology officer (CTO) or head of engineering) and how the manager directly oversees the work of the ST/T.

TNs are interesting in that they can be adjudicated by U.S. Citizenship and Immigration Services (USCIS), U.S. Department of State (DOS), and Customs and Border Protection (CBP). Canadian citizens do not need visas, so they can apply for TN status from CBP at a port of entry or through USCIS in the form of an initial application, change of status, or extension of previously approved TN status. Mexican citizens, on the other hand, do require visas; they can apply at a U.S. consulate or embassy for a visa, or with USCIS as a change of status if they are already in the United States in another status, or with USCIS as extension of status if they are already in the United States in TN status.

A Canadian citizen applying with CBP will present a paper application in person at a port of entry (land crossings, U.S. airports, foreign airports with U.S. preclearance). Along with proof of Canadian citizenship, the application must include a job offer letter from the U.S. employer. The letter should include the proposed job title, detailed job description, requirements for hire, an explanation of how it qualifies as a TN profession, address where the work will be performed, details on whether the position is part or full-time, the offered salary, and an explanation of how the beneficiary qualifies for the position. The job offer letter should have an original ink signature from the employer. The applicant should also present his or her original academic credentials (*i.e.*, original diploma) as proof of qualification. It is advisable to include proof that the U.S. company has the ability to pay the applicant the offered wage. Canadians applying at the border may request up to three years of TN status.

A U.S. company may also file a TN petition for a Canadian citizen who is abroad by filing an I-129 Petition for Nonimmigrant Worker and the Trade Agreement Supplement to Form I-129 with USCIS and paying the current $460 government fee. Similar to other nonimmigrant categories, TN petitions may be premium processed with USCIS by filing Form I-907 and paying an additional fee of $1,440 as it is currently. USCIS will adjudicate the petition, and if approved, the Canadian national may present the I-797 Approval Notice from USCIS at the port of entry and be admitted to the United States in TN status. The applicants may also request up to three years of initial TN status. Whether to apply for an initial Canadian TN with CBP or USCIS is a case-specific decision.

A Mexican citizen applying for a TN visa from abroad will apply through DOS at an embassy or consulate. To apply, the applicant must first complete Form DS-160 Online Nonimmigrant Visa Application. After completing the online form, he or she will pay the current $190 Machine Readable Visa (MRV) fee and schedule two appointments at a consulate in Mexico: one appointment for biometrics and one appointment for the TN application. At the biometrics appointment, DOS will simply collect fingerprints and a photo of the applicant. At the second interview, the individual will actually present his or her application for the TN visa. The application should contain the same evidence described above: proof of citizenship, job offer letter (with details above), proof of qualifications and education credentials, and company documents.

Like the CBP officer, the consular officer will ask questions about the offered employment and the individual's qualifications for the position. Once approved, the officer will keep the individual's passport so that the visa can be printed in it (typically three–seven days). Mexican TN visas are only issued for a period of one year. Once the passport is returned with the valid TN visa, the individual may travel to the United States and present the passport and visa to CBP at the port of entry to be admitted in TN status.

If a Mexican or Canadian national is already in the United States in another status, a U.S. company may petition to employ the individual on a TN by filing a *change of status* with USCIS. The U.S. employer does this by filing an I-129 Petition for Nonimmigrant Worker and the Trade Agreement Supplement to Form I-129 with USCIS and paying the $460 government fee. In this situation, however, the application is marked as a change of status since the individual is already in the United States in another status. These petitions also can be premium processed with USCIS by filing Form I-907 and paying the $1,440 fee. Mexican and Canadians applying for a change of status can request up to three years of TN status. If approved, USCIS will issue an I-797 Approval Notice that contains a new I-94 showing the individual's status has changed to TN and the date at which the status will expire.

Once a Mexican or Canadian national is in the United States working in TN status, he or she may simply extend that status through USCIS. This is also done by filing an I-129 Petition for Nonimmigrant Worker and the Trade Agreement Supplement to Form I-129 with USCIS and paying the $460 government fee, with the option of premium processing. By filing a timely extension with USCIS before the current TN expires, an individual will receive an automatic 240-day extension of TN status while the petition is pending. If USCIS denies the petition within the 240 days, the individual's work authorization ends at the time of the denial. All applicants for extension may request up to three years of additional TN status.

The last scenario many companies encounter is hiring an individual who is currently working in TN status for another U.S. employer. In this case, you may file with USCIS to transfer the TN to your startup. While you have the option to have the person travel abroad and use one of the previously described processes, it is common to file for a *change of employer* to avoid international travel. In this scenario, your company will file an I-129 Petition for Nonimmigrant Worker and the Trade Agreement Supplement to Form I-129 with USCIS and pay the $460 government fee. Here, however, the application is marked as a "Change of Employer" since the individual is already in the United States on a TN at another company. These cases can be premium processed to quickly onboard the new employee, and an extension of TN status of up to three years can be requested at the same time as the change of employer. Upon approval, the I-797 will contain the new employer's information and a new I-94 showing the date to which the TN status has been extended.

Despite the one-year limit on Mexican TN visas and the general limit on three-year periods of stay, there is no limit on the overall time a person may spend in TN status. So long as continued employment exists and the other qualifications for a TN are met, an individual can continue seeking TNs. A TN is not a dual-intent visa, so an individual cannot show the intent to immigrate to the United States permanently; however, this does not mean that a person cannot eventually seek permanent residence. What this means is that at the time an individual seeks a TN, he or she must not have the intent to remain permanently and thus should not have a green card or immigrant visa application filed on his or her behalf at that time. A person can come to the United States on a TN intending to remain temporarily and later be petitioned for permanent residence by an employer or family member.

The spouses and children of TN holders are eligible for *TD status* or visas. TDs are not authorized to work, but they are authorized to study while in the United States.

Treaty Visas Similar to H-1Bs: The H-1B1 and E-3

As previously discussed, a number of visa categories similar to the H-1B category are only available to nationals of certain countries. These categories came about through different trade deals and agreements with specific countries, including Australia, Chile, and Singapore.

The E-3 visa for "Certain Specialty Occupation Professionals from Australia" was enacted as part of "The Emergency Supplemental Appropriations Act for Defense, the Global War on Terror, and Tsunami Relief, 2005" (May 11, 2005). As with the other E visas previously discussed (see Chapter 5), E-3 came about as a result of a trade deal between the two countries: The Australia–United States Free Trade Agreement (AUSFTA). While Australians also have the benefits of E-1 Treaty Trader and E-2 Treaty Investor visas, the E-3 is a unique visa category only available to Australian professionals.

The H-1B1 visa for "Free Trade Agreement Workers in a Specialty Occupation from Chile and Singapore" came through a trade agreement signed by the United States and the respective countries in 2003 and which went into effect January 1 of the following year. The U.S.-Singapore Free Trade Agreement was notably the first trade agreement signed between the United States and an Asian nation. Both agreements included provisions on immigration resulting in a visa similar to the H-1B but available only for those countries.

As discussed in the H-1B chapter at great length (Chapter 4), only 85,000 new H-1Bs are approved each year, and due to the high demand for specialty occupation professionals, a lottery is held every April for those visas. Under the trade deals, 1,400 visas are available for professionals with Chilean citizenship and 5,400 for professionals from Singapore; these 6,800 total visas are deducted from the annual

85,000 H-1Bs available in the lottery. On the other hand, 10,500 E-3 visas are allotted annually to Australian specialty occupation professionals, and those are completely separate from the 85,000 H-1Bs. No lottery exists for the H-1B1 and E-3 categories because they have not historically been oversubscribed. The obvious benefit to a greater supply of visas than annual demand is that pursuing an E-3 does not come down to chance as it can with an H-1B, but another great benefit is that since E-3s and H-1B1s are not subject to a lottery, a person may apply any time during the year, as needed.

E-3s and H-1B1s are still based on whether the person is a professional and whether the position he or she is filling is a specialty occupation. The *Foreign Affairs Manual* explains:

To qualify for an E-3 visa, an Australian must:

1. Present an approved Labor Condition Application (LCA) issued by DOL;
2. Demonstrate that the prospective employment meets the standard of being "specialty occupation employment";
3. Demonstrate the necessary academic qualifications for the job have been met;
4. Submit evidence that the proposed stay in the United States will be temporary; and
5. Provide evidence of a license or other official permission to practice in the specialty occupation if required as a condition for the employment sought.[6] In certain cases, where such license or other official permission is not required immediately, the foreign national must demonstrate that he or she will obtain such licensure or permission within a reasonable period of time following admission to the United States.

To qualify for an H-1B1 visa, one must:

1. Be a national of Chile or Singapore and must meet the general academic and occupational requirements for the position pursuant to the definition cited. Proof of alternative credentials may be submitted for certain professions.
2. Submit evidence that his or her employer has filed an LCA with DOL covering the applicant's position. A certified Form ETA-9035 clearly annotated as "H-1B1 Chile" or "H-1B1 Singapore" must be submitted as evidence of filing.

---

[6] See 9 *Foreign Affairs Manual* (FAM) 402.9-8(H).

3. Submit evidence that the employer has paid any applicable fee imposed.

4. Submit evidence that his or her stay in the United States will be temporary (a letter or contract of employment should be evidence that the employment is being offered on a temporary basis).

5. Pay the MRV fee or provide proof of payment.[7]

As thoroughly discussed in the chapter on H-1Bs, a *specialty occupation* is defined as:

> An occupation that requires (A) theoretical and practical application of a body of highly specialized knowledge, and (B) attainment of a bachelor's or higher degree in the specific specialty (or its equivalent) as a minimum for entry into the occupation in the United States.[8]

In some cases, a co-founder may fall into a position where his or her degree is closely related to the field in which he or she works and can qualify as a specialty occupation. A common example is the co-founder and CTO who has a degree in computer science or mechanical engineering.

Similar to an H-1B, entrepreneurs face bigger challenges in the H-1B1 and E-3 context due to their equity ownership in the petitioning entity. However, a U.S. company may petition a person who owns a portion (or even the majority) of the company for an E-3 or H-1B1. Again, the main factor is the employer-employee relationship and who or what controls the beneficiary's employment. Relying again on the 2010 Neufeld Memo, the main factors to consider in determining whether a qualifying relationship exists include the following (with no one factor being decisive):

- Does the petitioner supervise the beneficiary, and is such supervision off-site or on-site?
- If the supervision is off-site, how does the petitioner maintain such supervision, *i.e.*, weekly calls, reporting back to main office routinely, or site visits by the petitioner?
- Does the petitioner have the right to control the work of the beneficiary on a day-to-day basis if such control is required?
- Does the petitioner provide the tools or instrumentalities needed for the beneficiary to perform the duties of employment?
- Does the petitioner hire, pay, and have the ability to fire the beneficiary?

---

[7] 9 FAM 402.10-5(H).

[8] Immigration and Nationality Act (INA) §214(i)(1).

- Does the petitioner evaluate the work-product of the beneficiary, *i.e.*, progress/performance reviews?
- Does the petitioner claim the beneficiary for tax purposes?
- Does the petitioner provide the beneficiary any type of employee benefits?
- Does the beneficiary use proprietary information of the petitioner in order to perform the duties of employment?
- Does the beneficiary produce an end-product that is directly linked to the petitioner's line of business?
- Does the petitioner have the ability to control the manner and means in which the work product of the beneficiary is accomplished?

Founders will have difficulties under any of these categories if they cannot show an "outside entity which can exercise control over the beneficiary." It is not always appropriate from a business law perspective and should be given significant consideration, but creating a board of directors that controls the individual's employment (*i.e.*, hire, pay, fire, supervise, or otherwise control the work of the foreign national) is the most common solution for entrepreneurs in this scenario.

As mentioned, the Trump administration has claimed that the degree the person holds must bear the name of the exact field as the position (as opposed to closely related fields that would also give a person the specialized knowledge needed for the position), often trying to rely on the DOL's *Occupational Outlook Handbook* only when it suits the examiner, although DOL never intended it for that purpose. The result has been increased Requests for Evidence and H-1B denials by USCIS based on specialty occupation challenges. A notable difference in the H-1B1 and E-3 context is that the DOS seems to have not adopted this extremist misreading of the regulations in contrast with USCIS, which is significant since these visas can be applied for at the consulate and without USCIS adjudication.

Whether applying at a consulate abroad or in the United States through USCIS, the process of applying for an E-3 or H-1B1 also starts with DOL and the filing of a labor condition application (LCA). The LCA solidifies the worksite, petitioning entity, wage, and other company related information. To complete the LCA, a DOL Standard Occupational Classification (SOC) code must be selected that most closely fits the duties of the position. Again, this is where a founder often has a hard time—finding an SOC code that fits his or her situation. Choosing a job code like Chief Executive is likely broad and will carry with it a high wage reflective of the DOL wage data for all C-level executives in the county where he or she will work.

However, given the size of an early startup, a more appropriate job code may relate to the engineering role or software developer role in which the founder is spending much more time while developing a product. The point is that determining the correct SOC code is a strategy that should be given proper consideration since it will lead to degree and wage requirements, and the typical co-founder titles are not always the most accurate.

Once the LCA is filed with DOL, the employer must post a *Notice of Filing* at the worksite. The posting must include the following information: job title; salary; start date; end date; and work location. This notice must be posted for 10 business days at the work locations. A company signatory must sign and date the notice and list the dates it was posted and taken down.

As with the H-1B, a company petitioning an E-3 or H-1B1 must also create a *public access file* (PAF) within one day of the filing of the LCA. The PAF must contain the following items:

- A copy of the filed LCA and cover pages (once the LCA is certified in about a week after filing, a copy of the signed certified LCA to the PAF is added).
- A copy of the LCA Instructions (10 pages).
- Documentation of the wage rate to be paid and a copy of the documentation used to establish the prevailing wage, which explains how the employer calculated the prevailing wage used in the LCA.
- A memorandum from the employer documenting that the H-1B beneficiary will be paid an amount equal to or higher than the actual wage paid to other employees with similar experience and qualifications and explaining the system used to determine the actual wage.
- Acknowledgment that the H-1B employee has received a copy of the LCA.
- Documentation that the LCA has been provided to the collective bargaining representative OR documentation that the LCA was posted at the work site or provided to employees' electronically.
- A summary of the benefits offered to the employer's U.S. workers in the same occupational classification as the H-1B worker. Any differences in benefits need to be explained.
- If the employer undergoes a change in corporate structure (such as a merger), a sworn statement from a responsible officer of the new employing entity that it accepts all the obligations, liabilities and undertakings under the LCAs filed by the predecessor employer, together with a list of each affected LCA, their date of certification and a description of the actual wage system and the Federal Employer ID Number of the new employer.
- Where the employer uses the IRS definition of a "single employer", a list of any entity included as part of the single employer when making H-1B determinations.
- For employers who are H-1B dependent or a "willful violator" and it indicates an employee is exempt from the dependency requirements on account of wage or degree, a list of exempt H-1B employees and a summary of recruitment methods used and the time frames of recruitment of U.S. workers.

The same rules must be followed for E-3 and H-1B1 PAFs in terms of retention, destruction, and availability. They should be treated the same as a PAF filed for an H-1B, which is detailed in the H-1B chapter.

Most applicants choose to file initial E-3 and H-1B1 applications at a U.S. consulate or embassy for reasons discussed. Additionally, a person who does not apply at a U.S. consulate will not receive an actual visa stamp in his or her passport that allows a person to travel internationally and continue to re-enter the United States in E-3 or H-1B1 status. When applying at a U.S. consulate, the applicant will need to complete a DS-160 Online Nonimmigrant Visa Application, pay the MRV fee, and schedule an interview.

At the interview, the applicant will present the signed, certified LCA, the DS-160 confirmation page, the MRV fee payment receipt, and the evidence that he or she qualifies for the respective visa. This usually comes in the form of the individual's passport (to prove treaty country nationality), education credentials (to prove qualifications, company financials (to prove ability to pay the offered wage), and a letter with supporting documents explaining how the position qualifies as a specialty occupation.

According to the H-1B regulations:

> [T]o qualify as a specialty occupation, the position must meet one of the following criteria:
>
> 1. A baccalaureate or higher degree or its equivalent is normally the minimum requirement for entry into the particular position;[9]
> 2. The degree requirement is common to the industry in parallel positions among similar organizations or, in the alternative, an employer may show that its particular position is so complex or unique that it can be performed only by an individual with a degree;[10]
> 3. The employer normally requires a degree or its equivalent for the position;[11] or
> 4. The nature of the specific duties is so specialized and complex that knowledge required to perform the duties is usually associated with the attainment of a baccalaureate or higher degree."[12]

---

[9] 8 CFR §214.2(h)(4)(iii)(A)(1).

[10] 8 CFR §214.2(h)(4)(iii)(A)(2).

[11] 8 CFR §214.2(h)(4)(iii)(A)(3).

Common evidence to present to the consular officer of specialty occupation includes:

- The DOL *Occupational Outlook Handbook* entry for the SOC code chosen demonstrating the applicant has the same type of degree normally required for the profession; or
- Advertisements for similar positions at similarly situated start-ups (comparable staff size, funding, industry, location, etc.) that show the same type of degree requirement;
- While the founder is typically in a unique position, evidence that the other company leadership holds degrees related to their respective positions or an organizational chart demonstrating the applicant founder's direct reports (if any) also have relevant degrees; or
- A breakdown of the duties and responsibilities of the position that explains how the tasks are complex and therefore would normally be associated with the requisite degree; it is helpful to include work product and a breakdown of how the individual will spend their time.

Once approved, Australians are granted a two-year E-3 visa that can be used for multiple entries. When entering the United States, CBP will generally admit Australians for a period of two-years. Unlike the H-1B, there is no cap on the number of E-3 visas a person can receive. So a person can continue to go for visa stamping every couple of years so long as they continue to qualify.

Nationals of Chile and Singapore will receive an 18-month H-1B1 visa, which can be used for multiple entries. CBP will generally admit H-1B1 holders for a period of one year per entry. Like E-3s, H-1B1 holders are also eligible for unlimited extensions so long as they continue to qualify.

Applicants already in the United States in another status, such as F-1 students, may choose to file a change of status to H-1B1 or E-3 with USCIS. Further, an entrepreneur already in the United States in H-1B1 or E-3 status may choose to extend his or her status through USCIS instead of traveling to a consulate. If applying through USCIS, the application is very similar to an H-1B. Once the LCA has been certified by DOL, the *Application for Change or Extension of Status* is filed using Form I-129 Petition for a Nonimmigrant Worker. An applicant will similarly need to provide his or her passport, education credentials, and a letter with supporting documents explaining how the position qualifies under the specialty occupation test above. As with other USCIS filings, there may be a Request for Evidence if additional evidence is needed. This is where current challenges to whether a position is

---

[12] 8 CFR §214.2(h)(4)(iii)(A)(4).

really a specialty occupation are likely to arise. Unfortunately, premium processing is not available for H-1B1 and E-3 applications.

A person already in the United States in H-1B1 or E-3 status who timely files an extension of status, will receive an automatic 240-day extension of the status while the adjudication takes place. The person is authorized to continue to work for the same employer during this period. The 240-day period ends at the time of a USCIS decision. USCIS will extend an individual's E-3 status up to two years per application, and H-1B1 status generally by one year.

The family members of an E-3 holder are eligible for E-3 visas and status. The main E-3 applicant's status allows for work authorization incident to status, meaning the person is authorized to work upon entering the United States in E-3 status. A spouse is also eligible for work authorization, but it is not incident to status. So a spouse must enter the United States and separately apply for work authorization using Form I-765 Application for Employment Authorization. While children are also eligible for E-3s, they are not eligible for work authorization. They can study while in the United States.

The family members of H-1B1 holders, on the other hand, are eligible for H-4 visas and status. Spouse and children on H-4s do not receive work authorization, but they may study while in the United States.

Family members in either status may, of course, seek independently to obtain their own work-authorized status through U.S. employment if they wish.

A final notable difference between the E-3 and H-1B1 as compared to the H-1B arises in the context of immigrant intent. The H-1B allows for dual intent, meaning a person can file a green card application and intend to remain in the United States permanently, and that does not prevent the issuance of future H-1B visas. E-3 and H-1B1 holders do not have that luxury, as they are not dual-intent visas and are subject to section 214(b) of the Immigration and Nationality Act. This comes up in two main contexts.

First, when applying for one of these visas at the consulate, a person must demonstrate to the satisfaction of the officer that he or she does not intend to remain in the United States permanently—often by showing ties to his or her own country.

Second: the green card application. The filing of an immigrant visa petition demonstrates immigrant intent and will often lead to consular officers denying future applications for E-3 and H-1B1 visas based on section 214(b) and immigrant intent. For this reason, an entrepreneur transitioning from an E-3 or H-1B1 to a permanent resident should have a clear strategy in place.

10

THE INTERNATIONAL ENTREPRENEUR RULE*

Entrepreneurs and co-founders are a group of foreign nationals that oftentimes do not fit well into one of the standard nonimmigrant visa categories. Though many issues can be resolved by creative lawyering, H-1Bs often lead to hurdles involving ownership issues, E visas are reserved for citizens of certain countries, O visas can be difficult for entrepreneurs to obtain, and L visas do not help new startups where the foreign national has not been previously working for a foreign company. Without a true startup visa or job creation visa in the nonimmigrant space, startup founders are often left trying to squeeze themselves into employee roles, make creative arguments in regards to their investment capital, or make stretch cases for extraordinary ability in their field.

The Obama administration created a number of initiatives to study and eventually try to help solve this glaring defect in the U.S. immigration system, which encourages foreign job creators to form their startups in more conducive (*i.e.*, outside the United States) environments. Two examples were the Entrepreneurs in Residence[1] initiative in 2011 and the Entrepreneur Pathways Portal[2] in 2012. While informative, neither of these ideas changed the legal gymnastics needed by most entrepreneurs or created a new pathway for a foreign entrepreneur to stay in the United States to run his or her new startup.

In November 2014, President Barack Obama delivered a televised address announcing a series of reforms to the immigration system that followed a failed nearly

---

* Thanks to James Hollis, https://www.linkedin.com/in/jameswhollis/, for his part in writing this chapter. This chapter is an update to an earlier version by this book's authors and Mr. Hollis and was included in the American Immigration Lawyers Association's *Immigration Options for Investors & Entrepreneurs*, 4th Ed. (2019).

[1] Visit https://bit.ly/2zWaNYf (last visited May 17, 2020).

[2] USCIS Press Release: Entrepreneur Pathways Portal (Nov. 28, 2012) (AILA Doc. No. 12112845).

two-year effort to pass a comprehensive immigration reform bill. At the time, much of the media coverage focused on a deferred action program for parents of undocumented immigrants, as well as changes to prosecutorial discretion rules to prioritize the deportation of violent criminals.

Lost in the coverage was an announcement that significant changes would be made to existing programs to help international entrepreneurs. The President noted that the reforms were designed to address some of the policy objectives addressed in the failed comprehensive immigration reform bill, and one of those was the "startup visa" that would have been created had the comprehensive bill passed.

Contemporaneously with the President's announcement, then–Department of Homeland Services (DHS) Secretary Jeh Johnson sent a memorandum to U.S. Citizenship and Immigration Services (USCIS) Director Leon Rodriguez and Immigration and Customs Enforcement (ICE) Acting Director Thomas Winkowski laying out a plan for a new entrepreneur parole program:

> Second, pursuant to the "significant public benefit" parole authority under section 212(d)(5) of the Immigration and Nationality Act (INA), USCIS should propose a program that will permit DHS to grant parole status, on a case-by-case basis, to inventors, researchers, and founders of startup enterprises who may not yet qualify for a national interest waiver, but who have been awarded substantial U.S. investor financing or otherwise hold the promise of innovation and job creation through the development of new technologies or the pursuit of cutting edge research. Parole in this type of circumstance would allow these individuals to temporarily pursue research and development of promising new ideas and businesses in the United States, rather than abroad. This regulation will include income and resource thresholds to ensure that individuals eligible for parole under this program will not be eligible for federal public benefits or premium tax credits under the Health Insurance Marketplace of the Affordable Care Act.[3]

On August 24, 2016, the Department of Homeland Security issued a proposed rule, the International Entrepreneur Rule (IER), implementing an entrepreneur parole program. After a 45-day comment period, the rule was modified in a few respects and on January 17, 2017, a final rule was released.[4] The rule called for the applications to begin being accepted beginning on July 17, 2017.

---

[3] U.S. Department of Homeland Security Memorandum, Policies Supporting U.S. High-Skilled Businesses and Workers (Nov. 20, 2014) (at https://bit.ly/2A55CVN (last visited May 17, 2020).

[4] International Entrepreneur Rule, 82 Fed. Reg. 5328 (Jan. 17, 2017) at https://bit.ly/2z669pY (last visited May 17, 2020).

On July 11, 2017, the Trump administration issued a delay rule indicating that it would not begin accepting applications until March 14, 2018, and that it intended to issue a rule removing the IER before that date.[5]

Shortly after DHS released its delay rule, the National Venture Capital Association and a group of individual plaintiffs filed a lawsuit.[6] The lawsuit challenged the process DHS used to delay the rule and requested the judge order the defendants to immediately implement the program. In December 2017, the plaintiffs were successful in their motion for summary judgment and a judge ordered the program to go forward. USCIS created an application form, issued instructions, and began accepting applications within a few weeks of the judge's order.

As of May 2018, 13 applications had been filed and no cases had been approved or denied. That information was conveyed in a letter from USCIS Director Lee Francis Cissna to Senator Charles Grassley (R-IA). That fact was cited in a motion for discovery from the plaintiffs in the lawsuit as a demonstration that the agency was not complying in good faith with the judge's order from the prior December. As of the time of writing this article, that motion had not been ruled on by the judge.

On May 29, 2018, DHS did issue a proposed rule removing the IER.[7] They offered a 30-day comment period that ended just prior to completion of drafting this article. The proposed removal rule cited three basic reasons to justify the about-face.

First, DHS argued that parole is not the proper vehicle for implementing and administering an entrepreneur immigration program. The agency mainly noted that the rule does not give any certainty to investors, entrepreneurs, and employees of the venture and the risks were too great to those parties.

Second, DHS argued that entrepreneurs could use existing immigrant and nonimmigrant programs like the E-2 nonimmigrant visa or the EB-5 immigrant investor program or U.S. Congress could create a startup visa.

Third, DHS argued that it lacked the resources and expertise to be able to adjudicate IER cases. If a final rule is, in fact, issued, and it calls for removal of the IER, further litigation is expected. While the Trump administration continues to indicate it is planning to rescind the IER rule, as of the summer of 2020, that had not yet

---

[5] International Entrepreneur Rule: Delay of Effective Date, 82 Fed. Reg. 31890 (July 11, 2017) at https://bit.ly/3eXh7xt (last visited July 16, 2018).

[6] See https://bit.ly/3cAMmNb (last visited July 16, 2018).

[7] Removal of International Entrepreneur Parole Program, 83 Fed. Reg. 24415 (proposed May 29, 2018) at https://bit.ly/2BzxDoN (last visited July 16, 2018).

happened. A few cases have been approved, but other cases remain pending. With the recent travel bans, it might become a more useful option for individuals who need to avoid depending on getting a visa stamp in an affected category.

The Application Process

On the most basic level, an application for Entrepreneur Parole requires filling out the Form I-941 and submitting it with supporting documentation and filing fees ($1,200 filing fee + $85 for biometrics per person).[8] The Form I-941 requests relatively basic personal information and then asks for detailed information about the investment or grant that forms the basis for the parole eligibility and continues with detailed questions for a re-parole filing. Parole can be granted for an initial period of 30 months, which can be extended for an additional 30 months upon proof that the parolee will continue to provide a significant public benefit based on his or her role in the startup. The applicant does not need to submit an additional application for employment authorization with his or her application for parole.

As with all immigration case types, filing the form is only part of the exercise. What matters most is the supporting documentation that an attorney gathers and creates with the client. While Entrepreneur Parole has some unique characteristics, it is helpful to consider creating an application for parole with reference to more common concepts that many practitioners are already comfortable with in business immigration law.

To obtain Entrepreneur Parole, it must be proven that the petitioning startup company exists, and that it was created within the last five years. It must be proven that an investment of at least $250,000 by a "qualified investor" was made into that business or the startup received a "qualified government grant or award" of at least $100,000 from a government agency. If the investment capital or grant threshold cannot be met, then the applicant can try in the alternative to establish compelling evidence showing a substantial potential for rapid growth and job creation; in these grants of discretion USCIS may consider the types of jobs created and the wage levels.

Furthermore, the invested capital must be coming from a "qualified investor." For IER purposes, a qualified investor must have invested a total of at least $600,000 in startups in three different calendar years (within the preceding five years), and at least two of the startups must have created at least five qualified jobs

---

[8] See www.uscis.gov/I-941 (last visited July 16, 2018).

or generated at least $500,000 in revenue with average annualized revenue growth of 20 percent or more.[9]

It also must be proven that the applicant owns a minimum of 10 percent of the startup company. This is much like an L-1A case in which the beneficiary is an owner. It must be proven that the entrepreneur is playing a central and active role in the business. This is much like the requirement in an E-2 case that the Treaty Investor is in a position to develop and direct the enterprise. It also must be proven that there will be a significant public benefit to the United States. This is much like the EB-2 National Interest Waivers (NIW) standard that the beneficiary's work will "substantially benefit prospectively the national economy, cultural or educational interest, or welfare" of the United States.

Finally, you must document the lawful source of funds and provide evidence that the investors in the case have made similar investments that created jobs or achieved annual recurring revenue. This is like the source of funds and job creation requirements in the EB-5 or E-2 context. Note that documentation of the "lawful source of funds" could be interpreted by USCIS as requiring submission of rigorous and detailed financial and background information from the investors (as with an EB-5), or as requiring a less intrusive showing (as with an E-2).

Below are the requirements of Entrepreneur Parole broken down into their constituent parts with recommendations for evidence that can prove each aspect of the case.[10]

Evidence Showing a Startup Meets the Definition of Startup Entity

- Organizational documents (such as articles of incorporation, bylaws, articles of organization, operating agreement, certificate of partnership, partnership agreement, etc.);
- Tax records;
- Financial records; or
- Other evidence establishing the company's potential for rapid growth and job creation.

---

[9] International Entrepreneur Rule, *supra* note 4; *see also* Form I-941 Instructions, *supra* note 8.

[10] *Id.*

Evidence Showing an Entrepreneur's Ownership Stake in the Startup Entity

- Organizational documents (such as articles of incorporation, bylaws, articles of organization, operating agreement, certificate of partnership, partnership agreement, etc.);
- Equity purchase or grant agreements;
- Equity ledger;
- Equity certificates;
- Ownership schedule; or
- Capitalization table.

Evidence Showing the Entrepreneur Is Playing a Central and Active Role in the Business

- Position description of the applicant's role in the operations of the company;
- Newspaper articles or other similar evidence that the applicant or the company has received significant attention or recognition;
- Degrees or other documentation indicating that the applicant has knowledge, skills, or experience that would significantly advance the company's business;
- Letters from relevant government entities, qualified investors, or established business associations with knowledge of the entity's research, products or services, and/or the applicant's knowledge, skills or experience that would advance the entity's business;
- Evidence that the applicant or the company has been recently invited to participate in, is currently participating in, or has graduated from one or more established and reputable startup accelerators;
- Patent awards or other documents indicating that the company or the applicant is focused on developing new technologies or cutting-edge research (supported by the applicant's efforts and expertise); or
- Any evidence that the applicant has played an active and central role in the success of prior startups.

Evidence the Startup Will Have a Significant Public Benefit

- Media coverage of the startup;
- Evidence of investments from any investors, government awards, or grants and the criteria used to make the investments, awards or grants;
- Evidence of revenue generation or job creation prior to filing;

- Evidence of participation in a reputable startup accelerator and the criteria for selection of the accelerator;
- Patent awards or related documents evidencing new technologies; or
- Letters from government agencies, qualified investors, or established business associations attesting to how the startup's research, products, or services, or the entrepreneur's knowledge, skills, or experience will result in a significant public benefit in the United States.

Evidence Showing the Investment Funds Received Came From a "Qualified Investor"

- If the investor is an individual, a clear and legible copy of a government-issued identity document showing the photograph, name, and date of birth of the investor, along with evidence showing that the investor is a U.S. citizen or lawful permanent resident of the United States;
- If the investor is an organization, such as a venture capital firm or other U.S. business investing in the startup entity, evidence that the organization operates through a legal entity organized under the laws of the United States (such as articles of incorporation, bylaws, articles of organization, operating agreement, certificate of partnership, partnership agreement, etc.), along with evidence showing that it is majority owned and controlled, directly and indirectly, by U.S. citizens or lawful permanent residents of the United States (such as an ownership structure chart outlining the direct and indirect ownership of the organization together with evidence that the individuals ultimately owning and controlling a majority of the organization are U.S. citizens or lawful permanent residents of the United States); and
- Evidence that the investor has, during the prior five years (1) made investments in other U.S. business entities in exchange for equity or convertible debt or other security convertible into equity commonly used in financing transactions within their respective industries comprising a total in such five-year period of no less than $600,000; and (2) subsequent to such investment by such individual or organization, at least two such entities each created at least five qualified jobs or generated at least $500,000 in revenue with average annualized revenue growth of at least 20 percent.
- To satisfy the investment requirement, such evidence may include such records as: bank records, wire transfers, debt agreements, equity purchase agreements, equity certificates, equity ledgers, or capitalization table. To satisfy the job creation or revenue generation requirement, such evidence may include such records as: tax and/or payroll records, I-9 records, or audited financial statements.

Evidence Showing a Qualified Government Grant or Award

- Copies of grant or award letters or other documents confirming the issuance of the award or grant, the amount of the award or grant, and the recipient of the award or grant;
- Documentation that the award or grant is for economic development, research and development, or job creation (or other similar money awards typically given to startups) made by a federal, state or local government entity that regularly provides such grants or awards to startups; and
- Bank records confirming the issuance and the receipt of the award or grant.

Evidence That the Startup Received Sufficient Minimum Investment or Government Funding

- Copies of the startup entity's bank records;
- Proof of investment instruments such as convertible notes or Simple Agreement for Future Equity (SAFE) agreements;
- Accounting documents;
- Corporate ownership records; and
- Documents showing receipt by the startup of a qualified grant or award from a government entity.

[*Note*: These documents must clearly show the trail of lawfully derived capital from the qualified investor to the startup. Furthermore, the documents should show the capital was used to purchase equity, convertible debt, or another security convertible into equity issued by the startup.]

Evidence That the Investment Funds Come from a Lawful Source

- Copies of the investor's bank records;
- Copies of the investor's tax records;
- Copies of the investor's wage records;
- Documentation on the investor's employment history; or
- Copies of evidence of the investor's assets or property

[Note – *As noted above, the burden is on the entrepreneur to show the trail of lawfully derived capital to the startup*]

Miscellaneous Issues

Length of Parole

No more than three entrepreneurs can gain parole based on the same startup entity. After the initial grant of up to 30 months of parole, the entrepreneur may obtain an extension of up to 30 additional months. Parole can be granted for a maximum of five years.

Family Members

The spouse and children of an entrepreneur applying for parole must qualify for parole independently from the entrepreneur. Spouses and children apply on Form I-131 showing documentation of the familial relationship. As a practical matter, spouses and children of entrepreneurs will likely be granted parole if the entrepreneur is granted parole. Spouses will be authorized to work but must apply for an employment authorization document, preferably at the same time as the entrepreneur's application for initial parole.

The fact that spouses are authorized to work is beneficial to the entrepreneur parolee because the regulations require that the household income of the entrepreneur must be maintained at or above 400 percent of the Federal poverty guidelines. This means that a household of two, for example, must maintain earnings at $65,840 or above to continue to qualify for entrepreneur parole (with an additional $17,280 in household earnings required for each additional household member).[11] This can be a significant hurdle given that many startup founders defer salaries in favor of using that capital for developing the business. If a spouse has not previously been authorized to work, satisfying this condition may be quite challenging.

Material Changes

Entrepreneurs with parole are required to immediately report material changes to USCIS. Material changes include any change in facts that could reasonably affect the outcome of the grant of parole including employment with the startup, ownership percentage of the startup, any criminal charges against the entrepreneur, judgments against the startup exceeding 10 percent of the startup's assets, cessation of

---

[11] Based on 2018 HHS Poverty Guidelines, published annually in March (available at www.uscis.gov/i-864p) (last visited July 16, 2018). Poverty guidelines are higher for Alaska and Hawaii.

operations, and bankruptcy. Note that parole is not renewable if the entrepreneur's ownership stake is diluted to less than 5 percent.

Parole can be terminated automatically and without notice if the parole expires, if the entrepreneur notifies USCIS that he or she will no longer be employed by the startup, or if the entrepreneur's parole no longer provides a significant public benefit.

Temporary Nature

In cases where parole is denied, there is no process of appeals or motions to reconsider. USCIS concluded that appeals would be contrary to the discretionary nature of IER, and inconsistent with how other forms or parole are treated. Applicants could use the normal customer service channels to address a denial and include facts that support their belief there was an error.

This broad ability of USCIS to terminate an entrepreneur's parole means that an entrepreneur's use of parole should be temporary whenever possible. A grant of parole should be used as a platform from which to make a case for a temporary classification like an O-1A or for a green card like the EB-2 NIW or the EB-1A that provide for self-petitioning.

Letters of Intent for Itineraries

In Entrepreneur Parole applications, an applicant will need to provide support letters which address the various requirements of the parole, including letters attesting to how the startup's research, products, or services, or the entrepreneur's knowledge, skills, or experience will result in a significant public benefit in the United States, letters attesting to the entrepreneur's central and active role in the development of the startup, and letters analyzing the startup's prospects for achieving rapid growth and job creation. In order to assist with writing a letter of this sort, it will help if the letter writer follows the guidelines below.

The letters should be written on letterhead and directed "To Whom it May Concern" or to "United States Citizenship and Immigration Services."

The text of recommendation letters should address the following points in any sequence the author desires:

> First paragraph: Introduce yourself and explain what this letter will be discussing, *e.g.*, "By this letter, I attest that [the Entrepreneur] plays a central and active role in the development of [Startup Name]".

Second paragraph: The author should include a description of him or herself, including his or her professional education and training, areas of expertise, present position, memberships in appropriate societies, organizations and associations relating to the applicant's field of endeavor, and whether serving in an official capacity in any society, organization or association. Attaching a copy of the letter author's current resume or other documentation of the letter author's credentials can be very helpful.

Third paragraph: The author should explain how he or she came to know the Entrepreneur (or whether they have never met but the author knows of the Entrepreneur's work) and describe the Entrepreneur's record of accomplishment and contributions in the applicant's field of endeavor. The author should provide comment on the quality of the Entrepreneur's abilities and accomplishments.

Fourth paragraph: The author should explain the purpose of the letter again and provide detailed analysis of that point. The more objective details (*i.e.*, statistics) that can be provided to back up statements arguing for significant public benefit to the United States and the startup's likelihood of achieving rapid growth and job creation, the better.

Authors should feel free to include any other comments which favorably reflect on the beneficiary or the beneficiary's background. Once complete, each letter should be signed by hand and sent or scanned and emailed to the attorney for inclusion in the application package.

Conclusion

As of the completion of the writing of this chapter, USCIS had yet to approve or deny any IER applications or even issue Requests for Evidence. Practitioners largely have only the IER rule and USCIS application instructions to guide them in preparing petitioners. With the uncertainty surrounding the future of the program, many lawyers are ignoring IER. However, the program may still be a good option worth considering when other options are unavailable, or a good backup option when other options are filled with uncertainty.

11

Introduction to Lawful Permanent Residency (the 'Green Card')

Startup founders in nonimmigrant categories choosing to remain in the United States indefinitely typically need to convert at some point to lawful permanent resident (LPR) status. This is the so-called "green card." The term "immigrant visa" refers to the visa used to enter the country as an LPR. The various terms—"lawful permanent residency," "permanent resident," "LPR," "permanent residency," "green card," and "immigrant visa" are used throughout this book and all refer to the same concept.

There are a number of avenues to obtaining a green card in the United States. Some are based on work. Others are based on family sponsorship. There are less common avenues to obtaining a green card, including investing a significant sum of money in a business that creates jobs for U.S. workers, entering an annual green card lottery, and filing for permanent residency after obtaining asylum status. This book examines obtaining permanent residency based on work.

Lawful Permanent Residency

As its name implies, lawful permanent residency allows individuals to remain indefinitely in the United States. Nonimmigrant status, on the other hand, requires the visa holder to meet requirements particular to the visa category and is limited in duration. The majority of permanent residents in the United States gain their status via family sponsorship or in an employment category.

While green card holders can remain in the United States and work in almost any kind of job without the need for employer sponsorship, there are several important differences between permanent residency (having a green card) and citizenship. Three of the most important are the following:

1. Citizens can vote and serve on juries.
2. Citizenship is truly permanent; lawful permanent residency can be lost if a person goes abroad for an extended period and is deemed to have abandoned U.S. residency or commits a criminal offense that makes one removable.
3. Citizens are given priority in terms of sponsoring family members for permanent residency.

The Categories of Permanent Residency

- *Family sponsorship*—U.S. citizens and LPRs can sponsor relatives in various categories; there are quotas for certain categories that can cause backlogs for many years.
- *Employment-based*—Individuals engaged in certain types of employment or investments can seek green cards in five employment-based preference categories. See Chapters 15–18.
- *Asylees and refugees*—Those admitted as refugees or granted asylum in the United States are eligible for permanent residency one year after receiving refugee or asylee status.
- *Registry*—Individuals in the United States continuously since 1972, and who can show good moral character, are eligible for permanent residency; note that those subject to the J-1 home-residency requirement are not eligible for the registry without a waiver.
- *Cancellation of removal*—Individuals in the United States for 10 or more years, who have good moral character and whose removal would cause an extreme hardship to a spouse, parent, or child, may seek permanent residency while in removal proceedings.
- *Diversity immigrant visas*—People from certain countries are eligible to participate each year in an annual green card lottery.
- *Legalization*—In 1986, a law was passed allowing certain individuals to apply for permanent residency if they had been in the United States for several years and were out-of-status. For the past 10 years, the U.S. Congress has debated creating a new legalization program.

The Family Green-Card Categories

The family green card program is divided between "immediate relatives" and various preference categories.[1] Immediate relatives include spouses of U.S. citizens,

---

[1] On April 22, 2020, President Trump issued the "Proclamation Suspending Entry of Immigrants Who Present Risk to U.S. Labor Market During the Economic Recovery Following the COVID-19 Out-

Continued

parents of adult U.S. citizens, and minor children of U.S. citizens. The following are the family preference categories:

- *First preference* (F1)—unmarried adult sons and daughters of U.S. citizens.
- *Second preference* (F-2A)—spouses and minor children of LPRs.
- *Second preference* (F-2B)—unmarried adult sons and daughters of LPRs.
- *Third preference* (F3)—married sons or daughters of U.S. citizens.
- *Fourth preference* (F4)—siblings of U.S. citizens.

A spousal relationship can serve as the basis for an immigrant petition if it involves a marriage that is legally valid, is recognized in the place where it was created, and the marriage is not one entered into solely for immigration reasons. Same-sex marriages may be recognized for immigration purposes if the marriage was legal in the place where the marriage occurred. Those who receive a green card based on a marriage to a U.S. citizen where the marriage is less than two years old at the time of being granted permanent residency will receive a two-year conditional green card. An unconditional green card can be sought after two years if the marriage is intact or, if the couple is no longer together, the green card holder can demonstrate that the marriage was not solely immigration-based.

A parent includes biological parents, stepparents when the stepparent relationship with the child was created before the child turned 18, and certain adoptive parents. Out-of-wedlock children can petition for their parents if they can document the parent-child relationship (such as by a DNA test or evidence the parent has supported the child).

For sibling petitions, the U.S. citizen needs to document that there is at least one common parent.

Children born out-of-wedlock may obtain immigration benefits from a mother. They also may obtain immigration benefits from a father, but only if the child is "legitimized" before the child turns 18. This may occur if the parents have since married or if the father is able to establish a "bona fide parent-child relationship," such as if the child and father live together or the father has been supporting the child financially before the child turned 21. A stepchild will be considered the same as a biological child if the relationship was created before the age of 18. The step-

break." The executive action bars the issuance of immigrant visas in the family preference categories as well as the parents of U.S. citizens' immediate relative category. The order is in effect until December 31, 2020, and has been the subject of litigation.

parent relationship will continue for immigration purposes even after a divorce, as long as the stepparent has maintained a parental relationship with the child.

Adopted children can receive immigration benefits if the adoption is before the age of 16 and the child has been in the legal custody of and resided with the adopting family for at least two years. The adoption age may be 18 if there are two or more siblings being adopted. U.S. immigration law also uses the term "orphans" to apply to a different group of individuals. Orphans are those whose parents have died, are missing, or have abandoned the child and there must be no surviving parent capable of providing for the child. If there is a surviving parent, the parent must relinquish the child for adoption. In orphan cases, the child must be under 16 and unmarried and will then qualify as an immediate relative of a U.S. citizen.[2]

The major advantage of petitioning for an immediate relative is that there is no cap or quota on the number of green cards that are available. That is in contrast to the family preference categories, which can be backlogged for years and even longer for certain nationalities seeking family-preference-category green cards. Note, however, that while there is no waiting on a quota number, processing of a green card for an immediate relative can still take a number of months.

While there is no limit on the number of immediate relative petitions that can be granted, there is a total cap of 480,000 on family-based numbers. Immediate relatives are subtracted from the 480,000 and the remainder may go to the preference categories. A minimum of 226,000 are to be made available in the preference categories, so if the number of immediate relatives exceeds 254,000, then the overall number of family-based green cards granted will exceed 480,000.

The family preference green card numbers are allocated as follows:

- First preference (F1) (unmarried sons and daughters of U.S. citizens)—23,400 per year, plus visas remaining from the fourth preference.
- Second preference (F-2A) (spouses and minor children of LPRs)—87,900 visas per year, plus numbers remaining from the first preference.
- Second preference (F-2B) (unmarried adult children of LPRs)—26,300 visas per year, plus any visas left over from the first preference.
- Third preference (F3) (married adult children of U.S. citizens)—23,400 visas per year, plus any visas left from the first and second preference categories.

[2] When immigration statutes refer to a "child," they are referring to a child who is unmarried and under the age of 21. Otherwise, the term "son or daughter" is used; however, to avoid confusion, when the law treats children differently depending on their age and marital status, this text will refer to them as a "minor child," "adult child," etc.

- Fourth preference (F4) (brothers and sisters of U.S. citizens over 21)—65,000 visas per year, plus any visas left over from the first through third preferences.

Unused employment-based green card numbers are added to the family-based categories in the following year, and unused family-based numbers in one year will roll into the next year.

Employment-Based Green Card Categories

Approximately 140,000 green cards are made available each year in various employment-based categories. They are the following:

- **EB-1**: This category is allotted 40,000 (28.6 percent) of the worldwide employment-based numbers plus any numbers not needed in the EB-4 and EB-5 categories. EB-1 includes three groups of workers—individuals with extraordinary ability in the arts, athletics, sciences, education, and business; multinational managers and executives; and outstanding researchers and professors.
- **EB-2**: This category is allotted 40,000 (28.6 percent) of the worldwide employment-based numbers plus any numbers not needed in the EB-1 category. It is open to members of the professions holding advanced degrees, persons of exceptional ability, and those seeking National Interest Waivers.
- **EB-3**: This category is allotted 40,000 (28.6 percent) of the worldwide employment-based numbers plus any numbers not needed in the EB-1 and EB-2 categories. It is open to skilled workers, professionals, and other workers.
- **EB-4**: This category is allotted 10,000 (7.1 percent) of the worldwide employment-based numbers. Certain types of religious workers primarily use it.
- **EB-5**: This category is allotted 10,000 (7.1 percent) of the worldwide employment-based numbers and is reserved for investors in businesses and projects that lead to the creation of jobs for U.S. workers.

Within each family-based preference green-card category (excluding the immediate relative category), there are limits on the number of green cards that can be granted to individuals in a particular nationality each year. There also are per country limits in the employment-based categories.

No more than 7 percent of visas in any of these categories can go to citizens of any country in a fiscal year (which runs from October 1 to September 30). This is not a separate allotment; rather, it is a limit on the allocations noted above. That is why the U.S. Department of State (DOS) will list separate waiting times for nationals of countries like Mexico in the family categories and India and China in the employment categories. The spillovers from other categories mentioned above are not, however, subject to per-country limits, so this actually can help alleviate the backlogs for some nationalities.[3]

Each month, DOS publishes a periodical called the *Visa Bulletin*, which lists each preference category and separates it out for countries that are hitting the per-country limits noted above.[4] For more information on the *Visa Bulletin*, refer to Chapter 12.

The *Visa Bulletin* lists "final action" dates in each of the family– and employment-based categories. An individual is granted a "priority date" based on when a green card or labor certification application has been filed. The final action dates tell what priority date a person must have to proceed with the final processing of a green card. In some cases, a category will have a "C" listed, which means it is current, and there is no waiting for a green-card number to become available. In some cases, a "U" will appear, meaning the category has been completely filled for the fiscal year.

For the various family– and employment-based green card cases, there are multiple stages to the green card process. In family cases, there is an application filed on Form I-130, Petition for Alien Relative, by the U.S. citizen or permanent resident relative on behalf of the family member and the application mainly focuses on documenting the qualifying relationship. Once a priority date is current, the relative will proceed with a final application for permanent residency via consular processing outside the United States or by applying for "adjustment of status" using Form I-485, Application to Register Permanent Residence or Adjust Status, in the United States. This phase of the case normally focuses on documenting that the individual is admissible to the United States. It is the phase where criminal background checks, medical exams, and similar screenings occur. For immediate relatives where there are no backlogs, the Forms I-130 and I-485 can be filed together.

For employment-based cases, there may be one to three stages to the case. Some employment-based green card applicants file for permanent residency in the EB-2 and EB-3 categories based on the filing of a labor certification application with the U.S. Department of Labor, which documents that an employer is offering a position for which there are no qualified U.S. workers who are readily available. Referred to as Program Electronic Review Management System (PERM) (and described in

---

[3] Numbers not used in family preference categories roll over to the employment categories for the following fiscal year. The same is true for unused employment numbers rolling over to family categories in the following fiscal year. There could be a sizeable number of unused green cards in fiscal year 2020 as a result of the slowdown in processing due to COVID-19 and also the April 22, 2020, presidential proclamation on immigrant visas.

[4] The *Visa Bulletin* can be found at www.travel.state.gov.

greater detail in Chapter 13), this process can take many months (six to 12 months is typical).

After this, an employer files an I-140, Immigrant Petition for Alien Worker, documenting that the "would be" immigrant meets the qualifications for the position certified in the PERM position and that the employer has the ability to pay the required salary. The third stage is the same as for the family-based categories—either consular processing or filing for adjustment of status.

If the applicant is not facing a backlog, then the I-485 adjustment-of-status application may be filed concurrently with the Form I-140.

Differences Between Consular Processing and Adjustment of Status

Consular processing is done through the DOS at a U.S. consulate in the applicant's home country. On rare occasions when there is no U.S. consulate in the home country or where the applicant would face danger returning to the country, a U.S. consulate in another country may agree to process the case. Consular processing of an immigrant visa involves initial data entry at DOS offices in the United States and then transfer of the process to the local U.S. consulate. The applicant will need to have a medical examination in the home country and be interviewed by a consular officer. After the officer approves the case, the applicant will be given a packet to take to the port of entry; upon entering the United States, the applicant will be considered an LPR. The green card will be mailed to the applicant within a few weeks of entry.

Adjustment-of-status applications are filed with U.S. Citizenship and Immigration Services (USCIS) in the United States. The applicant will need to visit a USCIS application support center to be photographed and fingerprinted. In most cases, there is no interview and the applicant will be sent the green card by mail after the case is approved. Occasionally, the applicant will be requested to visit a local office with documentation that he or she is either still employed by a petitioning employer or qualifies for portability, which allows for a change of employers.

Beginning in 2017, USCIS began requiring all employment-based adjustment of status applicants to interview at a local USCIS office before being granted permanent residency. This has led to much longer processing times.

As noted above, if one is eligible for adjusting status, then the individual can obtain an interim employment authorization document (EAD). This can be highly valuable in some cases, such as a nonimmigrant who is running out of L-1 time.

However, travel without advance permission can result in the adjustment-of-status application being denied due to abandonment. Advance permission is granted by filing for and obtaining an advance-parole travel document. This application can take four to six months to obtain, so good planning on the timing of filing an adjustment application is important.

Reasons for Green Card Denial

There are many reasons a green card can be denied. First and foremost, an immigration officer may determine that an individual does not qualify for the particular family– or employment-based category.

Applicants also may be deemed inadmissible for a variety of reasons. They include criminal violations; not satisfying the J-1 home-residency requirement; being deemed to have committed immigration fraud; having certain types of communicable diseases; and having past immigration overstays or status violations.

Some of these grounds of inadmissibility can be overcome by remaining outside the United States for an extended period or by obtaining a waiver of the ground of inadmissibility (such as a J-1 home-residency requirement waiver or a waiver of the bars based on visa overstays, which is tied to a hardship that would be faced by a qualifying American relative).

The process to obtain permanent residency typically takes anywhere from six months to several years depending on a variety of factors—

- The particular visa category and how many steps are required for processing;
- Whether a case is selected for a Request for Additional Evidence or an audit;
- Whether the particular green card category is backlogged or current;
- The nationality of the applicant and whether per-country limits apply to the applicant;
- Whether consular processing or adjustment of status is chosen; and
- Whether the applicant takes advantage of concurrent filing of an adjustment of status application if available.

12

UNDERSTANDING THE *VISA BULLETIN*: AN OVERVIEW

The U.S. Department of State (DOS), through the Bureau of Consular Affairs, publishes a monthly "*Visa Bulletin*." The *Visa Bulletin* lists the availability of "immigrant numbers" during the month of publication, and is intended as a guide for consular officials, attorneys, and others who would like to know if visas are immediately available for individuals in particular categories.[1]

The family, employment, and diversity visa (DV) green card categories have limits on the number of immigrant visas available; and within those categories, per country limits also apply. Because the demand exceeds availability in most categories, backlogs have developed in many of the categories.

The *Visa Bulletin* indicates the availability of visas for family– and employment-based preference categories, and separately lists countries that may have exceeded their allocation of visas. Countries that have exceeded their allocation of visas are "oversubscribed'' and individuals from those countries must wait before a visa can be issued.

If a category is "current" then visas are immediately available for issuance by the consulate, and tables on the *Visa Bulletin* indicate this fact with a "C" under the appropriate chargeability area. If a category is oversubscribed, tables on the *Visa Bulletin* indicate this fact with a date, such as 15MAR14, under the appropriate chargeability area.

When a category is oversubscribed, only individuals with a "priority date'' earlier than the one listed on the *Visa Bulletin* may be issued visas. The priority date is the date on which U.S. Citizenship and Immigration Services (USCIS) received the

[1] The *Visa Bulletin* is published on the State Department website at http://travel.state.gov.

application, either an I-130 application for an alien relative, an I-140 application for an immigrant worker, or in the case of a labor certification, it is when the PERM was submitted to the Department of Labor.

A priority date is assigned when an individual, who is qualified for the category of immigration requested, files a complete application. Individuals whose priority dates are after the one listed in the tables must wait until their priority dates are included in a table published in the monthly *Visa Bulletin*. Contrary to what one might believe, priority dates do not necessarily advance one month at a time and depend on the number of applications filed around the time of an individual's application. A surge in applications for a particular chargeability area at the time of filing could lead to priority dates advancing only one week per month. Similarly, a sharp drop in applications for a particular chargeability area when the application was filed might result in priority dates that advance two months at a time.

Family-Based Categories

Family-based immigration is divided into four preference categories and "immediate relatives" of U.S. citizens. Immediate relatives of U.S. citizens are parents, children under 21 and spouses. This category is not subject to any limits, and visas are always immediately available to those within it.

The first family preference is for unmarried (whether single, widowed, or divorced) children over 21 of U.S. citizens. The family 2A preference is for spouses and unmarried children under 21 of permanent residents. The family 2B preference is for unmarried children over 21 of permanent residents. The third family preference is for married children (any age) of U.S. citizens. The fourth and final family preference is for brothers and sisters of U.S. citizens (over 21).

Employment-Based Categories

Employment-based immigration is divided into five preference categories. The first preference category is for "priority workers'' such as outstanding professors and researchers, aliens of extraordinary ability, and multinational executives and managers. The second preference category is for members of the professions holding advanced (post-graduate) degrees, aliens of exceptional ability, and others whose immigration is in the "national interest." The third preference covers skilled workers, professionals, and other workers. The fourth preference is for "special immigrants" and includes certain U.S. government employees, religious workers, a small number of foreign medical graduates, employees of international organizations, juveniles, members of the U.S. Armed Forces, and limited number of other individuals. The fifth and final preference category is for "entrepreneurs," commonly known as immigrant investor visas. The investment typically required is $1,200,000 and requires the creation of at least 10 new full-time jobs in the United States for individuals other than the investor's spouse or children.

Diversity Immigrant (DV) Visa Availability

The 55,000 DV visas are allocated each year according to region and the *Visa Bulletin* lists a rank number for each region. Selected DV winners are eligible for an immigrant visa when the published rank number in a given region is higher than the winner's case number.

Why Are Their Two Charts for Family-Based Visas and Two Charts for Employment-Based Visas?

The *Visa Bulletin* includes a chart for "final action dates" for family and employment categories and "dates for filing" charts for family and employment categories. Final action dates mean that people with priority dates earlier than the listed date are authorized to have a green card issued. Green card processing can be completed for people with priority dates earlier than the listed date.

The State Department also has a chart that shows dates it anticipates having available for visa issuance before the end of a fiscal year. USCIS has the option to accept adjustment-of-status filings based on this alternative visa chart, which means that many applicants can get the benefits of filing much earlier.

The following example is based on the August 2019 *Visa Bulletin*:

Final Action Dates for Family-Sponsored Preference Cases

Family-Sponsored	All Chargeability Areas Except Those Listed	China-mainland born	India	Mexico	Philippines
F1	01JUL12	01JUL12	01JUL12	01AUG96	22FEB08
F2A	C	C	C	C	C
F2B	01JAN14	01JAN14	01JAN14	01JUN98	01APR08
F3	22JUN07	22JUN07	22JUN07	01DEC95	01OCT97
F4	01OCT06	01OCT06	15SEP04	01JAN97	01MAY98

Dates for Filing Family-Sponsored Visa Applications

Family-Sponsored	All Chargeability Areas Except Those Listed	China-mainland born	India	Mexico	Philippines
F1	01MAR13	01MAR13	01MAR13	01NOV99	22AUG08
F2A	01JUN19	01JUN19	01JUN19	01JUN19	01JUN19
F2B	01SEP14	01SEP14	01SEP14	01FEB99	01NOV08
F3	22DEC07	22DEC07	22DEC07	15JUL00	01APR98
F4	15DEC06	15DEC06	15MAY05	15DEC98	01NOV98

Final Action Dates for Employment-Based Preference Cases

Employment-based	All Chargeability Areas Except Those Listed	China-mainland born	El Salvador Guatemala Honduras	India	Mexico	Philippines	Vietnam
1st	01JUL16	01JUL16	01JUL16	01JAN15	01JUL16	01JUL16	01JUL16
2nd	01JAN17	01JAN17	01JAN17	02MAY09	01JAN17	01JAN17	01JAN17
3rd	01JUL16	01JUL16	01JUL16	01JAN06	01JUL16	01JUL16	01JUL16
Other Workers	01JUL16	22NOV07	01JUL16	01JAN06	01JUL16	01JUL16	01JUL16
4th	C	C	01JUL16	C	01JUL16	C	C
Certain Religious Workers	C	C	01JUL16	C	01JUL16	C	C
5th Non-Regional Center (C5 and T5)	C	15OCT14	C	15OCT14	C	C	15OCT14
5th Regional Center (I5 and R5)	C	15OCT14	C	15OCT14	C	C	15OCT14

Dates for Filing of Employment-Based Visa Applications

Employment-based	All Chargeability Areas Except Those Listed	China-mainland born	El Salvador Guatemala Honduras	India	Mexico	Philippines
1st	01SEP18	01OCT17	01SEP18	01OCT17	01SEP18	01SEP18
2nd	C	01FEB17	C	01JUN09	C	C
3rd	C	01JUN16	C	01APR10	C	C
Other Workers	C	01JUN08	C	01APR10	C	C
4th	C	C	01SEP16	C	C	C
Certain Religious Workers	C	C	01SEP16	C	C	C
5th Non-Regional Center (C5 and T5)	C	15NOV14	C	C	C	C
5th Regional Center (I5 and R5)	C	15NOV14	C	C	C	C

DV Category for the Month of August

Region	**All DV Chargeability Areas Except Those Listed Separately**	
Africa	CURRENT	
Asia	CURRENT	
Europe	CURRENT	
North America (Bahamas)	CURRENT	
Oceania	CURRENT	
South America and the Caribbean	CURRENT	

13

THE PATH TO AN EMPLOYMENT-BASED GREEN CARD: PERM

The most common path to an employment-based green card is this three-step process that is commonly known by the name of the online system in which it is filed—Program Electronic Review Management System (PERM). To start with, a company will complete the labor certification process through the Department of Labor's PERM system, Next, based on the approved PERM, the company will file an I-140 Immigrant Petition for Alien Worker with U.S. Citizenship and Immigration Services (USCIS) on behalf of the foreign national employee. Finally, based on the approved I-140, the beneficiary will apply for adjustment of status in the United States or process at a U.S. consulate or embassy abroad to become a lawful permanent resident (LPR).

The PERM process is well known for its many intricate rules and potential pitfalls. However, it is extremely effective when screened and managed by experienced practitioners. The labor certification is essentially a test of the U.S. labor market to establish there is not a U.S. worker willing, able, qualified, and available to fill the position at that time. In this context, U.S. workers include U.S. citizens, LPRs, and aliens who are legally authorized to work permanently in the United States. The process demonstrates to the Department of Labor (DOL) that U.S. workers are not being displaced or disadvantaged.

In general, labor certifications are not a viable path to permanent residence for company founders because the process does not allow for self-employment.[1] It also does not allow for part-time employment. Founders should still be familiar with the process for a couple of reasons; one is that the PERM process is prospective, meaning a company can complete the process based on a position the beneficiary will fill

[1] 20 Code of Federal Regulations (CFR) §656.3.

at the time he or she becomes a permanent resident. Therefore, another company could potentially petition the co-founder if he or she will eventually leave his or her venture and take up full-time employment with that other company.

Another reason founders should understand the process is because it is the most common path to an employment-based green card, so founders will regularly encounter it for the company's employees. The process cannot be used for contractors, but if the startup employs foreign nationals it will inevitably have to consider the labor certification process for the benefit and retention of the foreign national employees. It should also be noted that the company is responsible for all costs associated with the labor certification process, including legal fees and advertising; so it makes sense to be familiar with the immigration-related costs company owners will be taking on, knowing that they cannot be offset by the employees.

The PERM process is a true test of the labor market, meaning the company must advertise and determine whether there are willing, able, qualified, and available U.S. workers to fill the position before DOL will certify the position for a foreign national. The process generally starts by hammering out the specific job description for the position. This includes the title, duties, and the actual minimum requirements necessary to perform the job.

The details of the position cannot be tailored to the beneficiary. All of the duties and requirements should be normal to such a position or arise out of business necessity. DOL may challenge the duties or requirements of a position, and the burden is on the employer to prove that anything beyond the norm arises from a true necessity of the company:

> To establish a business necessity, an employer must demonstrate the job duties and requirements bear a reasonable relationship to the occupation in the context of the employer's business and are essential to perform the job in a reasonable manner.[2]

The company also cannot require any experience that it has previously provided through on-the-job training.

A common distinction in the PERM process is whether the position will ultimately qualify the beneficiary for EB-2 or EB-3 visa preference. Jobs requiring at least a bachelor's degree and five years of experience, or advanced degrees and any experience, will qualify for the employment-based second preference (EB-2) catego-

---

[2] 20 CFR §656.17(h)(1).

ry. Any positions requiring less than that will fall to the employment-based third preference (EB-3) category.

In the job description, the company will want to list the specific type of degree (bachelor's, master's, etc.) and the acceptable field(s) of study. If the company will accept equivalent foreign degrees, then that should be explicitly listed on the labor certification. This is also true if the employer will accept work experience in lieu of education. Lastly, the employer may also accept alternative education requirements, such as a bachelor's degree and five years of experience, or in the alternative, a master's degree and two years of experience. Either could be acceptable if explicitly stated, and both would qualify the beneficiary for EB-2.

Some minimum requirements for hire are considered inherent and do not have to be listed, such as speaking English. All other requirements should be explicitly described on the Notice of Filing. The PERM is a test for the minimum qualified candidate, not the perfect candidate; so it is best to just include the type of experience that is absolutely required for hire in the position and leave off skills that are "preferred" and other fluff you often see in job descriptions.

For example, "At least 5 years of experience in front-end development" clearly lays out a minimum requirement. Without that experience, the person would not be hired for the job. "Experience at financial technology company preferred" is not ideal, because it is not truly the minimum requirement since a person could be hired without that experience.

Lastly, requirements such as "Used to fast paced environment" or "Team player" is nonessential and could never actually be used to disqualify a U.S. worker, so there is no reason to include it. From a practical standpoint, the actual placing of ads are often billed by character—so brevity is best.

Every type of experience required for the position will ultimately have to be demonstrated by the beneficiary at the ensuing I-140 stage with USCIS. Beneficiaries document their experience for USCIS by submitting signed, detailed experience letters from their previous employers (or from their current employers in positions that are at least 50 percent different than the prospective PERM position). Most practitioners have PERM beneficiaries gather experience letters early in the process to prevent a situation in which months of work has been done toward the approval of a PERM only for the beneficiary to be unable to document his or her experience and thus get denied at the I-140 stage. When gathering the letters of support, beneficiaries of a PERM need to document word for word that they meet the minimum requirements of the PERM position.

They also need to be able to document the full number of years of experience required for the position. So, if the position requires five years of experience, a beneficiary who has spent two years with several employers each will need three experience letters to document that he or she is qualified for the position. Documenting experience is another potential pitfall in the process that further emphasizes the importance of clearly describing the details of the job description at the beginning of the process.

The first filing of the PERM process is called a Prevailing Wage Request. Historically, this electronic Form ETA-9141 was completed through DOL's online iCert system. As of mid-2019, the DOL Office of Foreign Labor Certification (OFLC) has moved the application to the Foreign Labor Application Gateway (FLAG) System. An employer or its legal representative must create an account in order to initiate the filing of a Prevailing Wage Request with the National Prevailing Wage Center (NPWC). Once in the system[3], the ETA-9141 requests, among other things, information about the proposed job including: title, duties, and experience and education required.

At the time of this writing, it generally takes three–four months for the application to be reviewed. Once reviewed, NPWC returns a Prevailing Wage Determination (PWD). According to DOL, "The prevailing wage rate is defined as the average wage paid to similarly employed workers in a specific occupation in the area of intended employment."[4] The purpose of the process is to set the minimum amount the employer may pay its employee.

Once a wage determination has been made, the employer must pay at least the determined wage or the amount already being paid to similarly skilled and qualified workers—whichever is higher. Remember, though, the PERM process is prospective; the beneficiary of a PERM does not have to be earning the determined wage at the time of the determination, but the employer must be willing to pay that wage to the beneficiary at the time he or she becomes a permanent resident. For some people, that may be just months away; for others who are subject to long country specific backlogs, it may be many years away.

If the wage comes back higher than the employee is earning, the employer essentially has four options:

---

[3] www.flag.dol.gov.

[4] www.foreignlaborcert.doleta.gov/pwscreens.cfm.

1. The employer can agree to the higher wage and pay that at the time the beneficiary becomes a permanent resident;

2. The employer can re-evaluate the filing to make sure only the minimum requirements were listed and there is not unnecessary language leading to a higher than warranted determination, and re-file a corrected job description if applicable;

3. The employer may file an appeal of the wage determination with the National Prevailing Wage Center and present further evidence of why the wage determination should be lower; or

4. The employer can choose to abandon the process at that stage and not make any adjustments to the beneficiary's pay.

Prevailing Wage Determinations are only valid for a set period of time. Each PWD will have an expiration date listed on it. A PWD will always be valid for at least 90 days from the date of the determination and will never be valid for more than one year.[5] The regulations state that in order to use a PWD before it expires, the employer must either file the PERM application before the PWD expires or start recruitment before the expiration date on the PWD. According to the Board of Alien Labor Certification Appeals (BALCA), starting recruitment means placing the first of any of the ads or forms of recruitment for the PERM.[6]

Once the employer has an acceptable wage determination, it is time to begin the recruitment process to test the labor market. The recruitment must be performed within the six-month period prior to filing the labor certification. In every recruitment for a professional occupation (those normally requiring at least a bachelor's degree), there are three forms of recruitment that are required by law and then three additional forms of recruitment that can be chosen from 10 acceptable options. The three mandatory methods include:

1. Placing a job order with the State Workforce Agency (SWA) for 30 days;

2. Placing newspaper advertisements in two separate Sunday editions of the local, major local newspaper, which is the "newspaper in general circulation" for the area of employment; and

---

[5] 20 CFR §656.40(c).

[6] *Matter of Horizon Computer Services, Inc.*, 2010-PER-00746 (May 25, 2011).

3. Posting of the Notice of Filing at the location(s) of employment in a visible place for at least 10 consecutive days or providing a copy of the notice to a local union if there is a collective bargaining agreement.

After the three mandatory methods, the employer must select three more from the ten acceptable options. The employer may:

1. Recruit in-person at a job fair;
2. Post the job opening on its company website;
3. Post the job opening on a known job search website that is not affiliated with the company;
4. Recruit by participating in on-campus recruitment at a school;
5. Place a notice of the opening in a relevant trade or professional organization's publication;
6. Retain a private recruitment firm to conduct a job search for applicants.
7. Post the position with a campus placement office;
8. Post a newspaper advertisement with a local or ethnic newspaper;
9. Recruit for the position on local radio or television; or
10. If the employer has an employee referral program that identifies specific incentives for making referrals than the employer may notify employees of that the position is available and part of the incentivized program.

To satisfy the requirements all of the ads that are posted must contain key information. The ad must:

1. Name the employer;
2. Direct applicants to report or send résumés, as appropriate for the occupation, to the employer;
3. Provide a description of the vacancy specific enough to apprise the U.S. workers of the job opportunity for which certification is sought;
4. Indicate the geographic area of employment with enough specificity to apprise applicants of any travel requirements and where applicants will likely have to reside to perform the job opportunity;
5. Not contain a wage rate lower than the prevailing wage rate;

6. Not contain any job requirements or duties which exceed the job requirements or duties listed on the ETA Form 9089; and
7. Not contain wages or terms and conditions of employment that are less favorable than those offered to the alien.[7]

The 30-day posting with the SWA is the longest running advertisement; therefore, all of the remaining steps can be done during that time, thus keeping the advertising period to 30 days. A mandatory 30-day wait period, in which the employer must continue to accept applications, begins the day after the last advertisement has come down. If everything is timed well, this means the total recruitment can be done in 60 days.

Next, the employer must assess applicants in order to determine whether any are able, willing, qualified, and available U.S. workers. Initially the employer can review the résumés of the applicants to identify which have the minimum required education and qualifying experience. The employer must interview candidates who appear to be qualified, as well as those about which a determination cannot be made simply by reviewing the résumé, in order to determine their qualifications.

The employer must complete this process, and the foreign beneficiary and attorneys cannot have any involvement. During the interview the employer must determine if there are "lawful job-related reasons" for rejecting a candidate.[8] This means the employer must find out whether the applicant meets the minimum education and experience requirements and is otherwise willing, able, and available to accept the position as offered. The employer may not reject a candidate simply for not currently possessing skills that could be acquired "during a reasonable period of on-the-job training."[9]

If the recruitment is being conducted for multiple open positions and an able, willing, qualified, and available U.S. worker exists, the employer may offer him or her one of the open positions and still continue with the labor certification process. If only one position is available and such a candidate is found, then the labor certification cannot move forward because the test of the labor market was not sufficient to demonstrate a lack of able, willing, qualified, and available U.S. workers.

At the end of every recruitment, the employer must sign a recruitment report. The report must include "the recruitment steps undertaken and the results achieved,

---

[7] 20 CFR §656.17(f).
[8] 20 CFR §656.17(g).
[9] 20 CFR §656.17(g).

the number of hires, and, if applicable, the number of U.S. workers rejected, categorized by the lawful job related reasons for such rejections."[10]

Once the recruitment has sufficiently demonstrated that there is not a U.S. worker willing, able, qualified, and available to fill the position, it is time to file the actual PERM using ETA Form 9089 Application for Permanent Employment Certification. As its nickname implies, PERM (Program Electronic Review Management System) is filed through an online application.

Setting up the online PERM account is a two-step process. First, the employer must set up a company profile. To complete this process, the employer will enter the company information, including the company name and matching Federal Employment Identification Number (FEIN), and accepts the conditions; this will generate two e-mails from DOL. The first e-mail will contain the company login and password, and the second e-mail will contain a pin number. The employer must return and login with the information from the first e-mail. Once in the account, the employer will add a new user, creating a profile for the attorney that represents the company and will be filing the PERM. Once that subaccount is created, the attorney can login to prepare the 9089 for review and submission. In some cases, a company may be unable to create a PERM account because DOL cannot confirm the company is real or the information is inconsistent with DOL records. This is generally not the case, but it does happen more frequently to small and early stage companies than larger, established companies.

The 9089 asks for information about the company and the person filing the PERM (generally the attorney). It also asks for information about the position, such as the title, duties, education requirements, experience requirements, training requirements, and alternative acceptable requirements. It asks very general information about the forms of recruitment used for the test of the labor market by only requesting the dates that the different advertisements were live, whether a Notice of Filing was posted, and the name and dates of the Sunday advertisements.

Lastly, it asks for basic biographic information about the beneficiary and has a section for documenting the previous work experience that qualifies the beneficiary for the PERM position. Submitting the application online will trigger automatic e-mails responses from DOL. One e-mail will require the employer to answer four questions that ensure the employer truly means to file the application and that the position is actually being offered to the beneficiary. Once the employer answers "YES" to all the questions, the 9089 will be officially submitted for adjudication.

---

[10] 20 CFR §656.17(g).

The 9089 is usually approved or DOL initiates an audit. Because the 9089 asks such basic information about the recruitment, some audits occur randomly to ensure that the recruitment was truly completed as indicated on the 9089 and that it contained the necessary language in accordance with the regulations. Some audits, however, ask for more than just the recruitment materials. For example, very early stage companies and small business are often asked for additional documents to prove the company is real. Also, an audit may ask for additional information to prove business necessity for the requirements of the position if the job requires higher than normal experience, foreign language skills, lots of travel or remote work, or in situations where the beneficiary is related to a company owner.

Employers are given 30 days to respond to a DOL audit. In general, the responses can be prepared quite quickly, because the attorney or employer is required to create an audit file while going through the PERM process so the materials around the recruitment are generally on hand. The audit file must contain: all of the recruitment materials (*i.e.*, dated screenshots of the advertisements from the day each went up and came down); the recruitment report; résumés received from applicants; the prevailing wage determination used on the 9089; all notices and postings; business necessity letters if necessary; and evidence of any relevant layoffs that occurred prior to the recruitment. The audit file must be maintained and stored for a minimum of five years.[11] If the recruitment was properly performed, then most cases are still approved after the audit, but the audit cases are notably slower than normal cases. At the time of this writing, 9089s are being processed in three–four months, but audits are adding an additional four months to the process.

The attorney filing the PERM will receive an e-mail notification once the case has been approved. DOL then sends an official copy of the approved 9089 in the mail. The next step in the PERM-based green card process is the filing of an I-140 Immigrant Petition for Alien Worker with USCIS. In general, the approved PERM must be used in the filing of an I-140 within 180 days of the PERM approval or it will expire. Production of the official approval cannot be expedited, even in cases involving children who may "age-out" before they can benefit from their parents' green card process. It is no longer possible to substitute the beneficiary of a PERM; it must be the same beneficiary of the I-140 that is listed on the labor certification. It is also no longer possible to amend or modify the labor certification once approved. If modification is needed, then the PERM must be withdrawn and a new application submitted.

[11] 20 CFR §656.10(f).

If the certifying officer denies the 9089, then the attorney will receive a Determination, which includes the reason for denial. The employer then has 30 days to request a review of the denial by the Board of Alien Labor Certification Appeals (BALCA). The employer also has the option to file a new application, but a new application cannot be filed while a request for review is pending with BALCA.

If the certifying officer finds that the employer failed to produce required documentation or submitted inadequate documentation, finds that a material misrepresentation was made, or finds it otherwise inappropriate, the employer may be required to conduct Supervised Recruitment in future labor certification filings for a period of up to two years from the date of the Final Determination.

Supervised Recruitment is exactly what its name implies; DOL actively takes part in a second recruitment for the position to ensure that it is done properly. When an employer receives a Notification of Supervised Recruitment, they are given 30 days to provide a draft of the job description and ad language to DOL. DOL then determines whether the language is satisfactory. Once the language is approved, DOL sends instructions on where and when to recruit for the position. The recruitment language will direct people to apply by submitting their résumés to OFLC or the Atlanta National Processing Center. DOL will then decide whether the recruitment yielded any able, willing, qualified, and available U.S. workers and/or whether the labor certification should be approved.

DOL will also notify the employer of the materials that should be included in the recruitment report. If the employer fails to comply with the Supervised Recruitment then they risk debarment. Debarment means the employer will be unable to receive future labor certifications from the OFLC.

I-140 Immigrant Petition for Alien Worker

As mentioned at the outset of the chapter, the PERM-based green card process is three steps (1) labor certification, (2) I-140, and (3) adjustment of status or consular processing. Up to this point, the discussion has all been around the first step, the PERM or Labor Certification. Once the PERM is approved by the Department of Labor though, the employer has six months to file an I-140 Immigrant Petition for Alien Worker with USCIS. The I-140 is the employer's permanent (or immigrant) visa petition on behalf of the foreign national.

While the filing date of the PERM becomes the foreign national's priority date for the *Visa Bulletin*, it is actually the filing of the I-140 that solidifies that priority date for the foreign national. Once the priority date is locked in, the foreign national always retains that priority date; even if used in combination with a future application by another employer, he or she can still rely on the priority date of the previous petition.

Form I-140 is used for all the different employment-based green card processes. The applicant indicates on the form what category they are applying under, which for PERM-based cases would either be EB-2 or EB-3. The application then asks for basic biographic information about the petitioner and the applicant. If currently in the United States, the applicant adds information on his or her current status in the United States and most recent entry. The form requires general information about the company, such as its type of business; the year it was created; number of employees; and gross and net annual income.

Next, the application asks for information about the position on which the PERM was based. The applicant must list the job title, SOC code from the Prevailing Wage Determination, a brief description of the duties, and the offered wage, and must answer "YES" or "NO" to whether the position is full-time, permanent, and new. The applicant must also list the worksite location for the position. Lastly, the foreign national's spouse and children are listed on the application.

The main challenges to the I-140 filing are showing that the company can really afford to pay the offered wage and that the beneficiary is actually qualified for the position. In order to demonstrate ability to pay, the regulations state:

> *Ability of prospective employer to pay wage.* Any petition filed by or for an employment-based immigrant which requires an offer of employment must be accompanied by evidence that the prospective United States employer has the ability to pay the proffered wage. The petitioner must demonstrate this ability at the time the priority date is established and continuing until the beneficiary obtains lawful permanent residence. Evidence of this ability shall be either in the form of copies of annual reports, federal tax returns, or audited financial statements. In a case where the prospective United States employer employs 100 or more workers, the director may accept a statement from a financial officer of the organization which establishes the prospective employer's ability to pay the proffered wage. In appropriate cases, additional evidence, such as profit/loss statements, bank account records, or personnel records, may be submitted by the petitioner or requested by the Service.[12]

Therefore, the company should ideally provide an annual report, federal tax return, or audited financial statement that shows sufficient ability to support the offered salary. If the person is already working for the company in the offered posi-

---

[12] 8 CFR §204.5.

tion, then it is also helpful to provide evidence that the company already has been paying the offered wage.

According to USCIS policy, the adjudicator will review the evidence submitted to determine whether the employer has demonstrated an ability to pay the offered wage in one of three ways[13]:

1. Net Income—The initial evidence reflects that the petitioner's net income is equal to or greater than the proffered wage.
2. Net Current Assets—The initial evidence reflects that the petitioner's net current assets are equal to or greater than the proffered wage.
3. Employment of the Beneficiary—The record contains credible evidence that the petitioner not only is employing the beneficiary but also has paid or currently is paying the proffered wage.

In many cases though, startups do not have any of these documents yet and must rely on the last line of the regulation that allows for "additional evidence." Startups can usually overcome the ability to pay hurdle by providing bank statements showing they have sufficient working capital to pay the proposed salary. If the company is funded by venture capital, then the applicant may also provide a copy of term sheets or the financial instruments (such as the Simple Agreement for Future Equity (SAFE)) to show sufficient funds exists in addition to the bank statements. These forms of evidence are discretionary though, and the USCIS adjudicator is not required to accept them.

If the startup is a sole proprietorship and the company is unable to produce such documents, then there is established precedent that USCIS should consider the individual founder's personal assets in determining whether the employer has the ability to pay.[14] The Administrative Appeals Office has also held that USCIS adjudicators must take a petitioner's business accounting practices into consideration of the totality of the circumstances when making ability to pay determinations; so he or she should consider the accounting practices of small and new businesses in making their determination. If the company cannot show sufficient finances, the applicant should submit the sole founder's federal income tax return so that USCIS may consider his or her total income and net current assets to demonstrate ability to pay. The

[13] William R. Yates, Memorandum, "Determination of Ability to Pay under 8 CFR 204.5(g)(2)" (May 4, 2004).

[14] See *Ranchito Coletero*, 2002- INA-105 (BLACA Jan. 8, 2004) (*en banc*).

adjudicator may also consider the totality of the evidence, taking into consideration a variety of factors including:

- The number of years the petitioner has been doing business;
- The established historical growth of the petitioner's business;
- The overall number of employees;
- The occurrences of any uncharacteristic business expenditure or losses;
- The petitioner's reputation within its industry;
- Whether the beneficiary is replacing a former employee or an outsourced service; and
- Any other evidence that USCIS deems relevant to the petitioner's ability to pay the proffered wage.

Demonstrating that the beneficiary of the I-140 truly qualifies for the position is a process that should be considered from the very outset of the PERM process. At the I-140 stage, the foreign national is expected to produce evidence that he or she has the education credentials and experience required by the position and listed on the PERM. Education is usually documented by submitting copies of the pertinent diplomas and college transcripts, plus any foreign degree evaluations that are needed in the case. Experience, on the other hand, is generally documented by providing experience letters from the beneficiary's previous employers to demonstrate that he or she gained the requisite experience while employed in previous roles.

These letters should be on company letterhead if possible. However, if the letter writer is no longer with that company, or the company no longer exists, a letter can be provided without letterhead but should still include: the writer's name, address, title with the company, the dates the beneficiary was in the role(s) with the company, and a specific description of the duties performed while in those roles. The last part is extremely important. The list of duties should document the exact skills needed for the position. Ideally, this description will be word-for-word or at least very close, so the adjudicator can clearly determine that the experience was acquired during the beneficiary's time with the previous company.

If the beneficiary gained the needed experience while self-employed, letters of support can still document the requisite experience. Beneficiaries in these cases can request letters from previous co-founders, members of the board of directors, or shareholders. Alternatively, a former entrepreneur could request a letter from other people intimately familiar with this previous role, such as a local chamber of commerce or company that worked closely with the beneficiary. In these cases, the specifics of the relationship should be explained. Previously self-employed individuals should also provide proof of their previous entity such as incorporation documents or business licenses.

Documenting the beneficiary's qualifying experience and the company's ability to pay are the two main cruxes of the PERM-based I-140 process. Under the Trump administration, USCIS has begun requesting documentation of the bona fide recruitment that was performed during the labor certification process. Historically, this was only requested by DOL during an audit since DOL oversees the recruitment process. This rarely should cause issues, since the audit file contains all documents needed to satisfy USCIS and must be maintained anyway.

Unlike the PERM, any party can pay the costs associated with the I-140. USCIS also allows for PERM-based I-140s to be premium processed for an additional government fee of $1,440, which means the case will be adjudicated within 15 calendar days. Once the I-140 is approved, the beneficiary's priority date is solidified, and he or she may complete the third and final step in the green card process.

Adjustment of Status or Consular Processing

Once the I-140 is approved, a beneficiary, spouse, and children under 21 may all apply for their green cards. This final step can occur through filing for adjustment of status with USCIS if the individuals are currently in the United States in a valid status, or by consular processing their immigrant visas with the Department of State at a U.S. consulate or embassy abroad. Every family member at this stage must file his or her own application. This final step in the green card process is the same for all employment-based green card processes that are discussed in this book; for more details on adjustment of status and consular processing, please refer to the general section on immigrant visas and employment-based green card processing.

14

An Alternative to PERM: The National Interest Waiver

In 1990, U.S. Congress created a new green card path for people whose work was deemed to be in the national interest. The National Interest Waiver (NIW) category has been both highly popular and nearly dead at various times over the last three decades depending on the views of the government at various moments in time. It is definitely alive today and is a category that will appeal to many startups.

Startup founders and entrepreneurs who own an equity interest in a business are closed out of the most common business immigration green card category. The vast majority of people who acquire green cards because of their work do so via the sponsorship of an employer and use a process called Program Electronic Review Management System (PERM) where an employer seeks a certification from the U.S. Department of Labor that they are offering a position for which no U.S. workers can be found who are available and qualified for the job. In most cases, owning any equity or having a family relationship with the employer are disqualifying in this category.

The NIW can be the ideal alternative to PERM. NIWs are part of the employment-based, second preference section of the Immigration and Nationality Act (*i.e.*, EB-2). As the name implies, an NIW is available to those "who are members of the professions holding advanced degrees" or who are foreign nationals of "exceptional ability" who can demonstrate that it is in the national interest for U.S. Citizenship and Immigration Services (USCIS) to "waive the requirements … that an alien's services in the sciences, arts, professions, or business be sought by an employer in the United States" for an EB-2 beneficiary (*i.e.*, waiving the PERM process).[1] U.S.

[1] Immigration and Nationality Act (INA) §203(b)(2)(B).

Congress did not define "national interest" nor has a regulatory definition ever been offered by USCIS. Instead, as discussed below, the category has been shaped by two major cases from USCIS's Administrative Appeals Office (AAO).

EB-2 immigrant visa applicants, including NIWs, must show that they are members of the professions holding advanced degrees or their equivalent or who possess exceptional ability in the sciences, arts, or business. Art, in the exceptional ability context, includes athletes and entertainers.[2] Regarding advanced degrees, the position must actually require an advanced degree and the person must possess the degree or its equivalent in education and work experience. A master's degree or higher is an advanced degree and a bachelor's degree plus five years of progressive experience in the field.

"Exceptional ability" is a degree of expertise significantly above that ordinarily encountered.[3] Any three of the following may be presented as proof of exceptional ability[4]:

- Degree relating to area of exceptional ability;
- Letter from current or former employer showing at least ten years of experience;
- License to practice profession;
- Person has commanded a salary or remuneration demonstrating exceptional ability;
- Membership in a professional association; or
- Recognition for achievements and significant contributions to the industry or field by peers, governmental entities, or professional or business organizations.

Comparable evidence may be submitted if the above categories are inapplicable. Note that USCIS will apply a two-step analysis first considering if three categories have been demonstrated and then determining if the evidence submitted is sufficient to demonstrate the beneficiary meets the required high level of expertise.[5]

While the NIW category was created by U.S. Congress in 1990, it only was in active use for a few years before a 1997 Administrative Appeals Office decision

---

[2] *Adjudicator's Field Manual* (AFM) at 22.2(j)(3).

[3] *Matter of Kim*, 12 I&N Dec. 758 (AC 1968).

[4] 8 Code of Federal Regulations (CFR) §204.5(k)(3)(ii).

[5] Referred to as the *Kazarian* standard USCIS confirmed it applies in the EB-2 exceptional ability context. Policy Memo, USCIS, PM-602-0005. Evaluation of Evidence Submitted with Certain Form I-140 Petitions.

called *Matter of NY State Department of Transportation*[6] made the category largely unusable for nearly two decades. NYSDOT, as the case became known, required applicants to demonstrate three requirements:

1. The applicant is working in an area that has "substantial intrinsic merit";
2. The benefit to be provided is "national in scope"; and
3. It would be contrary to the national interest to potentially deprive an employer of the applicant's services by requiring a labor certification.

NYSDOT said, in short, that an NIW would not be granted unless the applicant could demonstrate that the national interest would be served to a substantially greater degree than U.S. workers having the same minimum qualifications for the position, something few could easily do. USCIS denied most applicants who filed cases in the months that followed, and it had a chilling effect on the filing of applications.

In 2016, the AAO dramatically changed the NIW requirements in a case called *Matter of Dhanasar.*[7] There were three other cases simultaneously released that applied the standard set out in the *Dhanasar* case.[8] Dr. Dhanasar had a case that would have been easily approvable under the Pre-NYSDOT standard. He had done groundbreaking research in hypersonic propulsion systems, had funding from the U.S. Department of Defense and NASA, and the United States is facing challenges to our leadership in the field from the Chinese and the Russians.

The AAO specifically noted in the *Dhanasar* decision that among the reasons *NYSDOT* needed reworking was that it did not work for entrepreneurs:

> It has proven particularly ill-suited for USCIS to evaluate petitions from self-employed individuals, such as entrepreneurs. In NYSDOT, we even 'acknowledged that there are certain occupations wherein individuals are essentially self-employed, and thus would have no U.S. employer to apply for a labor certification. Nonetheless, we did not modify the test to resolve this scenario, which continues to challenge petitioners and USCIS adjudicators.'

Under *Dhanasar*, USCIS will now demand documentation of the following:

---

[6] *Matter of N.Y. State Department of Transportation* (NYSDOT), 22 I&N Dec. 215 (Acting AC 1998).

[7] *Matter of Dhanasar*, 26 I&N Dec. 884 (AAO 2016).

[8] The authors of this book were on the attorney team that worked on one of those cases, *Matter of E-C-H*, released on December 27, 2016, that happened to be approved using the new *Dhanasar* standard.

1. The applicant's planned work has substantial merit AND national importance;
2. The applicant is well-positioned to advance that endeavor; and
3. On balance, it benefits the United States to waive the job offer and labor certification requirements.

The AAO analyzed these requirements in the *Dhanasar* decision to help potential NIW applicants more easily determine if an NIW petition is appropriate. With respect to the first prong of *Dhanasar*, the AAO noted that in determining whether the requirement for "substantial merit," applicants can demonstrate merit in "a range of areas such as business, entrepreneurialism, science, technology, culture, health, or education." A significant economic impact may be viewed as favorable by USCIS, according to *Dhanasar*.

As for "national importance," *Dhanasar* notes that the requirement can be met if an undertaking will have national or even global implications within a particular field, such as those resulting from improved manufacturing processes or medical advances. The AAO de-emphasized focusing on geography:

> Instead, we look for broader implications. Even ventures and undertakings that have as their focus one geographic area of the United States may properly be considered to have national importance. In modifying this prong to assess "national importance" rather than "national in scope" as used in *NYSDOT*, we seek to avoid overemphasis on the geographic breadth of the endeavor. An endeavor that has significant potential to employ U.S. workers or has other substantial positive economic effects, particularly in an economically depressed area, for instance, may well be understood to have national importance.

With respect to the second prong, whether the applicant is well-positioned to advance the proposed endeavor, the AAO noted it would consider the following example factors:

- an individual's education;
- an individual's skills;
- an individual's knowledge;
- an individual's record of success in related or similar efforts;
- a model or plan for future activities;
- any progress toward achieving the proposed endeavor; and
- the interest of potential customers, users, investors or other relevant entities or individuals.

The AAO warned USCIS not to demand that entrepreneurs show an endeavor is going to succeed:

> We recognize that forecasting feasibility or future success may present challenges to petitioners and USCIS officers, and that many innovations and entrepreneurial endeavors may ultimately fail, in whole or in part, despite an intelligent plan and competent execution. We do not, therefore, require petitioners to demonstrate that their endeavors are more likely than not to ultimately succeed. But not withstanding this inherent uncertainty, in order to merit a national interest waiver, petitioners must establish, by a preponderance of the evidence, that they are well-positioned to advance the proposed endeavor.

The third prong of *Dhanasar* requires applicants to show, on balance, that it would be beneficial to the country to waive the requirements for a job offer and thus of a labor certification. The AAO specifically noted this third prong should make the application process much easier for entrepreneurs:

> We note that this new prong, unlike the third prong of *NYSDOT*, does not require a shoring of harm to the national interest or a comparison against U.S. workers in the petitioner's field. As stated previously, *NYSDOT*'s third prong was especially problematic for certain petitioners, such as entrepreneurs and self-employed individuals.

The actual *Dhanasar* case involved an aerospace scientist, so we need to look to cases applying the *Dhanasar* decision to entrepreneurs to understand how the decision works for startup founders.

As of August 2019, the authors identified eight national interest waiver appeals decided by the AAO regarding entrepreneurs and in each of these cases, the primary issue considered was whether the first prong of *Dhanasar* regarding national importance had been met. A few of the cases also addressed the question of whether the petitioner demonstrated possession of an advanced degree or exceptional ability, though in most cases, the petitioner won on that issue.

In seven of the cases, the AAO ruled against the entrepreneur. In some of the cases, the facts were, to be frank, weak and a denial under *Dhanasar* seemed inevitable. However, a few of the cases were stronger and there are some takeaways. So a brief summary of the decisions can be a helpful way to see what to avoid and what to emphasize when preparing these cases. One decision has been omitted because, in the authors' judgment, the facts were so weak and the case so inadequately documented, that the AAO had little choice but to deny.

Matter of A-R-A- (February 27, 2018)[9]

The petitioner in this case is the founder and CEO of a company in which he owns a 91 percent interest. The company purchases personal electronics products from U.S.-based distributors and sells them to national and international customers. The USCIS Texas Service Center director found that the petitioner showed substantial merit and the petitioner was well positioned to advance the endeavor, two of the requirements from *Dhanasar*, so the main issue in the case was whether the petitioner's proposed endeavor had national importance.

The petitioner provided a business plan, which outlined hiring and growth projections and industry analysis. He argued that the company's revenue, profit, payroll expenses, and corporate taxes would provide a substantial benefit to the U.S. economy. Also, the petitioner argued the company benefits its suppliers and contributes to the grown of other businesses, including freight forwarders and logistics partners. Revenue projections were provided showing expected growth from $476,104 in 2018 to $1,144,772 in 2021. Payroll would rise from $521,850 to $928,369 in the same period, according to the petitioner's projections. The employee headcount was anticipated to reach 17 by 2021 and the petitioner described plans to open a second location in Florida that would hire three others.

The AAO held the petitioner failed to show how the growth would offer a substantial economic benefit to the region or the nation. That included showing why employing 17 individuals stands to significantly impact employment levels in either location. And the company did not show it would represent a significant market share, according to the AAO.

Because national importance was not demonstrated, the AAO did not decide on the third prong of *Dhanasar*. The appeal was denied.

Matter of G-P-C-F-K- (March 8, 2018)[10]

The petitioner in this case was an aerospace engineer starting an engineering simulation business.

With respect to the first prong according to the petitioner, the business would provide engineering services for launch vehicles and the engineering of specific payloads. The AAO begins its analysis by noting that the petitioner failed to include

---

[9] https://bit.ly/A-R-A.

[10] https://bit.ly/G-P-C-F-K.

evidence of specific projects or scientific payloads other information about specific engineering research projects.

The petitioner offered a business plan for starting an enterprise in the category of "early stage innovation" in aerospace simulations. The petitioner provided letters from customers expressing their interest in purchasing engineering analysis services from the future company. Based on this evidence, the AAO found the petitioner's work had substantial merit.

With respect to the national importance requirement, the AAO took issue with the adequacy of the supporting documentation. The petitioner provided support letters describing his previous work, but the AAO noted the letters didn't address the national importance of his proposed endeavor. The AAO found that the petitioner had not established that his proposed work had implications beyond his company and its potential clients at a level sufficient to establish the national importance of the endeavor. Also, the AAO found that the specific work proposed by the petitioner did not offer original innovations to advance his industry or that it has wider implications in the aerospace simulation field.

The petitioner argued that his business had the significant potential to employ U.S. workers and intended to hire at least one additional employee. The AAO held that the record did not show hiring one worker represented a significant potential to employ U.S. workers or that it offers substantial positive economic effects for the nation. Therefore, the AAO held the national importance prong of *Dhanasar* was not met.

With respect to the second prong of *Dhanasar* regarding demonstrating the petitioner is well positioned to advance the proposed endeavor, the petitioner provided his resume, academic records, documentation of a postgraduate scholarship in his field and evidence of his graduate research work. With respect to the proposed business, the petitioner provided a business plan, financial forecasts and projections and a bank statement showing $20,501 in funds to start the business. He also provided support letters showing he had experience in payload design for space-based research and software. Despite this, the AAO held the record did not show his past experience rendered him well positioned to advance his proposed endeavor. They specifically cited his lack of a track record running a business.

With respect to the third prong of balancing factors to determine waiving the labor certification requirement, the AAO did not address this citing the failure to meet the first two prongs of *Dhanasar*.

Matter of K-S- (May 30, 2018)[11]

The petitioner in this case was a travel consultant who was planning to serve as the founder and executive manager of a destination management company engaged in the marketing and sales of experiential tour packages to East Asian nationals visiting the United States. She planned to provide tours to "diverse and unique target segments not available in the market including Amish residential, national parks and historical sites" including economically deprived areas of the United States. The petitioner planned on partnering with two Asian travel companies to sell travel packages to the South Korean market.

The petitioner provided copies of a business plan, feasibility analysis, and a monthly development plan for the business along with a description of the petitioner's job duties. She also provided an undated organizational chart listing four employees under her supervision. To support the national interest claim, the petitioner provided articles and research studies discussing the economic impact of travel and tourism on the U.S. economy, specifically tourism from South Korea. The AAO found that the petitioner's work had substantial merit.

To evaluate the national importance requirement, the AAO noted that it would look to the potential prospective impact of the petitioner's work. It is not enough that the field of industry that the foreign national will work in be important. In this case, the petitioner was arguing the business provided an economic benefit and the AAO noted that an endeavor that has the "potential to employ U.S. workers or has other substantial positive economic effects, particularly in an economically depressed area, for instance" may demonstrate national importance.

The petitioner addressed this requirement via her business plan, which showed a forecast of $886,750 in revenue in the first year of operation and $2.6 million by year five with a payroll growing from $168,833 to $299,483 by year five. The petitioner anticipated having eight employees by year five.

The AAO found that these metrics did not show the petitioner would offer "substantial economic benefits" in the region or in the nation. The petitioner did not specify where the business was to be located and where tours would take place so the specific economic impact of the business could not be evaluated. Furthermore, the petitioner did not show how the anticipated $2.6 million in revenue would provide a substantial benefit to the regional or national economy or how the business would have a meaningful impact on tourism in any of the states she noted she might

[11] https://bit.ly/K-S-.

provide tours. Also, while the business appeared to be growing, because she did not provide evidence that the location where the business is located is economically depressed or that the company would offer the region a substantial economic benefit through either its employment levels or tourism business. Finally, the petitioner did not show the business "would have broader implications within the field of tourism." Thus, the AAO found that the petitioner had not established that the endeavor is of national importance.

Having found that the petitioner did not meet the first prong of *Dhanasar* regarding national importance, the AAO did not consider the second and third prongs. The appeal was dismissed.

Matter of K-O-A-A- (June 21, 2018)[12]

The petitioner in this matter was an architect who had started a company that planned to design, produce, and market a multi-functional bag for retail customers, nonprofits, nongovernmental organizations, and humanitarian purposes (homeless and refugee populations). Her plans included partnering with a nonprofit organization to supply it with bags and form a "worker's cooperative" enlisting the "homeless who want to work."

The petitioner provided documentation of her agreement with the bag manufacturer, an organizational chart showing her managing four project team members, a letter from the petitioner's church pastor pledging money for the project, and various letters endorsing the project. Also included were background articles on the effects of homelessness. The AAO found that the petitioner's proposed work aiming to create jobs for the homeless and assisting them through her product met the requirement of showing substantial merit.

In an unusual move, the AAO withdrew the finding by the Texas Service Center director that the petitioner established the national importance of the proposed endeavor. According to the AAO:

> To evaluate whether the Petitioner's work satisfies the national importance requirement, we look to evidence documenting the "potential prospective impact" of the work. The relevant question is not the importance of the fields, industries, or causes for which the individual will work; instead we focus on the "specific endeavor that the foreign national proposes to undertake.

[12]https://bit.ly/KOOAMtr.

The AAO found that record in this case did not explain or document the potential prospective impact of the endeavor to support a finding that has national importance. The petitioner provided a budget showing $250,000 in start-up costs and projected sales of $250,000 in year one rising to $2,500,000 in year three. The bags' components would be manufactured in Ghana and Asia and the assembly would take place in the United States. The AAO noted that the petitioner failed to identify where the bags would be assembled in the United States nor how many jobs would be created. The petitioner did not show a homeless population needing work in the area in the United States where the business was to locate, nor did she show that the business would offer the region or its population a substantial economic benefit through employment levels or product sales. The petitioner also did not show that the benefits to the homeless population would be significant enough to merit a finding of national importance.

Having found that the petitioner did not meet the first prong of *Dhanasar* regarding national importance, it did not consider the second and third prongs and the appeal was dismissed.

Matter of E-J-C-D-H- (September 19, 2018)[13]

In this case appealed from the USCIS Texas Service Center, the petitioner proposed to continue developing and manufacturing liquid natural bio-stimulants derived from marine algae. He discussed his product's ability to provide similar benefits to pesticides without the dangers and how one of his products is helping fight serious crop threats from bacterial diseases. The petitioner provided news articles about the crop threats and the severe economic fallout facing the regions affected by the disease outbreak. The petitioner also included letters of support discussing the potential benefits of his work and the broader benefits to the industry. The AAO held that this was sufficient evidence to show the potential prospective impact of the petitioner's work and that the petitioner documented both substantial merit and national importance.

To demonstrate the petitioner was well-positioned to advance the proposed endeavor, the petitioner submitted his résumé, an advanced vocational diploma, a U.S. patent application, three U.S. trademarks, media coverage and documentation of his company's business plan and operations. Reference letters describing the petitioner's expertise as an agribusiness entrepreneur were also offered. The AAO found the

[13] https://bit.ly/E-J-C-D-H.

petitioner's experience rendered him well positioned to advance his proposed endeavor.

Finally, the AAO found that, on balance, it would be beneficial to waive the job offer and labor certification requirement. The AAO noted the petitioner had demonstrated providing "widespread benefits" and his being self-employed made it impractical for him to obtain a labor certification.

The AAO thus found that all three prongs of *Dhanasar* were met. As noted earlier, this is the only appeal by an entrepreneur the authors have found since *Dhanasar* that has been successful.

Matter of M-Z-H- (January 3, 2019)[14]

The petitioner in this case indicated he intended to work as a "self-employed consulting engineer/entrepreneur." He would be providing consulting engineering services and also extending engineering services for independent projects.

The AAO found substantial merit was demonstrated but questioned national importance. The petitioner argued that his undertaking would create jobs and have a substantial impact on the economy. He presented a business plan showing startup funding of $25,000 and plans to hire up to four staff in three years and achieve sales of $300,000 by year three. The petitioner also included articles on the economic impact of home building and school construction. And information regarding work on prior projects outside the United States was included.

The AAO noted the failure to identify any future U.S. projects. And they found that the petitioner had not offered sufficient information and evidence to demonstrate that the prospective impact of his proposed endeavor rises to the level of national importance. The AAO cited *Dhanasar's* finding that a classroom teacher's proposed endeavor is not nationally important because it will not impact the field more broadly to explain that the petitioner's work would not impact the industry more broadly. Also, the AAO did not agree that the number of jobs being created would have a significant economic impact.

Given the national importance requirement was not met, the AAO did not address the third prong of *Dhanasar*. The appeal was denied.

---

[14] https://bit.ly/M-Z-H.

Matter of S-J-H- (April 15, 2019)[15]

This petition was filed by a restaurant owner with a restaurant she owned in Alaska. USCIS's Nebraska Service Center agreed with the petitioner that the restaurant's positive impact on the small town where it was located met the "substantial merit" requirement.

However, the AAO did not agree that the endeavor meet the national importance requirement of the first prong of *Dhanasar*. The initial denial noted that the restaurant's impact would affect only the local community. On appeal, the petitioner argued that *Dhanasar* held that local businesses could be considered to have national importance and provided evidence of the local area being depressed and having a high unemployment rate. The restaurant employed 20 workers and paid out wages of $68,000. The petitioner noted an intention to hire five to 10 additional full-time employees, but the AAO noted that the petitioner did not explain the business need for additional workers. The AAO dismissed the benefit stating that 20 to 30 workers at the low rate of pay offered would not have a substantial impact in a community of 14,000 people. Also, the petitioner failed to show that the restaurant's benefits would not extend beyond the community or impact the restaurant industry more broadly. Thus, the AAO held that the first prong of *Dhanasar* was not met.

With respect to the second prong of *Dhanasar* requiring the petitioner be well positioned to advance the proposed endeavor, the petitioner submitted tax returns and a business plan. The AAO rejected the tax returns because they were incomplete and didn't include the petitioner's signature. Also, the petitioner's degree in communications was not viewed as being directly related to the proposed endeavor. The petitioner did present a résumé showing five years' experience managing a restaurant but did not include any documentation of the experience. The AAO found the second prong was not met.

The AAO chose not to address the third prong since the first two were not met and denied the appeal.

Takeaways

There are some takeaways from the cases that can help better strategize on NIW cases:

---

[15] https://bit.ly/S-J-H.

1. Basing a case on work that is already started rather than a plan for something that will be done entirely in the future is better.

2. Job creation is likely to be discounted unless the number of jobs being created is large and it will have a substantial impact on the employment rate in the local area. Also, if job creation is an argument, it helps to show the area where the jobs will be created is economically depressed.

3. If the NIW is based on strong projections for job growth or revenue growth, the evidence to document the projections are reasonable will need to be thorough and credible.

4. The documentation for the cases should be substantial as a general rule. All claims made need to be backed up by specific evidence.

5. Previous work should be closely related to what is the basis for the national interest argument.

6. Include evidence of specific projects and matters that demonstrate the work that is claimed to be of national importance.

7. Economic arguments based on the importance of an industry are not enough. The petitioner needs to show that his or her business will itself have a substantial economic impact on the regional or national economy or that the petitioner's business will have a major impact on the industry itself.

The *Dhanasar* decision was greeted with considerable optimism when it was released, particularly by immigration lawyers representing startup founders. However, as the AAO history shows, these cases are far from slam dunks. Waiting until a company is beyond its initial startup stage and spending the time to thoroughly document the cases may be the secret to successfully filing an NIW for a founder.

15

EMPLOYMENT-BASED FIRST PREFERENCE CATEGORIES: EB-1A EXTRAORDINARY ABILITY

Employment-based first preference, or EB-1A, is a green card category reserved for aliens of extraordinary ability in the sciences, arts, education, business or athletics.[1] This category is similar to the O-1A nonimmigrant visa category for aliens of extraordinary ability that was discussed thoroughly in a previous chapter. There are distinctions between the O-1A nonimmigrant visa and the EB-1A green card category, and this chapter will mostly focus on additional information needed for entrepreneurs pursuing this green card category, instead of repeating the suggestions from the O-1 chapter. It would be most beneficial to read the chapters together, even in the case of founders who are not making the common transition from an O-1A status to an EB-1A green card.

Since the labor certification process prohibits equity owners from pursuing employment-based green cards in the most common way,[2] many co-founders will look to the employment-based first preference categories and National Interest Waivers (NIW) as the most entrepreneur-friendly paths since they allow for "self-petitioning." Under the EB-1A extraordinary ability category, an individual may file an immigrant visa (green card) petition on his or her own behalf.[3]

Alternatively, a U.S. company may also serve as the petitioner for an EB-1A application, and unlike other visa categories, an approved EB-1A petition will remain the basis for a foreign national's green card application even if he or she does not

[1] Immigration and Nationality Act (INA) §203(b)(1)(A).

[2] 20 Code of Federal Regulations (CFR) §656.17.

[3] INA §204(a)(1)(E).

continue to work for the employer, so long as the foreign national will continue to work in the same field of extraordinary ability.[4]

In order to qualify for a green card as an alien of extraordinary ability, the following must be established:

(i) the alien has extraordinary ability in the sciences, arts, education, business, or athletics which has been demonstrated by sustained national or international acclaim and whose achievements have been recognized in the field through extensive documentation,

(ii) the alien seeks to enter the United States to continue work in the area of extraordinary ability, and

(iii) the alien's entry into the United States will substantially benefit prospectively the United States.[5]

The EB-1A process can be quite burdensome to document, and extraordinary ability at (i) is usually the crux of the matter. In order to demonstrate the alien has achieved extraordinary ability in his or her field, the entrepreneur must present evidence of one major international award (such as a Nobel Prize),[6] or much more commonly he or she must establish three of the ten following criteria:

1. Documentation of the alien's receipt of lesser nationally or internationally recognized prizes or awards for excellence in the field of endeavor;
2. Documentation of the alien's membership in associations in the field for which classification is sought, which require outstanding achievements of their members, as judged by recognized national or international experts in their disciplines or fields;
3. Published material about the alien in professional or major trade publications or other major media, relating to the alien's work in the field for which classification is sought. Such evidence shall include the title, date, and author of the material, and any necessary translation;
4. Evidence of the alien's participation, either individually or on a panel, as a judge of the work of others in the same or an allied field of specification for which classification is sought;

---

[4] INS Letter, E. H. Skerrett, "EB-1 Petition Valid With or Without Prospective Employer," AILA Doc. No. 93031040 (*posted* Jan. 25, 1993).

[5] INA §203(b)(1)(A).

[6] 8 CFR §204.5(h)(3).

5. Evidence of the alien's original scientific, scholarly, artistic, athletic, or business-related contributions of major significance in the field;
6. Evidence of the alien's authorship of scholarly articles in the field, in professional or major trade publications or other major media;
7. Evidence of the display of the alien's work in the field at artistic exhibitions or showcases;
8. Evidence that the alien has performed in a leading or critical role for organizations or establishments that have a distinguished reputation;
9. Evidence that the alien has commanded a high salary or other significantly high remuneration for services, in relation to others in the field; or
10. Evidence of commercial successes in the performing arts, as shown by box office receipts or record, cassette, compact disk, or video sales.[7]

Of these 10 criteria, eight are notably similar to the criteria available under the O-1A category, and two (7 and 10) are similar to the O-1B criteria for individuals with extraordinary ability in the arts. While performers and artists can benefit from the two criteria at (7 and 10), entrepreneurs cannot; therefore, this chapter will focus on the eight criteria a founder can use to demonstrate extraordinary ability in his or her field.

In the O-1A context, a foreign national is only required to meet three of the eight criteria. EB-1A varies greatly from O-1A because the applicant is subject to a two-step analysis. First, the entrepreneur must establish three of the regulatory criteria. Second, he or she must convince U.S. Citizenship and Immigration Services (USCIS) that a "final merits determination" of the totality of the evidence demonstrates the alien is among the small percentage at the very top of the field of endeavor.[8] This second test is known as *Kazarian* analysis and stems from a 2010 U.S. Ninth Circuit Court of Appeals case that USCIS has adopted as justification for placing additional scrutiny on EB-1A applicants.

---

[7] *Id.*

[8] *See Kazarian v. USCIS*, 596 F.3d 1115 (9th Cir. 2010).

Establishing the Regulatory Criteria

The analysis should still be just about presenting evidence that the founder meets each of the regulatory criteria that he or she is trying to establish. The USCIS *Adjudicator's Field Manual* (AFM) provides helpful insight on how this can be accomplished. For Part 1 of the analysis, the AFM explains:

> *Note*: While USCIS officers should consider the quality and caliber of the evidence when required by the regulations to determine whether a particular regulatory criterion has been met, USCIS officers should not make a determination regarding whether or not the alien is one of that small percentage who have risen to the very top of the field or if the alien has sustained national or international acclaim in Part One of the case analysis.[9]

Documentation of the alien's receipt of lesser nationally or internationally recognized prizes or awards for excellence in the field of endeavor[10]

The previous O-1 chapter goes into detail on the types of awards that an entrepreneur may present to establish this criteria. The AFM explains that in the EB-1 analysis, USCIS will consider two factors:

1. Determine if the alien was the recipient of prizes or awards.
2. Determine whether the alien has received lesser nationally or internationally recognized prizes or awards for excellence in the field of endeavor.[11]

In the first point, USCIS clarifies that the alien, not his or her employer, should be the recipient of any prizes or awards. However, in the case of a company founder, the company is the alien's "work;" thus, arguments can be made that awards won by the company the entrepreneur created are, at least in part, being awarded to the alien for his or her work in the field. It should be properly explained that there is no "employer" in a traditional sense, since the individual is self-employed.

To satisfy the second point, the AFM suggests the applicant include:

1. The criteria used to grant the awards or prizes;
2. The national or international significance of the awards or prizes in the field; and

[9] *Adjudicator's Field Manual* (AFM) Chapter 22.2(i)(1)(A).

[10] 8 CFR §204.5(h)(3)(i).

[11] AFM Chapter 22.2(i)(1)(A).

3. The number of awardees or prize recipients as well as any limitations on competitors (an award limited to competitors from a single institution, for example, may have little national or international significance).[12]

In many cases this information may be available directly from the institution that is presenting the award. In other cases, it is beneficial to include a letter of support from the institution specifically addressing the criteria used to choose a recipient as well as figures on the pool of potential applicants or winners. The more information you can provide on the number of people applying versus how many are being awarded, the stronger the evidence will be.

As with the O-1, purely academic awards are not given much weight. This is because academic awards are usually only available to students or faculty of the given institution. If an entrepreneur has received an award from an academic institution that was open to potential winners from outside of the student body, alumni, and faculty, this is more persuasive evidence of an award of national or international significance.

Lastly, as explained in the O-1 chapter, under the Obama administration, USCIS stated that the receipt of venture capital or angel investments could be presented as evidence of an award (of capital). The Obama-era language stated:

> *Note*: If you have received venture capital funding or have been awarded a grant, you may submit evidence of the funding or grant awarded, including the amount of the funding or grant and the criteria used in awarding the funding or grant. Evidence of other investments, such as those from an accredited angel investor, may also be submitted.[13]

As previously explained, the language was taken off the USCIS site during the Trump administration. In practice, this type of evidence remains more persuasive in the O-1 context than in EB-1A. That is not to say that the evidence should not be submitted, because it should. Entrepreneurs who relied heavily on this evidence to establish O-1 criteria, though, will want additional evidence of extraordinary ability and may be better served by using venture capital as supplemental evidence.

When presenting evidence of venture capital or angel funding, the applicant should include a detailed letter from the investor explaining what criteria were used for analyzing the entrepreneur and startup, how many companies were considered for such investment, and how many were chosen. It is also beneficial to explain who

---

[12] *Id.*

[13] Previously found at https://bit.ly/37bIMIm.

the investor or firm is and other companies that have been chosen for the portfolio especially if they have a well-known reputation.

Documentation of the Alien's Membership in Associations in the Field for Which Classification Is Sought, which Require Outstanding Achievement of Their Members, as Judged by Recognized National or International Experts in Their Disciplines or Fields.[14]

This criterion is often favorable for the entrepreneur given the number of relevant and prestigious organizations that exist. There are many organizations specifically for startup founders in general, as well as organizations within specific fields (*i.e.*, medtech, legaltech, etc.). Unlike many areas of business, the foreign national co-founder should have options out there for distinguished organizations to join, provided that he or she can meet the criteria for membership. As with prizes and awards, documenting the requirements for membership is the key to presenting successful evidence for this criterion. The other deciding factor is who is making the determination for membership. The AFM explains:

> The petitioner must show that membership in the associations is based on the alien being judged by recognized national or international experts as having attained outstanding achievements in the field for which classification is sought. For example, admission to membership in the National Academy of Sciences as a Foreign Associate requires individuals to be nominated by an academy member, and membership is ultimately granted based upon recognition of the individual's distinguished achievements in original research. See www.nasonline.org.[15]

Many of the distinguished entrepreneur-related organizations are invite-only, have extensive interview processes, or require current membership to vote on each new member. Applicants for EB-1A should present evidence of these barriers to membership since they further demonstrate that he or she has satisfied other distinguished founders who have similarly met the discernible criteria.

Organizations that simply require the payment of a fee or a certain number of years in an industry will not generally carry much weight. This even includes well-known professional organizations, such as the Chartered Financial Assistant Institute or the like. On this note, the AFM explains:

---

[14] 8 CFR §204.5(h)(3)(ii).

[15] AFM Chapter 22.2(i)(1)(A).

> Relevant factors that may lead to a conclusion that the alien's membership in the associations was not based on outstanding achievements in the field include, but are not limited to, instances where the alien's membership was based:
>
> – Solely on a level of education or years of experience in a particular field;
> – On the payment of a fee or by subscribing to an association's publications; or
> – On a requirement, compulsory or otherwise, for employment in certain occupations, such as union membership or guild affiliation for actors.[16]

Published Material About the Alien in Professional or Major Trade Publications or Other Major Media Relating to the Alien's Work in the Field for Which Classification Is Sought. Such Evidence Shall Include the Title, Date, and Author of the Material, and any Necessary Translation.[17]

As noted in the O-1 chapter, major media coverage of the entrepreneur is one of the stronger forms of evidence. Although not a requirement for establishing EB-1A, it does help with the overall narrative that a person is at the top of his or her field. Establishing this criterion is basically a two-step process: first, present evidence of the media coverage; second, explain how the coverage is considered major media.

The EB-1 regulation diverts slightly here from the language used in the O-1 context about the media coverage being "material about the alien[18]" and not "relating to the alien's work in the field."[19] This is an important distinction for an entrepreneur because his or her 'work' is the company and thus all of its accomplishments are arguably the accomplishments of its founders. Here, though, the AFM explains:

> The published material should be about the alien relating to his or her work in the field, not just about his or her employer or another organization that he or she is associated with.[20]

This means that stronger media coverage evidence will specifically identify the foreign national entrepreneur. This can be done different ways. For example, articles or stories may mention or quote the foreign national. It is particularly helpful if they

---

[16] *Id.*

[17] 8 CFR §204.5(h)(3)(iii).

[18] *Id.*

[19] 8 CFR §214.2(o)(3)(iii)(B)(3).

[20] AFM Chapter 22.2(i)(1)(A)

identify the co-founder's role or field. Obviously, language discussing the entrepreneur's extraordinary ability or accomplishments is even stronger.

Next, establishing that the media is major usually starts with identifying the scope of the media coverage. The media source can be major nationally within a single country and does not have to be from the United States, or it may be major internationally. The AFM suggests:

> Evidence of published material in professional or major trade publications or in other major media publications about the alien should establish that the circulation (online or in print) is high compared to other circulation statistics and show who the intended audience is, as well as the title, date and author of the material.[21]

Circulation, viewership, or traffic numbers can often be found from the media platform itself. If that information is not available, a number of third-party organizations can provide information to demonstrate the reach of the media outlet within its respective field and country.

Evidence of the Alien's Participation, Either Individually or on a Panel, as a Judge of the Work of Others in the Same or an Allied Field of Specialization for Which Classification Is Sought.[22]

Evidence that the foreign national has served as a judge of others in the field is another criterion that lends itself particularly well to entrepreneurs. As discussed in the O-1 chapter, this is because there are numerous examples of prestigious pitch competitions, business plan competitions, and hackathons around the world that successful entrepreneurs are often asked to judge. Entrepreneurs with academic backgrounds will find themselves in a good position since the AFM explicitly identifies academic peer review and PhD dissertation committees as acceptable forms of evidence.[23]

The main note under this criterion is that just an invitation for the foreign national to participate as a judge of others is not enough; he or she must actually accept the invitation and serve as a judge.[24] It is prudent to include evidence of whom the entrepreneur is judging, what applicants went through to be judged, who are the other

---

[21] *Id.*

[22] 8 CFR §204.5(h)(3)(iv).

[23] AFM Chapter 22.2(i)(1)(A).

[24] *Id.*

judges, and what criteria are the judges using to make their determination. Additional evidence of the distinguished nature of the competition or organization is also helpful.

Evidence of the Alien's Original Scientific, Scholarly, Artistic, Athletic, or Business-Related Contributions of Major Significance in the Field.[25]

Most startups are based on an innovative and original idea, but the bigger challenge is proving that the contribution is significant to the field or industry. In some cases, this can just be documented by meaningful intellectual property protections like patents or major media coverage about the significance of his or her impact on the industry. In more cases, though, the entrepreneur must rely on letters of support from other industry experts to explain to USCIS the significance of the contributions.

To that end, the AFM not only explains that this type of evidence should be accepted but also provides guidance on what these letters must include to be most persuasive. The AFM states:

> USCIS officers should take into account the probative analysis that experts in the field may provide in opinion letters regarding the significance of the alien's contributions in order to assist in giving an assessment of the alien's original contributions of major significance. That said, not all expert letters provide such analysis. Letters that specifically articulate how the alien's contributions are of major significance to the field and its impact on subsequent work add value. Letters that lack specifics and simply use hyperbolic language do not add value, and are not considered to be probative evidence that may form the basis for meeting this criterion.[26]

When requesting letters of support from fellow industry experts, the co-founder should ask for specific examples of how his or her work has influenced the work of others or the field as a whole. Peers, advisors, competitors, and customers may all have different but important ways of explaining the significance. These can all be valuable sources of expert analysis, and who should provide letters of support comes down to a case-by-case analysis. The substance of the letter though can be more important than the name recognition of the writer.

---

[25] 8 CFR §204.5(h)(3)(v).

[26] AFM Chapter 22.2(i)(1)(A).

Evidence of the Alien's Authorship of Scholarly Articles in the Field, in Professional or Major Trade Publications or Other Major Media.[27]

This is another example of the criteria being particularly kind to those with academic backgrounds. Co-founders who have published in scholarly journals related to their fields will benefit by presenting evidence of the articles and the journals that published them. USCIS will consider evidence of the journal's impact factor and rankings within its field to determine whether the academic publication is significant. For the entrepreneur who does not have an academic background, the question is whether he or she published in "major trade publications or other major media."[28]

Writing articles for business-related, startup-related, or industry-specific (*e.g.*, medtech, legaltech, etc.) publications can still satisfy this requirement. The analysis of "major media" under this criterion is similar to the documentation needed for showing major media coverage about the individual. Circulation, viewership, or traffic numbers can demonstrate that the platform publishing the entrepreneur's articles is significant.

There is no requirement that a person write a certain number of articles to establish this criterion. While more articles may be increasingly persuasive, any notable publications should be included.

Evidence that the Alien Has Performed in a Leading or Critical Role for Organizations or Establishments that Have a Distinguished Reputation.[29]

Every co-founder should be able to make the argument that his or her role is critical to the organization. Really, it should just be a matter of documenting that role, which may be possible through different forms of evidence, but should also be handled through letters of support. The AFM explains:

> This is one criterion where letters from individuals with personal knowledge of the significance of the alien's leading or critical role can be particularly helpful to USCIS officers in making this determination as long as the letters contain detailed and probative information that specifically addresses how the alien's role for the organization or establishment was leading or critical.

---

[27] 8 CFR §204.5(h)(3)(vi).

[28] *Id.*

[29] 8 CFR §204.5(h)(3)(viii).

> *Note*: 8 Code of Federal Regulations (CFR) §204.5(g)(1) states that evidence of experience "shall" consist of letters from employers.[30]

The note should be obvious, but someone at the company needs to draft a letter of support explaining the critical contributions and responsibilities the co-founder has made and continues to make to the organization. In general, another co-founder can provide examples of fundraising, leadership, or product development contributions made by the foreign national. If the entrepreneur does not have a co-founder than a company advisor or member of the board can provide the evidence.

Since every co-founder should be able to make the critical role argument, the crux of the matter is establishing that his or her organization has a distinguished reputation. This is similar to establishing that an entrepreneur's original contributions are significant to the field. In this context, there may again be major media, awards, or intellectual property to make this point obvious; but in most cases, the co-founder will continue to rely on letters of support from other industry experts. The AFM includes a note that is helpful for startup founders, which states:

> USCIS officers should keep in mind that the relative size or longevity of an organization or establishment is not in and of itself a determining factor. Rather, the organization or establishment must be recognized as having a distinguished reputation.

Thus, the company can still be young and growing while still satisfying USCIS that it has a distinguished reputation within its field.

Evidence that the Alien Has Commanded a High Salary or Other Significantly High Remuneration for Services, in Relation to Others in the Field.[31]

Co-founders at early-stage companies may not find this category as kind as others, since they often have C-level titles such as chief executive officer (CEO) or chief technology officer (CTO). In general, evidence is established under this criterion by comparing the foreign national's compensation to others in similar occupation categories and in the same geographical area (mostly county or nearby counties). This means the CEO applicant's salary will be compared to other chief executives in the county. Since most entrepreneurs are trying to keep their burn rate low, they are generally taking equity over high salaries. For that reason, this criterion can

[30] AFM Chapter 22.2(i)(1)(A).

[31] 8 CFR §204.5(h)(3)(ix).

be difficult to establish for young company owners. When trying to present evidence, it is best to start with government data if available. The three most common sources are included in the AFM:

- The Bureau of Labor Statistics (BLS): http://www.bls.gov/bls/blswage.htm
- The Department of Labor's Career One Stop website: http://www.careeronestop.org/SalariesBenefits/Sal_default.aspx
- The Department of Labor's Office of Foreign Labor Certification Online Wage Library: http://www.flcdatacenter.com[32]

The AFM also notes:

> Aliens working in different countries should be evaluated based on the wage statistics or comparable evidence in that country, rather than by simply converting the salary to U.S. dollars and then viewing whether that salary would be considered high in the United States.[33]

While this evidence can be more difficult to gather, the co-founder who has earned significant income in other roles abroad should include documentation of how that stacked up against peers.

When trying to establish that the total compensation is highly valuable, the foreign national will need to formally document the value of the stock as well. This can be done through evidence of the post–money valuation and through signed affidavits.

If the Standards Do Not Readily Apply to the Beneficiary's Occupation, the Petitioner May Submit Comparable Evidence to Establish the Beneficiary's Eligibility.[34]

In order to present persuasive "comparable evidence" under this criterion, the foreign national must include an explanation of how the criteria "do not readily apply to the alien's occupation." For most entrepreneurs, this is generally not true for all of the reasons mentioned above, as well as those in the O-1 chapter. Many of the criteria do apply to fields related to entrepreneurship; in fact, many lend themselves well to the co-founder foreign national applying for EB-1A.

There may be some fields, though, where the regulatory criteria are not a good fit, and then the applicant is free to present evidence that demonstrates extraordinary

---

[32] AFM Chapter 22.2(i)(1)(A).

[33] *Id.*

[34] 8 CFR §204.5(h)(4).

ability in a way not described. The AFM only gives examples of Olympic coaches and members of Olympic teams and does not give examples of comparable evidence in the business-related fields. Some people argue that being invited to give major speeches and presentations should be classified as comparable evidence. This is a strategy decision best left to the attorney to decide whether this type of evidence can fall under another category. General letters of support are not accepted as comparable evidence for establishing the criteria.[35]

In the EB-1 context, since the foreign national has to establish at least three of the defined criteria and satisfy the *Kazarian* analysis, many will choose to add the less clearly defined evidence in the greater "final merits determination" that the totality of the evidence demonstrates the alien is among the small percentage at the very top of the field of endeavor.[36]

The Process

The EB-1A application is filed using USCIS Form I-140 Immigrant Petition for Alien Worker. In the labor certification green card process, the foreign national first goes through the Program Electronic Review Management System (PERM) process, then files an I-140, and then finally applies for a green card in the third and final step. In the EB-1A context, it is a two-step process.

The I-140 is filed with all of the evidence to establish extraordinary ability. USCIS then can approve, deny, or send a Request for Evidence (RFE) if more evidence is needed to prove the entrepreneur has risen to the level of extraordinary ability under EB-1A. This type of I-140 can be premium processed with USCIS, so the foreign national can pay an additional fee of $1,440 and the case will be adjudicated in 15 days.

The date the I-140 is filed becomes the foreign national entrepreneur's priority date on the *Visa Bulletin*; once approved, this date is secured. Once the I-140 is approved and the priority date is current, the founder and his or her family (spouse and children under 21) may all file for green cards either through the adjustment-of-status process in the United States or consular processing at a U.S. consulate or embassy abroad. Both processes are covered in more detail in the general chapter on immigrant visas.

---

[35] *Id.*

[36] *See Kazarian v. USCIS*, 596 F.3d 1115 (9th Cir. 2010).

16

Employment-Based First Preference Categories: EB-1C Multinational Executives and Managers

Often thought of as the green card counterpart to the L-1 nonimmigrant visa, the EB-1-3 (commonly referred to as EB-1C)[1] permanent residency category is available to certain multinational executives and managers. The Immigration and Nationality Act (INA) describes those who are eligible:

> Certain multinational executives and managers.—An alien is described in this subparagraph if the alien, in the three years preceding the time of the alien's application for classification and admission into the United States under this subparagraph, has been employed for at least one year by a firm or corporation or other legal entity or an affiliate or subsidiary thereof and the alien seeks to enter the United States in order to continue to render services to the same employer or to a subsidiary or affiliate thereof in a capacity that is managerial or executive.[2]

But just as the O-1 is not the same as the EB-1A extraordinary ability category, having an L-1 is no guarantee that a beneficiary will succeed with an EB-1C multinational executive/manager I-140 petition. A higher standard is generally applied and there are a few key differences in the categories discussed below.

What are some of the reasons why the EB-1C category might be considered attractive to a startup founder? First, it's in the EB-1 category which, by virtue of being at the top of the employment-based preference category food chain, tends to have no backlogs or shorter backlogs. For Indian and Chinese nationals facing years-long backlogs in the EB-2 and EB-3 categories, this is pretty important.

---

[1] The authors will refer to the EB-1-3 category as EB-1C in this chapter.

[2] Immigration and Nationality Act (INA) §203(b)(1)(C) [U.S. Code §1153(b)(1)(C)].

Second, the EB-1C category doesn't have a labor certification requirement. This means there is no need to go through a recruiting process to demonstrate to the U.S. Department of Labor that there are no U.S. workers with the minimum qualifications readily available. Labor certifications are not available to employees who have an equity stake in the employer so this will often mean the startup founder can't look to that category. There is no such bar on holding equity in the EB-1C category. Also, the labor certification process can add a year or more to the green card timeline.

Third, if one is in the United States on an L-1A working for the startup already, the EB-1C may be a more natural fit. While there are a few key differences between the two categories, often meeting the requirements for an L-1A is a good indicator of qualifying for EB-1C.

Finally, EB-1C cases come with the ability to concurrently file an adjustment of status petition with the I-140. This might be useful if one's seven years of L-1 eligibility is running out or if a person is in a category (like an O-1 or H-1B) where a spouse or child isn't eligible to work and would like to more quickly secure an employment authorization document. Also, for those from countries where administrative processing and other delays are a real risk in nonimmigrant visa processing, being able to re-enter the United States on an advance parole document is potentially very helpful.

As for the downsides of EB-1C, there are a few. First, the category requires foreign employment abroad for a company related to the U.S. petitioner, something that might not be available to many. And even if such foreign employment exists, the foreign company must continue doing business and continue being related to the U.S. enterprise until at least the I-140 is approved. And, unlike the L-1, the business in the United States must be operating for at least a year before the I-140 petition can be filed.

Second, there is no premium processing available to EB-1C applicants and current I-140 processing times are getting longer and longer. So it could be many months before a petitioner finds out that the case is approved, denied, or will require additional evidence. If premium processing were available, a decision could be known in as little as 15 days.

Finally, the statute is not supposed to be harder on small businesses, but U.S. Citizenship and Immigration Services (USCIS) interprets the rules regarding demonstrating managerial and executive duties in a way that seem to favor larger organizations with multiple layers in the organizational hierarchy. That obviously means startup businesses face more of a challenge.

The Employer Requirements

Qualifying Relationship

For an employer to meet the EB-1C requirements, there must be a qualifying relationship between a foreign company and an employer that is currently or will be doing business in the United States. Like the L-1, there is no requirement that the U.S. and foreign businesses need not be in the same field.

A key concept in EB-1C cases is ownership and control and whether the U.S. entity and the foreign entity that is transferring the beneficiary to the United States are properly related. The statute requires the beneficiary have worked previously for an affiliate or subsidiary of a U.S. firm or corporation, or other legal entity, prior to entering the United States. While the statute doesn't mention the foreign entity being the parent of a U.S. entity, USCIS has historically permitted this. The USCIS *Adjudicator's Field Manual* confirms this very clearly:

> When an employer wishes to transfer an alien employee working abroad to a U.S. company location as an EB-1-3 immigrant, a qualifying relationship must exist between the foreign employer and the U.S. employer. A qualifying relationship exists when the U.S. employer is an affiliate, parent or a subsidiary of the foreign firm, corporation, or other legal entity, as specified in 8 [Code of Federal Regulations] CFR 204.5(j)(2). To establish a "qualifying relationship" under the Act and the regulations, the petitioner must show that the beneficiary's foreign employer and the proposed U.S. employer are the same employer (*i.e.*, a U.S. entity with a foreign office) or related as a "parent and subsidiary" or as "affiliates.[3]

Joint ventures may also qualify under the USCIS regulation's definition of "subsidiary":

> Subsidiary means a firm, corporation, or other legal entity of which a parent owns, directly or indirectly, more than half of the entity and controls the entity; or owns, directly or indirectly, half of the entity and controls the entity; or owns, directly or indirectly, 50 percent of a 50-50 joint venture and has equal control and veto power over the entity; or owns, directly or indirectly, less than half of the entity, but in fact controls the entity.

And, as noted in this definition, the rules allow for a broader reading of "control" to include a stake less than 50 percent if one entity has effective control over the other. Importantly for startups, USCIS's *Adjudicator's Field Manual* allows for

[3] *Adjudicator's Field Manual* (AFM) 22.2(i)(3)(B).

"self-incorporated" petitioners with as few as one owner or employee to seek an EB-1C as long as the corporate is a "separate and distinct legal entity from its owners or stockholders."[4]

If a company ceases foreign operations before the beneficiary has completed immigrant visa processing, the immigrant visa will be denied.[5] However, if at least one of the company's qualifying overseas entities continues to be doing business, it is possible to complete immigrant visa processing.[6]

Unlike L-1 petitions, the prospective U.S. employer must have been "doing business" for at least one year.[7] Hence, a brand-new startup will not be able to seek a green card for a founder under this category if it has just started operations. "Doing business" is defined as "the regular, systematic, and continuous provision of goods and/or services by a firm, corporation, or other entity and does not include the mere presence of an agent or office.[8]" That provision of goods can be within the company and need not be with third parties.[9]

Petitioning employers in employment-based green card petitions are required to demonstrate they have the ability to pay the offered salary. The regulations state:

> Any petition filed by or for an employment-based immigrant which requires an offer of employment must be accompanied by evidence that the prospective United States employer has the ability to pay the proffered wage. The petitioner must demonstrate this ability at the time the priority date is established and continuing until the beneficiary obtains lawful permanent residence. Evidence of this ability shall be either in the form of copies of annual reports, federal tax returns, or audited financial statements. In a case where the prospective United States employer employs 100 or more workers, the director may accept a statement from a financial officer of the organization which establishes the prospective employer's ability to pay the proffered wage. In appropriate cases, additional evidence, such as profit/loss statements, bank account records, or personnel records, may be submitted by the petitioner or requested by the Service.[10]

---

[4] AFM 22.2(i)(3)(B)(3).

[5] AFM 22.2(i)(3)(C)(2).

[6] *Id.*

[7] 8 Code of Federal Regulations (CFR) §204.5(j)(3)(i)(D).

[8] 8 CFR §204.5(j)(2).

[9] *Matter of Leacheng International, Inc.* 26 I&N Dec. 532 (AAO 2015).

[10] 8 CFR §204.5(g)(2).

For startups, this can be challenging. Founders are often paid little in the early stages of a new company because investors tend to react negatively when early-stage employees are taking too much money home in salary. Yet being paid a low salary could be an indicator to a USCIS examiner that the position is not a high-level manager or executive.

The Employee Requirements

The beneficiary of the immigrant visa petition must have been employed full-time by an overseas entity described above for a period of at least one year during the three years before the date the immigrant visa petition is filed.[11] If the beneficiary is already working in the United States for the company, then the test is whether the beneficiary has worked for the employer for one year in the three years before he or she entered the United States to begin work for the employer.[12] Note that the work in the United States can be in any category and not just an L-1 (though that is probably the most common route for most).

The work abroad must have been in a managerial or executive capacity. This is a requirement that is somewhat different than the L-1 nonimmigrant category. L-1s can come to the United States as managers, executives or specialized knowledge employees. EB-1C applicants can only be managers or executives. In the L-1 context, an applicant can work abroad in any of the three capacities even if it is not the category they'll be working in the United States. For example, one who worked as a specialized knowledge employee abroad can enter the United States on an L-1 to work as a manager. With respect to EB-1C, the beneficiary must have worked only in a managerial or executive position abroad and must be entering to accept a managerial or executive position.[13] An L-1B in the United States can seek an EB-1C-based green card in the United States if they worked abroad as a manager or executive, but petitioners should expect these cases to be closely scrutinized with respect to both the job duties abroad and whether the U.S.-based position is truly that of a function or personnel manager.

Like the L-1A, the EB-1C must be coming to the United States to work in a "managerial" or "executive" capacity. The regulations defining these terms are largely the same for the EB-1C as they are for the L-1A. With respect to personnel managers, the rule reads as follows:

---

[11] 8 CFR §204.5(j)(3)(A).

[12] 8 CFR §204.5(j)(3)(B).

[13] INA §203(b)(1)(C).

Managerial capacity means an assignment within an organization in which the employee primarily:

(A) Manages the organization, or a department, subdivision, function, or component of the organization;

(B) Supervises and controls the work of other supervisory, professional, or managerial employees, or manages an essential function within the organization, or a department or subdivision of the organization;

(C) If another employee or other employees are directly supervised, has the authority to hire and fire or recommend those as well as other personnel actions (such as promotion and leave authorization), or, if no other employee is directly supervised, functions at a senior level within the organizational hierarchy or with respect to the function managed; and

(D) Exercises direction over the day-to-day operations of the activity or function for which the employee has authority.

A first-line supervisor is not considered to be acting in a managerial capacity merely by virtue of the supervisory duties unless the direct reports are professionals.[14]

"Function managers" may also qualify for EB-1C. According to the AFM, "functional" or "function manager" applies generally when a beneficiary does not supervise or control the work of a subordinate staff but instead is primarily responsible for managing an "essential function" within the organization.[15] A manager may qualify as a "function manager" if the beneficiary will be primarily managing or directing the management of a function of an organization, even if the beneficiary does not directly supervise any employees.[16] A function manager will have the following characteristics:

- Manages the organization, or a department, subdivision, function, or component of the organization;
- Manages an essential function within the organization, or a department or subdivision of the organization;
- Functions at a senior level within the organizational hierarchy or with respect to the function managed; and
- Exercises discretion over the day-to-day operations of the activity or function for which the employee has authority.[17]

---

[14] INA §101(a)(44)(A).

[15] AFM 22.2(i)(3)(E).

[16] *Id.*

[17] *Id.*

USCIS examiners typically look at function manager petitions with considerable scrutiny so petitioners will want to carefully document the case. In a recent precedent decision from USCIS's Administrative Appeals Office (AAO) discussed function managers in the L-1A context, but the same criteria apply to EB-1C petitions:

> Ultimately, we must determine whether the petitioner has demonstrated that the beneficiary will primarily manage, as opposed to perform, the essential function. While an L-1A function manager may use his or her business expertise to perform some operational or administrative tasks, he or she must primary manage an essential function.[18]

"Executive capacity" is defined by the Immigration and Nationality Act as an assignment within an organization in which the employee primarily

- Directs the management of the organization or a major component or function of the organization;
- Establishes the goals and policies of the organization, component, or function;
- Exercises wide latitude in discretionary decision-making; and
- Receives only general supervision or direction from higher level executives, the board of directors, or stockholders of the organization.[19]

With respect to startups and their founders, AFM cautions:

> An individual will not be deemed an executive under the statute simply because they have an executive title or because some portion of their time is spent "directing" the enterprise as the owner or sole managerial employee; the focus is on the primary duties of the individual. In this regard, there must be sufficient staff (*e.g.*, contract employees or others) to perform the day-to-day operations of the petitioning organization in order to enable the beneficiary to be primarily employed in the executive function... The petitioner must also establish that the U.S. entity itself is in fact conducting business at a level that would require the services of an individual primarily engaged in executive (or managerial) functions. In making this determination, you should consider, as appropriate, the nature of the business, including its size, its organizational structure, and the product or service it provides.

That is not to say it is impossible to qualify as an executive if the beneficiary is the sole employee of a company. But it is certainly harder to get a case like that approved than for a company that has a larger team.

---

[18] *Matter of Z-A-*, Inc. Adopted Decision 2016-02 (AAO April 14, 2016). The decision also cited prior cases noting that the beneficiary must be engaged in overseeing essential functions of the business rather than performing them herself and not merely be performing the functions of the company.

[19] INA §101(a)(44)(B).

Whether the position is managerial or executive in nature, a winning petition is likely going to get very specific about job duties, the percentage of time being spent on each job duty, how the employee is going to manage a function or a department or how an executive's senior-level role is reflected in his or her day-to-day specific job duties. A detailed organization chart should also be provided documenting this. The petition must also show that there are sufficient employees below in the hierarchy managing everyday operations and that the manager or executive is not also filling those roles.

In addition to a support letter from the U.S. employer, the EB-1C petition should also be accompanied by a letter from the foreign entity verifying a year of full-time employment outside the United States and, ideally, outlining the nature of the work performed abroad by the petition beneficiary and the salary paid. The foreign company's organization chart showing the beneficiary's role and documentation of the beneficiary's earnings abroad with the foreign employer can also help bolster a petition.

Differences Between L-1 Petitions and EB-1C Petitions

While the L-1 nonimmigrant visa and the EB-1C petitions have a close resemblance and the EB-1C is a common green card strategy for L-1s, there are some important differences which include:

1. The U.S. entity must be doing business for at least a year before the EB-1 petition is filed. L-1s may be filed by new offices. Note that the entity must be "doing business" versus merely existing.[20]

2. The employment abroad for one year out of the prior three need not be continuous for EB-1C. As the AFM notes:

    > Under 8 CFR §204.5(j)(3)(i)(A), the petition must demonstrate that the beneficiary was employed abroad by a qualifying organization for one year out of the previous three years. Note that, unlike the L-1 nonimmigrant classification, the year of qualifying employment does not have to be "continuous." Compare section 101(a)(15)(L) (requiring that the alien have been employed "continuously" abroad for the one-year period) with section 203(b)(1)(C) of the Act (requiring that the alien be employed overseas for "at least one year."

[20] 8 CFR §204.5(j)(3)(i)(D).

3. USCIS's policy is that there are no "successor-in-interest" provisions that allow an EB-1C petition to survive mergers, acquisitions and other major corporate changes. That's contrary to the L-1 category which does allow for this. In a 2009 USCIS memorandum, the agency noted:

   > Successorship-in-interest determinations are principally relevant to the continuing validity of a labor certification. Successor-in-interest petitions are not required to reaffirm the validity of the initial I-140 petition for petitions that are filed requesting visa preference categories that do not require a labor certification, such as the EB-1 Alien of Extraordinary Ability and the EB-2 National Interest Waiver (Non-NIW Physician cases). An employer seeking to classify the alien as an EB-1 Multi-National Executive of Manager or EB-1 Outstanding Professor or Researcher, must file a new I-140 petition and establish the alien's eligibility under the requested category's specific eligibility requirements.[21]

   One exception to this appears to be where the beneficiary's foreign employer is no longer in operation but this occurred after the I-140 immigrant visa application is approved but before the beneficiary's adjustment of status application is adjudicated.[22]

4. In the EB-1C context, the U.S. entity cannot be an unincorporated branch. The AFM explains:

   > Branch Offices: While the L-1 nonimmigrant visa regulations allow for a "branch office" to petition for a manager or executive, the EB-1-3 immigrant visa regulations do not provide for a foreign branch office as a petitioner. The nonimmigrant regulations define the term "branch" as "an operating division or office of the same organization housed in a different location."[23]
   >
   > Neither an unincorporated branch office of a foreign employer nor a nonimmigrant alien is competent to offer permanent employment to a beneficiary for the purpose of obtaining an immigrant visa for the beneficiary under section 203(b)(1)(C) of the Act.[24] The petitioner must be a U.S. citizen, corporation, partnership, or other legal entity to file this immigrant visa petition. Thus, a U.S. corporation with an overseas

---

[21] Memorandum from D. Neufeld, Acting Associate Director, Domestic Operations, USCIS, HQ 70/6.2. AD 09-37, "Successor-in-Interest Determinations in Adjudication of Form I-140 Petitions," AILA Doc. No. 09090362 (*posted* Aug. 6, 2009).

[22] INS Memorandum, Y. LaFleur, "Impact of Overseas Affirmation on I-485", AILA Doc. No. 96061590 (*posted* July 15, 1996).

[23] 8 CFR §214.2(*l*)(1)(ii)(J).

[24] *See Matter of Thornhill*, 18 I&N Dec. 34 (Comm. 1981).

branch may file an EB-1-3 petition, but a foreign corporation with a branch office in the United States may not.[25]

5. One of the major differences between the L-1 and the EB-1C is that the transferred employee cannot be filling a "specialized knowledge" role. In other words, there is no EB-1C counterpart to the L-1B nonimmigrant category. The AFM points this out but notes that not all L-1Bs are barred from seeking an EB-1C:

> Unlike in the case of the L-1B nonimmigrant classification, there is no provision of law that allows an individual who was/is employed in a purely specialized knowledge capacity abroad to be classified as a "specialized knowledge" EB-1-3 immigrant. However, it should be noted that some EB-1-3 beneficiaries who are classified as L-1B nonimmigrants might qualify for the EB-1-3 classification because their specialized knowledge employment abroad also would have qualified as managerial or executive employment and because the petitioners intend to employ them in managerial or executive positions on a permanent basis.[26]
>
> Similarly, an L-1B nonimmigrant may have held both specialized knowledge and managerial positions abroad at different times.

6. USCIS generally applies a tougher standard on EB-1C cases than L-1. While the statute and regulations don't address this, USCIS's Administrative Appeals Office has confirmed this to be a reality in a liaison meeting with the American Immigration Lawyers Association:

> Does the AAO take into consideration prior corresponding nonimmigrant (L-1 or O-1) approvals in reviewing EB-1 appeals?
>
> Please note that each individual adjudication (nonimmigrant and immigrant) has its own record of proceeding. We review the EB-1 case on its own merits, so we don't think it will be particularly helpful to insist on this. I-140 petitions are not based on an earlier nonimmigrant petition. We see INA §204 as a more exacting standard.[27]

Finally, it is worth noting that while most EB-1C applicants are already working in the United States, that is not a requirement. Individuals currently working abroad can be the beneficiaries of a petition and can process an immigrant visa at a U.S. consulate abroad. Because premium processing is not available for EB-1C cases, the wait for consular processing could be some time—likely well over a year. And if

---

[25] AFM 22.2(i)(3)(B)(3).

[26] AFM 22.2(i)(3)(H).

[27] "AAO/AILA Liaison Meeting Minutes" (Mar. 15, 2007), AILA Doc. No. 07051068.

EB-1 visa availability dates retrogress and waits develop (something that is becoming increasingly likely), the wait to enter the United States could grow even longer.

17

EMPLOYMENT-BASED FIRST PREFERENCE CATEGORIES: EB-1B OUTSTANDING PROFESSORS AND RESEARCHERS

The EB-1-2[1] preference category, commonly referred to as EB-1B, for outstanding professors and researchers may not be one that immediately comes to mind for entrepreneurs and startup companies, but it is sometimes worth considering. The category is mainly used by universities, but for-profit employers, particularly in the pharmaceutical and biotech industries, often file using the category. It has a few key advantages over other categories:

- There's no need for a labor certification.
- It is in the EB-1 category so backlogs are generally shorter than the category for national interest waivers and labor certifications.
- When the category is current, which is often the case for non-Indians and non-Chinese, you can file an adjustment application along with the I-140 and get a work authorization document much more quickly than may be the case in other categories.
- It generally has a lower proof standard than the EB-1 category for individuals with extraordinary ability.
- For those with children nearing age 21 who are in danger of "aging out," premium processing of the I-140 petition may allow for a faster way to lock in a priority date and preserve the child's eligibility to immigrate under the Child Status Protection Act.[2]
- If the six-year limit on staying in H-1B status is running out, getting an I-140 approved for an outstanding researcher may be faster than getting an I-140 approved based on a labor certification (potentially allowing for a rush AC21 H-1B extension).

[1] The authors will refer to the EB-1-2 category as EB-1B in this chapter.

[2] Pub. L. No. 107-208 (Aug. 6, 2002).

EB-1B Requirements

So, what is required to be an outstanding researcher or professor? According to U.S. Citizenship and Immigration Services (USCIS):

> The statutory provision for the Outstanding professor or researcher immigrant classification at Immigration and Nationality Act (INA) §203(b)(1)(B) requires that the alien be recognized internationally as outstanding in a specific academic field. Outstanding professors or researchers should stand apart in the academic community through eminence and distinction based on international recognition. The regulation at 8 Code of Federal Regulations (CFR) §204.5(i)(3)(i) requires a petition for an outstanding professor or researcher to be accompanied by evidence that the professor or researcher is recognized internationally as outstanding in the academic field specified in the petition. This evidence must consist of at least two out of the six types of evidence listed in the regulation (*e.g.*, major prizes, membership in associations).[3]

While many think of the category as one for university petitioners, it can be used by private companies as well. The basic requirements for the category are

1. The applicant is internationally recognized as outstanding in his or her area.
2. The applicant has three years' experience teaching or researching in the academic area and the research has been recognized as outstanding in the academic field.
3. The applicant is seeking entry for:
   - a tenure or tenure-track position at a university;
   - comparable position at a university to conduct research; and
   - a comparable position to conduct research with a private employer who employs at least three full-time researchers and has achieved documented accomplishments in the academic field. Note that this research doesn't include engineering or product design.
4. The research position must be for a permanent position (in other words, not for a temporary period).

To demonstrate recognition as being outstanding in one's academic field, an applicant must show at least two of the following:

---

[3] Policy Memo, USCIS, PM-602-0005.1, Evaluation of Evidence Submitted with Certain Form I-140 Petitions, AILA Doc. No. 11020231 (*posted* Dec. 22, 2010) at 2, 56 FR 30703 (July 5, 1991).

Documentation of the alien's receipt of major prizes or awards for outstanding achievement in the academic field;

The USCIS *Adjudicator's Field Manual* (AFM) notes that the emphasis needs to be on prizes or awards won by the beneficiary and not the beneficiary's employer or institution. If the employer or institution was awarded the prize, it may still be possible to claim this category provided the award or prize can be directly attributed to the beneficiary.

Documentation of the alien's membership in associations in the academic field which require outstanding achievements of their members;

The AFM lists factors that demonstrate a membership in an association was NOT based on outstanding achievements in an academic field, including membership being based: a) solely on a level of education or years of experience in a particular field; or b) on the payment of a fee or by subscribing to an association's publications.

Published material in professional publications written by others about the alien's work in the academic field. Such material shall include the title, date, and author of the material, and any necessary translation;

USCIS requires publications submitted in this category to be about the beneficiary's work and not just about the beneficiary's employer or another organization with whom the beneficiary is associated. And a publication that merely cites the beneficiary's work as one of multiple footnotes or endnotes is not considered generally to be "about" the person's work. Evidence in this category must also cite the publication's circulation data (online or in print) and the intended audience of the publication as well as the title, date and author of the article.

Evidence of the alien's participation, either individually or on a panel, as the judge of the work of others in the same or an allied academic field;

While the EB-1A category allows entrepreneurs to use their judging of entrepreneurial competitions (like pitch events), this category is limited to judging the research of others in an academic field. Traditionally, this has included peer review work, serving on a dissertation panel, judging poster competitions at academic conferences, etc.

Evidence of the alien's original scientific or scholarly research contributions to the academic field;

This is a broad category and one often demonstrated through support letters from experts in the academic field.

Evidence of the alien's authorship of scholarly books or articles (in scholarly journals with international circulation) in the academic field; or

AFM first instructs USCIS examiners to look at whether the article "reports on original research, experimentation, or philosophical discourse" and is one "written by a researcher or expert in the field who is often affiliated with a college or university." The publication should have "footnotes, endnotes, or a bibliography" and may include "graphs, charts, videos, or pictures as illustrations of the concepts expressed in the article."

Beyond that, the petitioner should identify the circulation data (online or in print) and the intended audience of the publication. USCIS examiners are reminded that scholarly articles use technical jargon and normally include an abstract, a description of methodology, footnotes, endnotes and a bibliography.

Comparable evidence when the other evidence categories do not readily apply.

A petitioner showing an applicant meets two of these criteria has only partly met the test; however, like the EB-1A Extraordinary Ability category, a secondary test must also be met. Called the *Kazarian*[4] standard based on a 2009 case of that name applying to EB-1A petitions, the U.S. Ninth Circuit Court of Appeals held that USCIS is entitled to conduct a "final merits determination" and essentially decline to approve a case even when they rule that the required evidence categories have been met.

So in the EB-1B context, USCIS could decide that even though a petitioner has shown a beneficiary has satisfactorily documented two of the six evidence categories to show outstanding ability, it could nonetheless deny the case saying that it ultimately does not believe outstanding ability has been demonstrated. Critics of the decision say USCIS has broad authority to apply a vague standard that essentially permits them to ignore the evidence scheme Congress set up in the category.

---

[4] *Kazarian v. USCIS*, 596 F.3d 1115 (9th Cir. 2010).

Startup Companies and the EB-1B Outstanding Researcher/Professor Category

While an employer is required for an outstanding researcher/professor petition, a labor certification is not required. But like a labor certification-based case, the employer must show an ability to pay the offered salary.[5]

Another subject that must be considered is whether the person has outstanding ability in an "academic field." USCIS rules define "academic field" as a "body of specialized knowledge offered for study at an accredited U.S. university or institution of higher education."[6] AFM also notes that the field must be larger than a very small area of specialization where only a single course is taught or which is the subject of a very specialized dissertation.[7]

There are a couple of major caveats to using the outstanding researcher and professor category. For one—and it seems obvious—the applicant must be a researcher or professor, something that will be a challenge for many, if not most, startup founders. USCIS also notes that the beneficiary must "stand apart" in their "academic community"[8] which is not defined. Perhaps it's possible to meet the category without any reputation within the world of higher education, but an applicant who can show a prior background serving as a researcher in a university setting may find better footing.

Nevertheless, founders who are scientists and engineers, as well as individuals engaged in research in other fields, may be able to consider the category. For example, many technology-focused employees of companies in the United States and abroad are interested in starting companies that apply their skill set. It's not unusual for a founder to have a background that includes patent filings and publications of research findings; and some university professors start companies while they're teaching, sometimes in cooperation with their institutions, and might be able to pursue a green card under this category.

The outstanding researcher and professor category also requires an employer to serve as a petitioner. Because no labor certification or demonstration of prior recruiting is required, an applicant can own an equity stake in the business. The bene-

---

[5] 8 Code of Federal Regulations (CFR) §204.5(g)(2).

[6] 8 CFR §204.5(i)(2).

[7] AFM 22.2(i)(2)(A).

[8] Policy Memo, USCIS, PM-602-0005.1, Evaluation of Evidence Submitted with Certain Form I-140 Petitions, AILA Doc. No. 11020231 (*posted* Dec. 22, 2010) at 2, 56 FR 30703 (July 5, 1991)..

ficiary may even be able to own all of the business as long as he or she is an employee of the company and another person can sign an I-140 on behalf of the company.

Petitioning employers in employment-based green card petitions, including the EB-1B outstanding researcher category, are required to demonstrate ability to pay the offered salary. The regulation states:

> Any petition filed by or for an employment-based immigrant which requires an offer of employment must be accompanied by evidence that the prospective U.S. employer has the ability to pay the proffered wage. The petitioner must demonstrate this ability at the time the priority date is established and continuing until the beneficiary obtains lawful permanent residence. Evidence of this ability shall be either in the form of copies of annual reports, federal tax returns, or audited financial statements. In a case where the prospective United States employer employs 100 or more workers, the director may accept a statement from a financial officer of the organization which establishes the prospective employer's ability to pay the proffered wage. In appropriate cases, additional evidence, such as profit/loss statements, bank account records, or personnel records, may be submitted by the petitioner or requested by the Service.[9]

For startups, this can be challenging. Founders are often paid little in the early stages of a new company because investors tend to look negatively upon early stage employees who take too much money home in salary. Yet an outstanding researcher being paid a low salary could indicate to a USCIS examiner that the employee is not really all that outstanding.

The rules also require a private employer to employ at least three full-time researchers, and the employer must have documented accomplishments in the academic field. This could be a difficult test for a new company that has few employees and hasn't had a chance to develop its own reputation. Nevertheless, if a founder has been able to spend time on a nonimmigrant visa building the company and has started building out a research and development team, this could be possible. Also, if there are individuals who have joined a new company and these individuals already have documented accomplishments, one could argue that the company, by extension, has accomplishments. But expect USCIS to argue that the company itself must have accomplishments.

So why would an entrepreneur use the outstanding researcher category? For one, the standard for qualifying is easier than a category like EB-1 extraordinary ability.

---

[9] 8 CFR §204.5(g)(2).

Only two categories need be shown, and those categories are reviewed under an easier standard than EB-1A. For example, EB-1A applicants who argue membership in an association requiring outstanding achievements of their members must demonstrate that eligibility for such membership has been determined by national or international experts. And while the EB-1B category requires a demonstration that research is of "major significance," the outstanding researcher category only says that the beneficiary has made "contributions" to the field.

This category has fewer criteria to claim than EB-1 extraordinary ability. But the "other comparable evidence" standard may be a way to present evidence that could have been presented in the EB-1 extraordinary ability category.

Here are some notes of caution for an employer looking at this category—

1. The employer must be employing at least three people engaged in full-time research in an area other than product design or engineering. Ideally, the company has a research and development department.

2. The company can't be a brand-new startup because the employer must have already achieved documented accomplishments in the field. An exception might apply in the case of a joint venture with an academic institution or another employer that has a longer track record. Also, if the founder is a high-profile individual in the field and the company is closely associated with that person, a case might be made that the startup can show documented achievements because the company is essentially synonymous with the founder.

3. The applicant must be internationally recognized as outstanding and have at least three years' experience teaching or researching in the field, and the research must have been recognized as outstanding.

4. The category can be used by both a founder as well as a key employee engaged in research. Note that the application must be filed by an employer, which means that a founder must also be an employee of the company and have some control exercised over him or her (such as from an outside board).

5. A university spinning off a company or participating in a venture with a privately held company might be able to pursue an EB-1B for a faculty member if the category's conditions are otherwise met.

The use of the EB-1B category by a startup is pretty unusual, but if a company is in a field that is by nature heavily focused on research and has employees with solid academic credentials, the category may be worth exploring.

18

'SCHEDULE A' EXCEPTIONAL ABILITY FOR STARTUPS

In 2005, the U.S. Congress created an additional 50,000 green cards per year in the EB-2 category for those who fall under "Schedule A." Schedule A includes two categories or groups. Group I is reserved for occupations that U.S. Congress has acknowledged a shortage of in the United States, specifically nurses and physical therapists. Group II is for aliens of exceptional ability in the sciences or arts, including university teachers who can demonstrate "widespread acclaim and international recognition."[1]

The exceptional ability green card category under Schedule A Group II shares some similarities with the EB-1A extraordinary ability category and the Program Electronic Review Management System (PERM)–based green card process. In terms of using it for company founders, the EB-2 exceptional ability category poses many of the same problems as labor certification. The most notable similarity to labor certification is that the Schedule A process does not allow for self-sponsorship or for the foreign national to own equity in the petitioning company.[2] The process requires U.S. employment, which according to the regulations means: "Permanent, full time work by an employee for an employer other than oneself."[3] So this category will really only benefit founders previously petitioned by another company, prospectively petitioned by a company that they will eventually join, or it may just come up for a founder in the context of another key employee.

Unlike the EB-1A extraordinary ability category, the Schedule A Group II notably leaves out 'business' as one of the fields in which a foreign national can demonstrate his or her abilities. This means the category is better reserved for those with science backgrounds (again, helpful for startups in the pharmaceutical and biotech

[1] 20 Code of Federal Regulations (CFR) §656.15(d)(1).

[2] 20 CFR §§656.10(a)(3) and 656.3.

[3] 20 CFR §656.3.

industries) or at least for members of the team working on the technical side of the business.

All Schedule A I-140s are filed entirely with USCIS, and an application for exceptional ability must include the following[4]:

1. USCIS Form I-140.
2. An uncertified Form ETA-9089, in duplicate, signed in the original by an authorized official of the petitioning organization, the alien, and the representative, if any.
3. A wage determination issued by the State Workforce Agency (SWA) having jurisdiction over the proposed area where the job opportunity exists or by the SWA having jurisdiction over the petitioner's headquarters if the prevailing wage will be derived from the area of the employer's headquarters in the situation of roving employees.
4. A copy of the notice sent to an applicable collective bargaining unit, or a copy of the notice posted with attestation of posting for at least ten consecutive business days within the period between 30 and 180 days preceding the petition filing.
5. Copies of any and all in-house media, whether electronic or printed, in accordance with the normal procedures used in the employer's organization for the recruitment of similar positions to the position specified in the Form 9089.
6. Evidence of widespread acclaim and international recognition accorded the alien by recognized experts in the alien's field and evidence that alien's prior and intended work requires exceptional ability.

The main challenge lies in the last requirement, showing that the person has achieved exceptional ability. In order to establish exceptional ability in one's field, a foreign national must submit evidence that he or she meets two of seven possible criteria.[5]

(i) Documentation of the alien's receipt of internationally recognized prizes or awards for excellence in the field for which certification is sought;

---

[4] *Adjudicator's Field Manual* (AFM) Chapter 22.2.

[5] 20 CFR §656.15(d)(1).

(ii) Documentation of the alien's membership in international associations, in the field for which certification is sought, which require outstanding achievement of their members, as judged by recognized international experts in their disciplines or fields;

(iii) Published material in professional publications about the alien, about the alien's work in the field for which certification is sought, which shall include the title, date, and author of such published material;

(iv) Evidence of the alien's participation on a panel, or individually, as a judge of the work of others in the same or in an allied field of specialization to that for which certification is sought;

(v) Evidence of the alien's original scientific or scholarly research contributions of major significance in the field for which certification is sought;

(vi) Evidence of the alien's authorship of published scientific or scholarly articles in the field for which certification is sought, in international professional journals or professional journals with an international circulation;

(vii) Evidence of the display of the alien's work, in the field for which certification is sought, at artistic exhibitions in more than one country.

These seven criteria are similar to the ten possible criteria to establish extraordinary ability under EB-1A, but under exceptional ability only two (not three) of the criteria must be met. Unlike EB-1A, exceptional ability places a much greater emphasis on the international nature of the person's accomplishments. International awards, international memberships, and journals of international circulation are distinctly different, because under EB-1A an applicant can produce evidence of national significance in the United States or any other country in the world. Another glaring difference between the two categories is that Schedule A Exceptional Ability requires that the foreign national demonstrate that his or her work over the last year has required a person of exceptional ability and that the proposed work in the offered position requires exceptional ability.

Despite this difference, establishing the criteria is very similar. Examples of how to establish similar criteria are detailed in Chapters 7 and 15, but some suggestions are included below. As with those categories, letters of support from other experts in the field will serve as persuasive evidence that the foreign national has received "widespread acclaim and international recognition."[6]

---

[6] *Id.*

Documentation of the Alien's Receipt of Internationally Recognized Prizes or Awards for Excellence in the Field for which Certification Is Sought.[7]

Chapter 7, "Foreign Nationals with Extraordinary Ability: The O-1 Visa," goes into detail on the types of awards that a foreign national may present to establish this criteria. The main difference, again, is that in the Schedule A context, the award must be international in scope. When presenting evidence of an international award, it is key to explain how the award is related to the person's field and provide any discernible criteria that is used in order to decide winners of the award. The best source of criteria is often from the organization granting the award, either through a letter of support or published material on the award if the criteria are publicly discussed. Documenting the distinguished judges that choose winners is helpful, as is listing previous award winners who are also at the top of their field and if they are spread across multiple countries. Also useful are statistics on the acceptance rate or number of winners to show how hard it is to win such an award.

Documentation of the Alien's Membership in International Associations, in the Field for Which Certification Is Sought, Which Require Outstanding Achievement of Their Members, as Judged by Recognized International Experts in Their Disciplines or Fields[8];

As the O-1 chapter discusses, whether the organization is distinguished can be established by media coverage on the organization or by showing the elite membership that comprises the organization. This is often accomplished by including a strong letter of support from the organization. It is advisable to include the criteria required for membership either in the letter of support or in the organization's constitution or bylaws, if available. Again, include information on the judges deciding on membership and what that process entails. Is the membership by invitation only? Do current members vote new members in? Is there an interview process? Lastly, include any available information or statistics on acceptance rate to show its distinguished nature.

---

[7] 20 CFR §656.15(d)(1)(i).

[8] 20 CFR §656.15(d)(1)(ii).

Published Material in Professional Publications About the Alien, About the Alien's Work in the Field for Which Certification Is Sought, Which Shall Include the Title, Date, and Author of Such Published Material.[9]

This criterion interestingly does not suggest the evidence must be international in nature, as with other exceptional ability criteria. Similar to the O-1 criteria, the exceptional ability criterion does allow for media coverage "about the alien" and "about the alien's work in the field." This means that entrepreneurs and other key employees can submit evidence of the coverage of their businesses or products and connect the dots that those are the "work" of the beneficiary. Media coverage will always be stronger if it lists the person by name (and even better by title), but this coverage of the individual's work should still be included. Aside from listing the "title, date, and author of such published material" an applicant should also explain the significance of the media source. This is best handled by presenting evidence of circulation numbers or traffic data. This information is often available from the media sources themselves but then can be supported by additional evidence from third party sources such as website traffic analytics companies.

Evidence of the Alien's Participation on a Panel, or Individually, as a Judge of the Work of Others in the Same or in an Allied Field of Specialization to that for Which Certification Is Sought.[10]

Since many of the people at startups using Schedule A will be in the sciences, this is a good opportunity to rely on those with similar academic backgrounds. Evidence of peer review or serving on dissertation committees is great evidence of judging the work of others in a field. With peer review, it is wise to include evidence of the significance of the journal that has invited the foreign national to serve as a reviewer, which can be done by documenting the journal's impact factor or its rankings in a given field. Impact factor is a measure of the average number of citations that articles in a journal have received in a given year. Those without academic backgrounds can include evidence of judging competitions or peers in other capacities such as within a previous organization. In these cases, a letter of support from the organization or competition is generally the most thorough way to document why the foreign national was asked to be a judge, who he or she was judging, what criteria were used to judge, how many people were judged, and what was the result of the judging (*i.e.*, awards). As with most categories, purely student related ven-

---

[9] 20 CFR §656.15(d)(1)(iii).

[10] 20 CFR §656.15(d)(1)(iv).

tures will receive less weight unless students were competing nationally or internationally.

Evidence of the Alien's Original Scientific or Scholarly Research Contributions of Major Significance in the Field for Which Certification Is Sought.[11]

As previously discussed, some forms of evidence clearly establish an original contribution, such as patents. Those without protected intellectual property will generally need to rely on letters of support from other people in the field who can explain the foreign national's contributions and their significance. These letters should explain how people in the industry perceived the contribution and how it differed from or affected the way the work was previously performed. Explain if the work has been heavily cited or copied. If customers or competitors now purchase or rely on the work then that is also great evidence, and a letter of support from a distinguished competitor or customer explaining the significance of the contribution to their company can go a long as way as well.

Evidence of the Alien's Authorship of Published Scientific or Scholarly Articles in the Field for Which Certification Is Sought, in International Professional Journals or Professional Journals with an International Circulation.[12]

This criterion is notably different from the O-1 and EB-1, as it leaves out those who have published articles in major media sources and only allows for those who have authored work in scholarly and professional journals. This is another example of exceptional ability being less business-friendly and more science-focused than O-1A and EB-1A. Again, those with backgrounds in the hard sciences will probably benefit most from this possible criterion. For those with academic backgrounds, it is suggested they submit evidence of the publications and an explanation of how it relates to the person's field. The applicant should also include evidence about the international circulation or scope of the journal. Using materials from the journal itself and again presenting evidence of the journal's impact factor and international ranking can most likely accomplish this, but letters of support from other experts in the field may help corroborate the evidence.

---

[11] 20 CFR §656.15(d)(1)(v).

[12] 20 CFR §656.15(d)(1)(vi).

Evidence of the Display of the Alien's Work, in the Field for which Certification Is Sought, at Artistic Exhibitions in More Than One Country.[13]

This criterion is used for people trying to qualify for Schedule A exceptional ability in the arts and does not normally help startup founders or key employees, with a few exceptions for those working in fields such as graphic design who have had some of their work on public display. A person who falls under a category like that, needs to submit evidence of the artistic exhibitions that have featured his or her work and evidence that it has been exhibited in multiple countries. This can be done with photographs, press releases, media coverage, and detailed letters of support.

Similar to the labor certification process, the company must detail the job description for the offered position. The job description should include the title of the position, the duties and responsibilities, and the education and experience requirements for hire. In this context, it often includes details on how exceptional or ability is required to fill the position. The company then submits the job description to the State Workforce Agency (SWA) with jurisdiction over the area where the person will work.[14] The SWA then returns a dated Prevailing Wage Determination (PWD) that sets the minimum wage the company may pay the beneficiary. This differs from the labor certification where the company is obtaining the prevailing wage from a National Processing Center of the Department of Labor. The State agencies tend to receive far fewer requests for prevailing wage determinations and therefore, process them much quicker.

Once the PWD has been obtained, the company must either give notice to a collective bargaining representative or, more commonly, post a Notice of Filing at the worksite for ten days which documents the details of the offered position, including the salary. The Schedule A petition may not actually be filed until 30 days after the Notice of Filing and any other recruitment postings come down.

The company must also collect and submit any recruitment materials normally used in recruiting employees for similar positions. These materials can include electronic or prints ads the company usually relies on.

To prepare the filing, the company must actually complete an ETA 9089 as in the labor certification process. However, under Schedule A, the ETA 9089 is not filed with or certified by the Department of Labor. In this case, the ETA 9089 is simply

[13] 20 CFR §656.15(d)(1)(vii).

[14] 20 CFR §656.15.

completed with all the details of the company, position, and beneficiary. Then two copies of the uncertified Forms ETA 9089 are signed by an authorized official of the petitioning organization, the alien, and the representative and then submitted to USCIS with the rest of the required evidence.

An applicant under Schedule A exceptional ability must have a bona fide job offer from a U.S. employer. The details of the job offer must be documented on USCIS Form I-140 filed in the Schedule A application.

All of the supporting documents are submitted to USCIS (not the Department of Labor) along with a signed Form I-140 detailing the bona fide job being offered to the foreign national. The date the I-140 is filed with USCIS becomes the foreign national's priority date on the *Visa Bulletin*. Once the Schedule A I-140 is approved, the priority date is locked in under the EB-2 category.

If visas are currently available for the birth country of the foreign national, or once visas become available for that priority date, the foreign national may file the last step and complete the green card process by filing for Adjustment of Status in the United States or consular processing at a U.S. consulate or embassy abroad. It is at this final step that the beneficiary's spouse and children under 21 may also benefit by applying for their own green cards based on the primary family member's approved Schedule A I-140.

19

EMPLOYMENT-BASED FIFTH PREFERENCE IMMIGRANT VISA CATEGORY: THE IMMIGRANT INVESTOR PROGRAM

History of the Program, Broad Requirements, Recent Changes, Political Issues

In 1990, the U.S. Congress created the Immigrant Investor Program and it is classified as the employment-based fifth preference immigrant visa category (EB-5). The program is aimed at benefiting the U.S. economy by providing an incentive for foreign investment that creates or preserves jobs for U.S. citizens and lawful permanent residents.

Since the program was created, it has had the same limit of 10,000 visas per fiscal year. That includes spouses and children under the age of 21. In 1993, the program was modified so that 3,000 of the visas would be reserved for investors in U.S. Citizenship and Immigration Services (USCIS)-designated regional centers as opposed to direct investments in a business. Regional centers are organizations set up to pool investor funds and invest in in projects designed to promote economic growth. While regional center investing is an option for startup founders, this chapter will primarily focus on direct investing, particularly as it relates to investing in the founder's startup.

Applicants must have invested or be actively in the process of investing funds directly in a new commercial enterprise or indirectly through a regional center. The required investment is $1,800,000 or $900,000 (for investments in certain rural or high unemployment areas)[1]. The petitioner must document the invested funds are

[1] The investment amounts were adjusted by U.S. Citizenship and Immigration Services (USCIS) in November 2019 after being at the same $500,000/$1,000,000 threshold for nearly three decades. Un-

Continued

from a lawful source and the investment must be at risk versus having a guaranteed return.

The EB-5 enterprise must create "full-time employment for not fewer than ten U.S. citizens or aliens lawfully admitted for permanent residence or other immigrants lawfully authorized to be employed in the United States (other than the immigrant and the immigrant's spouse, sons, or daughters)."[2] In the case of certain troubled businesses, an applicant can show that the investment will lead to the number of existing employees being maintained at no less than the pre-investment level for a period of at least two years.[3]

Investors initially file a Form I-526, Immigrant Petition by Alien Investor. If the I-526 is approved, the investor receives a conditional green card valid for a two-year period. After the two-year period, if the investment has been sustained and the required number of jobs have been created, the immigrant will apply for the conditions to be removed using a Form I-829, Petition by Investor to Remove Conditions on Permanent Resident Status. If approved, a ten-year unconditional green card will be granted, which is renewable indefinitely as long as the permanent resident continues residing in the United States and does not commit any acts that would lead to removal (such as committing certain crimes).

The EB-5 category may be a workable green card strategy for some startup founders. The investment can be either in the startup itself or in another business. Unlike PERM cases, the applicant need not be an employee of the business and can have an equity stake. And unlike the EB-1 extraordinary ability, EB-2 outstanding researcher and EB-2 national interest waiver categories, the applicant need not document subjective criteria like showing one is at the top of their field or the work they are doing is providing a significant national benefit.

But the category does have drawbacks. It is slow. The initial petition could take as long as four years to approve.[4] That means investors must hold their investments in much longer, thus raising the risks if the business fails or the investor is forced to withdraw the investment. Required investment amounts have risen significantly and new rules mean that the amounts will continue to rise regularly. The required em-

---

der the new rule that raised the required investment in 2019, every five years the required investment amount will adjust based on a methodology to be determined by USCIS.

[2] Immigration and Nationality Act (INA) §203(b)(5)(A)(ii).

[3] 8 Code of Federal Regulations (CFR) §204.6(j)(4)(ii).

[4] On December 1, 2019, USCIS was reporting that the average processing time for an I-526 Immigrant Petition by Alien Entrepreneur, the initial form filed in an EB-5 petition, was 31.5 to 52 months, the longest wait time ever seen in the nearly three decades this program has existed.

ployment requirement could be a problem for startups that don't grow rapidly. And documenting the legal source of funds can be a challenge.

Eligibility Requirements

Investment of "Capital"

Immigrant investors must invest "capital." The term is defined broadly to mean not just cash, but also equipment, inventory, other intangible property, cash equivalents and indebtedness secured by assets owned by the immigrant investor, provided the immigrant investor is personally and primarily liable and that the assets of the new commercial enterprise are not used to secure the debt. The invested capital must be valued at fair market value in U.S. dollars.[5]

The investor must also demonstrate that he or she is the legal owner of the invested capital and the funds were obtained lawfully.[6] To demonstrate capital was obtained lawfully, the *USCIS Policy Manual* lists the following types of documents that can be provided:

- Foreign business registration records;
- Business and personal tax returns, including income, franchise, property, or any other tax returns of any kind filed within five years in or outside the United States by or on behalf of the immigrant investor;
- Evidence identifying any other source(s) of capital; or
- Certified copies of any judgments or evidence of all pending governmental civil or criminal actions, governmental administrative proceedings, any private civil actions involving judgments against the immigrant investor from any court within the past 15 years.[7]

An immigrant investor will not get credit for funds that are loaned to the business. But that's not to say that debt can't be the source of capital in other respects. For example, an immigrant investor's promissory note is a permissible form of investment capital as long as the immigrant investor is personally and primarily liable for the debt and his or her assets secure the note. Other characteristics of the promissory note, according to the *USCIS Policy Manual*, include the following:

- The security interest must be perfected to the extent provided for by the jurisdiction where the asset is located;

---

[5] 8 CFR §204.6(e).

[6] *Id.*

[7] *USCIS Policy Manual*, Volume 6, Part G, Chapter 2.

- The assets securing the debt cannot include the assets of the company in which the immigrant is investing;
- The assets securing the debt must be specifically identified as securing the promissory note;
- The assets must be amenable to seizure by a U.S. noteholder.[8]

Similarly, proceeds from a loan may be used as the capital invested in the EB-5 business. USCIS' Policy Manual notes the following requirements to use loan proceeds as capital:

- The immigrant investor is personally and primarily liable for the debt;
- The indebtedness is secured by assets the immigrant investor owns; and
- The assets of the new commercial enterprise are not used to secure any of the debt.[9]

As far as the collateral securing the debt is concerned, the immigrant investor must show that the collateral's value is enough to meet the minimum investment amount.

Investors may not be guaranteed a return on any of the invested capital since the investment must be at risk. To the extent a person is guaranteed the right to eventual ownership or use of an asset in exchange for the capital invested, the expected present value of that ownership or asset will be deducted from the amount invested. The *USCIS Policy Manual* provides the example of an investor being given a right to own real estate and having the value of that real estate counted against the investment amount.[10]

The payment of distributions to an investor is not necessarily a problem as long as such distributions happen during the two-year conditional residency period. But the distribution cannot count toward the minimum investment amount not can the distribution be guaranteed.[11]

An investor may not be provided with a right to be repaid their investment since that would mean the investment was not at risk and is to be treated the same as a loan. So mandatory redemptions and options exercised by the investor are impermissible. But an option by the enterprise to buy back the shares of the investor *is*

[8] *Id.* Referencing *Matter of Hsiung*, 22 I&N Dec. 201, 202–203 (Assoc. comm. 1998).

[9] *USCIS Policy Manual*, Volume 6, Part G, Chapter 2.

[10] *Id.*

[11] *Id.*

permissible if the investor has no control over whether the option is exercised or not.[12]

The Investment Must Be in a New Commercial Enterprise

The rules governing EB-5s require an investment to be in a commercial enterprise which is defined to be:

> ... [A]ny for-profit activity formed for the ongoing conduct of lawful business including, but not limited to, a sole proprietorship, partnership (whether limited or general), holding company, joint venture, corporation, business trust, or other entity which may be publicly or privately owned. This definition includes a commercial enterprise consisting of a holding company and its wholly-owned subsidiaries, provided that each such subsidiary is engaged in a for-profit activity formed for the ongoing conduct of a lawful business. This definition shall not include a noncommercial activity such as owning and operating a personal residence.[13]

The definition is broad and should include most startups. As for what is a "new" commercial enterprise, it's not all that new. It applies to any business created after November 29, 1990, and even businesses created before that date qualify as new if the business is being restructured or expanded through the investment of the EB-5 applicant's capital.

Sole Proprietorships

Startup founders operating sole proprietorships can face challenges. The founder can get credit for the amount invested in their business, but they cannot get credit for funds held in their personal bank accounts.

Also, merely investing capital in the business is not enough if the business is not yet active. In a case called *Matter of Ho*, the Administrative Appeals Office noted:

> Even though the petitioner owns only half of the authorized shares in King's Wheel, he is the sole shareholder thus far. He is also the only officer of the corporation. As such, the petitioner exercises sole control over the corporation's activities; whether the business proceeds according to plan or whether, for example, the business returns the petitioner's money is the petitioner's de-

---

[12] *Id.*

[13] 8 CFR §204.6(e).

> cision alone. Therefore, the petitioner cannot meet his at-risk requirement by merely depositing funds into a corporate account.[14]

> *Matter of Ho* goes on to state that:

> Simply formulating an idea for future business activity, without taking meaningful concrete action, is similarly insufficient for a petitioner to meet the at-risk requirement. Before it can be said that capital made available to a commercial enterprise has been placed at risk, a petitioner must present some evidence of the actual undertaking of business activity; otherwise, no assurance exists that the funds will in fact be used to carry out the business of the commercial enterprise.[15]

Escrow Funds

An investor's funds may be temporarily held in an escrow account as long as the investor can document that the funds must be released upon the approval of the I-526 Immigrant Petition by Alien Investor and issuance of the immigrant visa and admission to the United States as a conditional permanent residence or approval of the investor's adjustment of status petition. Documentation must be included in the I-829 petition that the escrow funds were released and the investment was sustained for the period of the immigrant investor's residence in the United States.[16]

Escrow funds can be held in either a U.S. or foreign account, but they are typically held in the United States because of currency fluctuation risks. The *USCIS Policy Manual* states that USCIS will look at the currency rate at the time of the I-526 adjudication.[17]

Keeping funds in escrow will likely only be an issue for startup founders seeking an EB-5 through an investment in another enterprise than the startup.

Documenting the Investment

To show the EB-5 investor has committed the required amount, evidence submitted with the I-526 may include (but isn't limited to) the following:

- Bank statements showing amounts deposited in U.S. business accounts for the enterprise;

[14] *Matter of Ho*, 22 I&N Dec. 206, 209 (1998).

[15] *Id.* at 210.

[16] *USCIS Policy Manual*, Volume 6, Part G, Chapter 2.

[17] *Id.*

- Evidence of assets which have been purchased for use in the U.S. enterprise, including invoices, sales receipts, and purchase contracts containing sufficient information to identify such assets, their purchase costs, date of purchase, and purchasing entity;
- Evidence of property transferred from abroad for use in the U.S. enterprise, including U.S. Customs and Border Protection commercial entry documents, bills of lading, and transit insurance policies containing ownership information and sufficient information to identify the property and to indicate the fair market value of such property;
- Evidence of monies transferred or committed to be transferred to the new commercial enterprise in exchange for shares of stock (voting or nonvoting, common or preferred). Such stock may not include terms requiring the new commercial enterprise to redeem it at the holder's request; or
- Evidence of any loan or mortgage agreement, promissory note, security agreement, or other evidence of borrowing secured by the immigrant investor's assets, other than those of the new commercial enterprise, and for which the immigrant investor is personally and primarily liable.

Use of the Invested Funds

100 percent of the invested capital must be used to support business activities (*e.g.*, activities that result in the creation of jobs). That means that fees associated with EB-5 processing do not count toward meeting the required investment amount. In the regional center context, it is common for investors to be paying costs like administrative fees, finders' fees, syndication fees and attorney fees. Those expenses must be paid by the investor on top of the minimum investment amount.

For funds to be considered properly invested and at-risk, USCIS notes that the following requirements apply:

- The investor must have placed the required amount of capital at risk for the purpose of generating a return on the capital placed at risk;
- There must be a risk of loss and a chance for gain;
- Business activity must actually be undertaken; and
- The full amount of the investment must be made available to the business(es) most closely responsible for creating the employment upon which the petition is based.[18]

[18] *Id.*

The Role of the Investor

An immigrant investor must be engaged in the management of the new business either through day-to-day management activities or by playing a policy-making role. To demonstrate this, an EB-5 application must be accompanied by

- A statement of the position title that the petitioner has or will have in the new enterprise and a complete description of the position's duties;
- Evidence that the petitioner is a corporate officer or a member of the corporate board of directors; or
- Evidence that the petitioner is engaged in policy making activities. For purposes of this section, a petitioner will be considered sufficiently engaged in policy making activities if the petitioner is an equity holder in the new commercial enterprise and the organizational documents of the new commercial enterprise provide the petitioner with certain rights, powers, and duties normally granted to equity holders of the new commercial enterprise's type of entity in the jurisdiction in which the new commercial enterprise is organized.[19]

Under the prior rules, mention was made of an investor qualifying if he or she was a limited partner with the rights, powers and duties granted under the Uniform Limited Partnership Act (ULPA). The 2019 rule broadened this to include anyone granted an equity stake in the business and not just individuals covered by ULPA guidelines.

The Investment Amount

The standard amount required to be invested to qualify for EB-5 is $1,800,000. However, investors in businesses located in "targeted employment areas" or "TEAs" can invest $900,000.[20] USCIS regulations define TEAs:

> **Targeted employment area** means an area that, at the time of investment, is a rural area or is designated as an area that has experienced unemployment of at least 150 percent of the national average rate.[21]
>
> A "rural area," under the rules, is:
>
> Any area other than an area within a standard metropolitan statistical area (as designated by the Office of Management and Budget) or within the outer

[19] 8 CFR §204.6(j)(5).

[20] Under the new USCIS rules relating to EB-5, both the $1,800,000 and the TEA rate are subject to rise every five years. The next increase is scheduled to take effect Oct. 1, 2024.

[21] 8 CFR §204.6(e).

> boundary of any city or town having a population of 20,000 or more based on the most recent decennial census of the United States.[22]

In other words, the population of the town where the business is located must be under 20,000 and the town cannot be adjacent to a metro area.

The business cannot just be located in the TEA. It must also principally be doing business in the location including providing goods or services that support job creation. If the business is operating in more than one location, the location most significantly related to the job creation will be the location which determines if the TEA investment amount is available.[23] According to USCIS, the following factors are used in considering where the business is "principally doing business":

- Any jobs directly created by the new commercial enterprise;
- Any expenditure of capital related to the creation of jobs;
- The new commercial enterprise's day-to-day operation; and
- The new commercial enterprise's assets used in the creation of jobs.[24]

With respect to showing the TEA has an unemployment rate of 150 percent of the U.S. national unemployment rate, the local unemployment rate can be used or USCIS can make a case-specific designation. The new EB-5 rule states:

> USCIS may designate as an area of high unemployment (at least 150 percent of the national average rate) a census tract or contiguous census tracts in which the new commercial enterprise is principally doing business, and may also include any or all census tracts directly adjacent to such census tract(s). The weighted average of the unemployment rate for the subdivision, based on the labor force employment measure for each census tract, must be at least 150 percent of the national average unemployment rate.[25]

This modifies the longstanding prior rule which allowed state governments to designate TEAs in census tract locations. USCIS now has that authority.

The TEA determination is made at the time of the investment or at the time of the filing of the I-526. The fact that an area was previously designated a TEA is not relevant. However, loss of TEA designation after the I-526 is filed will not cause the later filed I-829 to be denied.

---

22 *Id.*

23 *USCIS Policy Manual*, Volume 6, Part G, Chapter 2.

24 *Id.*

25 8 CFR §204.6(i).

Lawful Source of Funds

EB-5 investors must demonstrate that their invested funds were obtained through lawful means. Any funds that cannot be shown to be obtained lawfully cannot be counted toward the minimum investment amount. To document the lawful source of funding, an EB-5 petition must be accompanied by:

- Foreign business registration records;
- Corporate, partnership (or any other entity in any form which has filed in any country or subdivision thereof any return described in this subpart), and personal tax returns including income, franchise, property (whether real, personal, or intangible), or any other tax returns of any kind filed within five years, with any taxing jurisdiction in or outside the United States by or on behalf of the petitioner;
- Evidence identifying any other source(s) of capital; or
- Certified copies of any judgments or evidence of all pending governmental civil or criminal actions, governmental administrative proceedings, and any private civil actions (pending or otherwise) involving monetary judgments against the petitioner from any court in or outside the United States within the past 15 years.[26]

Furthermore, the *USCIS Policy Manual* states that an investor is required to submit evidence identifying any other source of capital including the following:

- Corporate, partnership, or other business entity annual reports;
- Audited financial statements;
- Evidence of any loan or mortgage agreement, promissory note, security agreement, or other evidence of borrowing which is secured by the immigrant investor's own assets, other than those of the new commercial enterprise, and for which the immigrant investor is personally and primarily liable;
- Evidence of income such as earnings statements or official correspondence from current or prior employers stating when the immigrant investor worked for the company and how much income the immigrant investor received during employment;
- Gift instrument(s) documenting gifts to the immigrant investor;
- Evidence, other than tax returns, [45] of payment of individual income tax, such as an individual income tax report or payment certificate, on the following:
    - Wages and salaries;
    - Income from labor and service or business activities;

---

[26] 8 CFR §204.6(j)(3).

- Income or royalties from published books, articles, photographs, or other sources;
- Royalties or income from patents or special rights;
- Interest, dividends, and bonuses;
- Rental income;
- Income from property transfers;
- Any incidental income or other taxable income determined by the relevant financial department;

– Evidence of property ownership, including property purchase or sale documentation; or
– Evidence identifying any other source of capital.[27]

Job Creation

Enterprises receiving EB-5 funds must demonstrate that the enterprise will directly create at least 10 full-time jobs for U.S. worker. Full-time employment means employment in a job requiring a minimum of 35 working hours per week.[28] A variation on this rule applies to Regional Center EB-5 petitions, which can qualify by showing jobs requiring 35 working hours being created indirectly through revenues generated from the Regional Center Program. Job sharing arrangements where the workers hours add up to more than full-time work qualify, but part-time positions do not (even when combined).[29] To demonstrate that a job-sharing arrangement qualifies, the following evidence are examples of what may be presented:

– A written job-sharing agreement;
– A weekly schedule that identifies the positions subject to a job-sharing arrangement and the hours to be worked by each employee under the job-sharing arrangement; and
– Evidence of the sharing of the responsibilities or benefits of a permanent, full-time position between the employees subject to the job sharing arrangement.[30]

Jobs that are intermittent, temporary, seasonal, or transient in nature do not count.[31]

---

[27] *USCIS Policy Manual*, Volume 6, Part G, Chapter 2.

[28] 8 CFR §204.6(e).

[29] *Id.*

[30] *USCIS Policy Manual*, Volume 6, Part G, Chapter 2.

[31] *Id.*

USCIS considers jobs expected to last at least two years to be sufficient.[32] When there are multiple investors in a business, the job creation credit will be split only among those seeking an EB-5.[33] So, for example, if 40 jobs are created, there are ten investors, and three are EB-5 applicants, then each investor will be okay. If there are ten investors and five EB-5 applicants, then there will not be enough and one of the EB-5 applicants will not be able to meet the filing requirements. For certain troubled businesses, the job requirement can be met by showing that the number of pre-existing employees in the business will be maintained for no less than the pre-investment level for a period of two years.[34]

The requirement can also be met by showing that ten jobs have been preserved, created or some combination of the two.[35]

The regulations defined a "troubled business" as having the following characteristics:

- Has been in existence for at least two years;
- Has incurred a net loss for accounting purposes (determined on the basis of generally accepted accounting principles) during the 12 or 24-month period prior to the I-526 filing date; and
- The loss is at least equal to 20 percent of the troubled business's net worth prior to such loss.[36]

Successors in interest to a business get credit for the two years as long as the business they succeeded existed more than two years before the I-526 is filed.[37]

To show that a business is a "troubled business," an EB-5 applicant should provide photocopies of tax records, Forms I-9, or other relevant documents for the qualifying employees and a comprehensive business plan.[38]

"Employee" is defined by the EB-5 rules to mean an individual who provides services or labor for the new business and who receives wages or other remuneration directly from the new business. Employees of third parties would not qualify since they are not paid directly. And independent contractors would also not qualify

---

[32] *Id.*

[33] 8 CFR §204.6(g).

[34] 8 CFR §204.6(j)(4)(ii).

[35] *USCIS Policy Manual*, Volume 6, Part G, Chapter 2.

[36] 8 CFR §204.6(e).

[37] *Id.*

[38] 8 CFR §204.6(j)(4)(ii).

since they are, by definition, not employees. However, contractors may be counted in regional center job creation calculations.

Workers must also be "qualifying employees" for EB-5 applicants to get credit. This means that the worker must be

> … a United States citizen, a lawfully admitted permanent resident, or other immigrant lawfully authorized to be employed in the United States including, but not limited to, a conditional resident, a temporary resident, an asylee, a refugee, or an alien remaining in the United States under suspension of deportation. This definition does not include the alien investor, the alien investor's spouse, sons, or daughters, or any nonimmigrant alien.[39]

To satisfy USCIS that the enterprise will create not fewer than ten full-time positions for qualifying employees, applicants need to present one of the following:

- photocopies of relevant tax records, I-9 Forms, or other similar documents for ten qualifying employees, if such employees have already been hired following the establishment of the new business; or
- copy of a comprehensive business plan showing that, due to the nature and projected size of the new business, the need for not fewer than ten qualifying employees will result, including approximate dates, within the next two years, and when such employees will be hired.

Submitting a comprehensive business plan is a critical part of the I-526 petition because if USCIS is not satisfied that the business is likely to create ten jobs, then the petition could be denied.

The Administrative Appeals Office decision in *Matter of Ho* in the 1990s still guides USCIS today and its discussion of business plans should guide applicants:

> According to 8 Code of Federal Regulations (CFR) §204.6(j)(4)(I) and (B), if a petitioner has not already met the employment-creation requirement, he must submit a comprehensive business plan from which it is clear that the business will in fact require ten qualifying employees within the next two years. To be "comprehensive," a business plan must be sufficiently detailed to permit the Service to draw reasonable inferences about the job-creation potential. Mere conclusory assertions do not enable the Service to determine whether the job-creation projections are any more reliable than hopeful speculation.
>
> A comprehensive business plan as contemplated by the regulations should contain, at a minimum, a description of the business, its products and/or ser-

[39] *Id.*

vices, and its objectives. The plan should contain a market analysis, including the names of competing businesses and their relative strengths and weaknesses, a comparison of the competition's products and pricing structures, and a description of the target market/prospective customers of the new commercial enterprise. The plan should list the required permits and licenses obtained. If applicable, it should describe the manufacturing or production process, the materials required, and the supply sources. The plan should detail any contracts executed for the supply of materials and/or the distribution of products. It should discuss the marketing strategy of the business, including pricing, advertising, and servicing. The plan should set forth the business's organizational structure and its personnel experience. It should explain the business's staffing requirements and contain a timetable for hiring, as well as job descriptions for all positions. It should contain sales, cost, and income projections and detail the bases therefor. Most importantly, the business plan must be credible.

Certainly, no astute investor would place half a million or a million dollars into a business that he had not thoroughly researched. Creating a comprehensive business plan as described above is normal practice for any businessman seeking to operate a viable business. Without knowing whether a business is feasible and has the potential for long-term survival, neither the petitioner nor the Service can reasonably conclude that it will create permanent, full-time employment. It is not too onerous to ask a petitioner who has not yet met the employment-creation requirement to submit to the service a real business plan. Other administrative agencies, such as the Small Business Administration, and private financial institutions routinely require the submission of detailed business plans before extending loans to businesses. Permanent resident status is no less significant a matter than a loan.

The petitioner's four-page "business plan" is wholly inadequate and fails to meet the petitioner's burden of showing that he will create 10 permanent, full-time positions within the next two years.[40]

Removal of Conditions

After the I-526 is approved, the investor receives conditional permanent residency that expires after two years. To remove the conditions on permanent residency and get unconditional permanent residency, an application to remove conditions on permanent residence status must be submitted using Form I-829.

The I-829 must be accompanied by

---

[40] *Matter of Ho*, 22 I&N Dec. 206, 209 (1998).

- Evidence that the immigrant investor invested, or was actively in the process of investing the required capital and sustained the investment throughout the period of the immigrant investor's residence in the United States; and
- Evidence that the new commercial enterprise created or can be expected to create, within a reasonable time, at least ten full-time positions for qualifying employees. In the case of a troubled business, the investor must submit evidence that the commercial enterprise maintained the number of existing employees at no less than the pre-investment level for the period following his or her admission as a conditional permanent resident.[41]

Evidence of the investment can be made by providing an audited financial statement.[42] To demonstrate the investment has been sustained throughout the conditional resident period, the following evidence may be submitted:

- Bank statements;
- Invoices;
- Receipts;
- Contracts;
- Business licenses;
- Federal or state income tax returns; and
- Federal or state quarterly tax statements.[43]

It is possible to get an I-829 approved even if the full capital investment has not yet happened as long as the investor can show that it is more likely than not that the investor is in substantial compliance with the capital requirements.[44]

For non-regional center EB-5 cases, whether regular investments or investments in troubled businesses, job creation can be shown by providing payroll records, relevant tax documents and I-9 forms. For regional centers, applicants will provide reasonable methodologies, including multiplier tables, feasibility studies, analyses of foreign and domestic markets for the goods or services to be exported, and other economically or statistically valid forecasting devices.[45]

As long as the jobs were created by the business as a result of the investment, USCIS does not require the jobs still be in existence at the time the I-829 is adjudicated.[46] Also, as long as the I-829 petition can demonstrate jobs will be created with

---

[41] 8 CFR §216.6(a)(4)(iv).

[42] 8 CFR §216.6(a)(4)(ii).

[43] 8 CFR §216.6(a)(4)(iii).

[44] *USCIS Policy Manual*, Volume 6, Part G, Chapter 5.

[45] *Id.*

[46] *Matter of Ho*, 22 I&N Dec. 206, 209 (1998).

a "reasonable time," the petition can be approved. USCIS will look to the totality of the circumstances in approving the delay. The *USCIS Policy Manual* notes that jobs projected to be created more than three years after the investor's admission in, or adjustment to, conditional permanent resident status are usually not considered to be created in a reasonable time unless extreme circumstances are present.[47]

Full-time positions will be allocated to an EB-5 investor at the date the I-829 was filed. If there are multiple investors in a business, the order of the receiving of the I-829 will determine the order in which jobs are allocated.

Upon the filing of the I-829, conditional permanent residency status is automatically extended while the I-829 is pending. The receipt notice along with the immigrant's permanent residence card provides the needed documentation for travel, employment or other instances when evidence of conditional permanent residence status is required.[48]

Material Changes

While following the business plan is important in EB-5 cases, USCIS recognizes that plans change and an investor may not have control over those circumstances. An I-829 petition may still be approved if the capital was further deployed in a manner that satisfies the requirement to sustain the capital at risk. As long as the following can be demonstrated, an I-829 may still be approved:

- The required funds were placed at risk throughout the period of the petitioner's conditional permanent residence in the United States;
- The required amount of capital was made available to the business or businesses most closely responsible for creating jobs (unless the job creation requirement has already been satisfied);
- This at-risk investment was sustained throughout the period of the petitioner's conditional permanent residence in the United States; and
- The investor created (or maintained, if applicable), or can be expected to create within a reasonable period of time, the requisite number of jobs.[49]

Evaluating the Pluses and Minuses of the EB-5

Whether a startup founder is a good candidate for the EB-5 depends on a number of factors. Among them are the following:

---

[47] *USCIS Policy Manual*, Volume 6, Part G, Chapter 5.

[48] *USCIS Policy Manual*, Volume 6, Part G, Chapter 5.

[49] *Id.*

- Can the founder easily document the source of the funds being used to meet the EB-5 capital investment requirements?
- Is the investment requirement manageable?
- Can the investor wait the number of years required to eventually get to unconditional permanent residency?
- Are the job creation requirements realistic for the startup?
- Are there currency export, sanctions or other rules that will make it difficult to move capital?

The EB-5 program is one that has been in a state of change for many years and there is no reason to believe it has reached a period of stability despite the issuance of long-awaited rules. Applicants should approach the category cautiously.

INDEX

Alphabetization is word-by-word (e.g., "R visas" precedes "REAL ID Act")

A

E

F

J

K

L

M

N

Made in the USA
Monee, IL
05 November 2026

67845322R10151